FREE

························

FALL

A LATE-IN-LIFE LOVE AFFAIR

an erotic
memoir

rae padilla francoeur

SEAL PRESS

Published by
Seal Press
A Member of the Perseus Books Group
1700 Fourth Street
Berkeley, California

Library of Congress Cataloging-in-Publication Data

Francoeur, Rae Padilla, 1948-
  Free fall : a late-in-life love affair / by Rae Padilla Francoeur.
     p. cm.
  ISBN 978-1-58005-304-4
  1. Francoeur, Rae Padilla, 1948---Sexual behavior. 2. Middle-aged
women--Sexual behavior--United States--Biography. 3. Older
people--Sexual behavior--United States--Biography. I. Title.
  HQ30.F73 2010
  306.77092--dc22
  [B]
                                    2009048170

9   8   7   6   5   4   3   2   1

Interior design by Tabitha Lahr
Printed in the United States of America
Distributed by Publishers Group West

To Jim and Eli, with love and respect

CONTENTS

INTRODUCTION

O ne chilly Thursday night in late October 2006, Eli and I find ourselves approached by a handful of National Guard troops at Boston's international airport. Several nervous-looking young men with rifles and a German shepherd halt a few yards away from us—not a situation you want to find yourself in at Logan, still rattled and wary after its disastrous role in 9/11. This incident occurs as we're preparing to board a nearly empty, late-evening flight to La Guardia.

Eli and I have plans to join his mother and brother for a birthday dinner in Greenwich Village the next night. Then on Saturday night we've scheduled our semiannual dinner with Jim, a lively friend of Eli's whom I know mostly from these occasional get-togethers. The two men first met as students at Columbia University while protesting the Vietnam War. I don't know it at the time, of course, but this de rigueur journey to Manhattan changes everything for Jim, Eli, and me.

Other events intervene, as well. In just a few weeks, Eli will languish in intensive care, hallucinating and wild with fever. "It's going to be a long haul," one of the doctors tells me. She sketches his digestive tract and indicates where the cancer has spread. To keep his stomach empty and to prevent what seems to be failure of his kidneys, the doctors have withdrawn all his psych meds, most significantly lithium, and Eli, who's bipolar, falls into a state of unrelenting delirium and depression. He embarks on a year of utter hell—hell for all of us—highlighted by nine hospitalizations and numerous threats of suicide.

"I can't take him home like this," I will eventually tell every doctor, every social worker. "I'm not safe."

So what was I to do—just weeks after this exhausting trip to New York City with its unexpected consequences—when I realized that I must choose between my own survival and that of Eli's? How could I ever betray Eli that way? How could I consign him to what I pictured as the inevitable—homelessness, the realm of the crazy people no one wants?

Few people come forward to help.

Jim hears the stories of Eli's worsening condition over the telephone. He lowers his voice, compressing the emotion, turning steely and uncompromising. "It's you or him. You have to choose you."

I choose myself and in doing so, I choose Jim.

How can I regret what I have done? Jim's kisses bore in, suck, probe, penetrate. It goes on and on, this aggressive taking over. I don't see it at first, but in time I realize that his kisses tell me exactly what's going to happen to me.

I open my eyes and glimpse a bit of his face pressing hard against mine. His jaw is cocked open and I see a deep line along the side of his face. I am amazed by the intensity and drive. My sexual fantasies about Jim often start there, the place where the laugh line turns hard and rigid and intent upon wearing me down till I am totally lost to him and whatever it is he wants to do next.

. . . .

That night at Logan things start to go very wrong when a small pocket-knife Eli forgot about sets off the metal detector. I'm stepping onto the plane when I hear shouts. It has to be Eli. His bipolar disorder is always right on the surface when we travel. He has trouble with transitions. After eighteen years with him, I'm as aware of his vulnerabilities as I am of those qualities I treasure in him.

Despite how well I know Eli and how good I am at anticipating trouble, I'm stunned by what I see when I get back to the security gate. Guards are nearby and there's a lot of yelling. I rush to Eli, grab his arm, and squeeze hard. His loud, near-pleading screams alarm me. "Stop it right now," I shout into his face. "Everything's going to be okay." Like lurching for a child who's toddling into traffic, I yank at Eli, try to pull him out of this mess.

He's hopelessly flummoxed. I see that he's dumped his jacket on the floor, and his briefcase and its contents are also strewn around his shoeless feet. He's clutching a wad of papers in his right hand, including a bunched-up boarding pass. A guard says something about a driver's license, which Eli may have been trying to search for. He's confused and flustered. He can't figure out what to do with the stuff in his hand so he drops the whole parcel and begins a frantic search of his pockets.

"We need that boarding pass and your license," the guard at the security gate says.

"Just leave me the fuck alone," he cries, and his plea does sound like crying. Eli is so disturbed he has no sense of the danger he's in— the danger we're both in. I again insist that he calm down and he turns to me and yells, "Just shut up and leave me alone."

I understand what's happening. He just wants time to get calm and regroup, but he doesn't have a way to say that or to do that in the face of all this pressure.

Eli turns to leave and I block his exit. "We've paid and we're going." My legs shake so hard I can barely stand. I catch movement and turn to see the young men inch perceptibly closer. "Eli," I shout. "You've got to stop this. Just hold still a minute."

It's almost 9 PM, the time the plane is scheduled to take off, and we've been told that this will be the last flight of the evening. I'd raced from work to home to the airport in three hours. There'd been no time for dinner and I'd just spent the last half hour driving frantically around the congested construction zone of a long-term parking lot trying to find any empty space. In the midst of all that, I'd managed an increasingly irritated sixty-one-year-old man who wanted to see his mother like he wanted to have a colonoscopy.

I summon bluster and bravado. My instincts tell me to take charge and sound in control. I realize I need to do this more for the guards than Eli. Those men are just kids, kids with guns. How trained can they be? They are scared to death. They aren't even making eye contact. They're edging ever closer. They're going to lose it and shoot.

I'm fifty-eight years old. Kent State is seared into my soul, one of the top ten pivotal events in my lifetime. Kent State for me wasn't a shooting, it was a life lesson, an example of how bad things can get in a nanosecond when you mix unrelenting tension and awful fear and lack of training.

I look around. Something tells me I am the only one in control and, then, just barely. My knees feel like they're going to buckle any second. I'm terrified. It's not just the crisis at hand, but everything. I can't. I just can't. I just can't do this anymore.

Just minutes earlier, Eli, the guards, and I had all chatted and laughed with actor Richard Dreyfuss, who stood beside me at the ticket counter talking about a movie he was making. He was upbeat, full of energy, bald, and rumpled looking in loose-fitting blue jeans and a sweatshirt, and he would have been unrecognizable were it not for his signature, nasal-sounding voice.

It was a quiet night because of the icy conditions in Boston and New York City. The remaining shuttles had already been canceled. What had seemed like an intimate evening with all of us gathered in the dim light around a natural-born storyteller had turned into trouble for Logan and Eli and me.

But that's how it often was with Eli. His ability to provoke danger seemed to be escalating with his advancing age and his worsening mental condition.

I find Eli's driver's license and boarding pass and hand them over to the security guard. The knife will be mailed back to Rockport and Eli gets through the metal detector this time without incident. He moves onto the boarding ramp and I pick up his belongings and hand them to a flight attendant, who's been called over to help.

Eli boards the plane, leaving me to submit to a second search, as well, since I'd gone back through the security checkpoint to help him. Still mindful of the armed guards and the dog, I grit my teeth as a female security guard approaches and pats me down as if I were a criminal. It hurts when she squeezes my breasts and prods my crotch in front of everyone. Afterward, she says, "Don't ever let that man fly again."

Poor Eli. It's as if they can smell him coming.

. . . .

My love affair with Jim does not begin that Saturday night in Chinatown. Possibility happens. But for someone like me, for whom hope is the only currency I've ever had, possibility is all I need. If I have any sense of what is to come, it is this—a split-second awareness, an instantaneous energy flaring, then going dark.

At the time I wonder, did something just happen or did I imagine it? I look at Jim. No, there's nothing of note. Everything's steady, everything's normal.

. . . .

Our weekend struggles continue on Friday night at the birthday dinner. Eli's mother complains often during the delicious repast, held in a private room in an upscale Village restaurant. Eli's brother Simon tries to excuse her, "She hates her birthday." Not to mention that the Alzheimer's, even at this early stage, has altered her behavior. At the start of the evening she turns to me, seated to her right at the table crowded with friends and family, and snipes, "Couldn't you dress up a little bit for this?"

"Never again," I tell Eli. "I'm never traveling with you again and I'm never coming with you to visit your mother." After a summer of intensifying frustrations, I pull further away from him and his family.

Few people understand my unwavering allegiance to Eli, in part because no one dares ask. For me the early attraction was sexual, intellectual, and rooted in a certain welcome simpatico. Eli was forty-two and a working poet when I met him. I liked his dark Semitic looks, his quiet sense of humor, his rare ability to be both candid and kind simultaneously, and his enviable facility with language. There was also a dark side to the psychological attraction, though I never looked in that direction early on.

I wish people could know Eli as I do, but people are not always open to him. In Al-Anon there's a saying—*Take what you like and leave the rest.* Eli offers up plenty that I like. And where would my daughter and I be without him?

Eli was there when my larger-than-life younger brother died of a drug overdose after a weeklong binge in an L.A. hotel room. "You'll be okay," Eli said. "I'm right here."

Just a year later, he shared the weight of my wretched ambivalence when my mother died. It was self-inflicted, as well, though her death was wielded like a weapon—angrily, resolutely aimed at her small, disappointing family. She swallowed drugs and alcohol in her Beverly Hills condominium after sending a spate of nasty letters. We drove to the mountains to grieve her. At a small Vermont restaurant near the Canadian border, Eli, a practicing Buddhist, picked up his wineglass and toasted her: *To Muriel. May her next life be a happy one.*

Eli's family resented him, especially early on. He often needed money because he had a hard time supporting himself. Like most people, his family took him at face value and blamed him for his deficiencies. In an ironic bit of bad luck, he was endowed with above-average intellect; thus, much was expected of Eli. Why wasn't he a doctor like his cousins? A famous poet? Self-supporting would certainly have helped appease his mother. Eli shared their frustrations and wondered why he couldn't do better.

I could help some, but my wages as a journalist and editor were meager and I had a daughter who went to college and graduate school and then embarked on a modestly paid career as a department manager in a library. She and I saw Eli as a good and caring man whose integrity was beyond question. For eighteen years Eli kept house and ran all the errands while I worked long hours as a writer, editor, and creative services director at an art museum. Though he didn't like gardening, he weeded and watered my vegetable garden because I was too busy. He made my coffee every morning and handed me a thermos to take to work with me. And he had hot meals waiting every evening because he felt bad about my four-hour-a-day commute to and from Boston.

Could any man be more considerate? When I turned fifty, he gave me a fabulous birthday party that concluded with big fluffy bowls of tapioca pudding. He'd remembered that this was my favorite dessert from childhood.

What I liked best about my life with Eli, though, were the quiet nights we spent together as we read, chatted, and soaked up companionship and serenity—essential nutrients for hurts we'd both suffered over the years.

People know Eli as a talented, quirky poet who can be counted on to say something coyly irreverent. He grew up in the Bronx and blames the fact that he skipped two grades in elementary school for most of his social ills. He is known for his entertaining, affecting poetry readings. His vast store of knowledge and emotional intelligence are assets he shares with me, to my great advantage. Perhaps he is a bit of a savant. Or perhaps he's just typically crazy in the way so many bipolar poets are. We lived for a long time without television, without the clamor of commercialism, without noise and affectation—except for his occasional rages, so devastating, unpredictable, and ultimately impossible to endure.

I bore witness to the horrific injustices and continual suffering those with mental illness—in particular Eli—had to accept. Eli never complained. He just tried harder. I saw all of this and privately vowed never to abandon my true friend.

As change neared, I also saw—with growing clarity—that my friends were uncomfortable with Eli's moods. No doubt they also wondered about me, someone who purported to find refuge and emotional sustenance with a man they viewed as a misfit. I saw, as well, the exorbitant price I was paying in terms of my own health and emotional well-being. It was almost as if Eli were an extravagance I could no longer afford.

. . . .

The tension continues to build for Eli over the long weekend that he and I are in Manhattan. His mother seems unusually hostile to Eli, who she sometimes sees as one of her disappointments in a life characterized by compromise. He employs a very effective self-defense. He shuts down, falls asleep, pretends not to hear.

So I'm not surprised when he gets us lost walking around the back streets of the Village as we attempt to meet up with Jim on Saturday night. Eli has reached some sort of stimuli overload and can barely function. It's as if there's stress-induced static building in his brain. He stutters. He trips over his own feet.

What's supposed to be the fun part of our trip—Saturday night dinner with Jim in Chinatown—is turning out to be another fiasco. We're cold. We're tired. We've been walking around the Village for forty minutes and we still can't find the corner where we're supposed to meet Jim. He'll be there any minute and we have no clue where *there* is.

Jim calls Eli. He takes a sounding and gives Eli directions. They are in cell phone communication repeatedly. Talk. Walk. Talk. Walk. Still, we stay lost. Eli is just hopeless, half listening, forgetting what Jim says before we get to the next intersection. These are Eli's old stomping grounds but the weekend's stressors are making everything much harder to negotiate.

We discover we're walking in circles. I cannot believe this. Eli by now is agitated and limping. He's got a blister that's bleeding and infected. He says he can't go on for much longer. We're both hungry and we've both had enough. As always in these situations, I fight back the panic with something falsely cheerful like, "We'll find him any minute." It's so disingenuous I can't stand the sound of my own voice.

Then I hear Jim's laugh on Eli's cell phone. "What the fuck?" Jim chides Eli. At least Jim's reaction sounds relaxed, normal, honest. I find myself thinking: Once we get there, I'll let down and relax. I'm going to let Jim deal with Eli for a while.

In some ways, Jim and Eli haven't changed since the anti–Vietnam War riots. They're passionate about politics and critical of authority. I love this about them. While they were facing down riot police at Columbia, I was trying to protect myself from one of several SWAT teams in Harvard Square. The police, looking ruthless and robotic in full-body armor that glinted in the streetlights, wielded clubs against antiwar protesters. Struck at and kicked at, I rolled under a hedge to protect myself from serious injury. When I stood up again, I was fully radicalized. If people can feel like home, then Jim and Eli do that for me.

Tonight there's another war to rail about and several months to catch up on, since Jim lives in Chelsea and Eli and I live in Rockport, Massachusetts, 250 miles away. I look forward to these semiannual check-ins. I'm especially looking forward to seeing Jim this evening, when I will give him his old friend and say, "Here, you take over for a while."

* * * * * * * * * * * *

Jim and I often say we were separated at birth. Our compatibility feels cultural, like maybe we grew up as neighbors or maybe we experienced the same womb. We savor avocados and could subsist on tuna sandwiches if he weren't worried about the toxins and I weren't opposed to all that bread. We love sex and laughing and our kids. We grew up on the West Coast but got away as fast as we could. The East Coast feels more like home. He once hated flying and so did I, though now we look forward to taking trips together. He loves to tell stories and he gravitates to storytellers and so do I. We're tall. We're comfortable as leaders. We're way left of center.

But we're not a perfect fit. He was sixty-seven and I was fifty-eight when we began our love affair. Age and experience shaped us as they do everyone, gave us jagged edges that, when placed up against the other, did not smoothly align. Time teaches tolerance, on the other hand, and I see that we're both good at letting go.

Jim left his home in Southern California in his teens just as I did. He joined the Army. After his discharge, he traveled to Manhattan, took a room for $13.50 a week, and began an apprenticeship as a stained-glass artisan. He also took advantage of his veteran's benefits and got a college education. He never looked back.

For twenty-five years he belonged to the Gurdjieff Work, an international spiritual practice with a following in Manhattan. Through education, the work in the program, and meditation he developed an incredible ability to stay in the moment. Early on he would caution me, "We are good now, in this moment."

What? Fuck off, you Alpha Male.

When I stopped resenting the "moment," I picked up a few helpful tips on living a more peaceful life.

Jim's two ex-wives both have law degrees and both of them have other fields of expertise as well. He has three grown children, all living and working in New York City. When Jim told his oldest son that he and I were thinking of living together, the forty-two-year-old reacted with alarm: "But you're a bachelor. What about how much you like your freedom?"

Jim tells me that story and I cringe. Well, I think, by the time we're tired of each other, we'll be on our deathbeds. We both like to look on the bright side.

. . . .

Jim's voice on Eli's phone sounds cheery. Perhaps he's unaware of what's happening with his old friend; more likely, he's just ignoring it. On other occasions I've noticed Jim look past Eli when Eli was misbehaving. I glom on to this carefree attitude. I take comfort in that deep calm voice coming from Eli's phone. Yes. Absolutely. I'm turning this whole mess over to Jim. Voilà! Suddenly a fantasy, only one of two I've allowed myself since meeting Jim twenty years earlier, has taken hold—Jim stepping in, throwing out his long arms, taking me into his zone of safety.

I spot him, finally, on a corner, looking right at us. Jim's a watcher. He's seen us long before we see him. He's a beacon, six foot five, erect under a streetlight, grinning. His striking mane of white curly hair is heads above the Saturday night crowds. He beckons us in all the sly ways he has of drawing people to him. With a laugh Jim admonishes Eli for his lousy sense of direction. We all hug, relieved and a little bit on edge, and head down the street in search of dinner.

The burden of Eli lifted, I feel like a kid. I'm out in front of the two men, perusing restaurant menus affixed to window storefronts. I glance behind me and Jim's saying something to Eli while watching me. I catch his eye and we smile. Neither of us lets go.

I choose the first restaurant that looks good. Vietnamese pho soups. It's cold outside and we're all shivering. Steaming bowls of Vietnamese rice noodle soup seem right, but so does stopping and sitting down and immediately ordering drinks.

We barely talk at first. The waiter brings us our wine and beer and our heads drop over our menus, where we hover in silence. Thinking about what to order is my excuse for a respite from all the noise, confusion, and pent-up anxiety. I drink the wine like it's medicine and feel myself start to relax for the first time in days. I tell myself I'll just sit, get drunk, and slurp the delicious salty soup while the two of them catch up. I don't need to talk. I don't need to focus. I drink more wine and weigh whether I want rare or well-done steak in my pho soup. Life is so much simpler when all I have to worry about is what kind of soup to eat.

I start to notice what's going on around me. It's a small restaurant and it's sweaty hot. Young Thai couples enjoy outsize bowls of noodle soup into which they've floated tiny, fiery green peppers, handfuls of fresh basil leaves, and even bigger fistfuls of crunchy young mung sprouts. Using chopsticks, they extract pieces of beef from the soup and dip the beef into a searing red-pepper sauce. Everyone's faces are flushed pink and they glisten with sweat.

When our food shows up we dive in. The windows are fogged, Jim and Eli have stripped down to shirtsleeves, and there's moistness to everything I touch. Aromatics like the basil, lime, and long-simmering chicken stock are so thick in the humid air you can taste them.

As the wine kicks in and the soup warms me from the inside, I sit back and finally take a good look at Jim. Good lord. What a gorgeous man he is and so surprisingly unself-conscious about it. He picks up a napkin and wipes the sweat off his face, motions to a waiter for a stack of napkins, and repeats the gesture throughout the meal.

Everyone inside this little restaurant is sweating. I'm reminded of the ceremonial sweat lodges I've heard about and imagine how intimate the experience must feel at times—just like this.

· · · · · · · · · · · ·

In that moment of companionable warmth I have no inkling that, one night a few months from then, I will slide right off Jim's torso, he is so slick with sweat. We are so wet with each other's sweat, in fact, that we wrestle and writhe and roll right off the bed, bringing the mattress down with us. We are shocked by the abrupt dumping, the hardness of the floor. Our lovemaking turns hilarious then.

There's no heat in my tiny attic bedroom and a fierce winter storm rocks my three-story house likes it's bobbing at sea. We literally sway to and fro and I feel slightly seasick. We lie, spent, and listen. The waves pound the sand on Front Beach. Our sweat begins to chill and we climb under the heavy down comforter.

"I can't really see very far into the future," Jim says that night. "But I do see us here in this bed this summer. We'll be totally covered in sweat. It will be one hundred degrees in here and we're going to be drippy wet. I'm going to like that."

My craving for him seems to have no bounds. He may have no vision of the future, he may be locked into the moment, but I am not Jim in those ways. I see the future. I see us locked together. I see nothing big enough, save death, to get in my way.

I am shameless. I will slide over every inch of him, kissing him back, wrestling in all that sweat to stay on top. I am sure I will never get enough of him. He will find this out and, being the man he is, he will revel in trying to find the outer limits of my stamina and prowess. He never will.

. . . .

We say little as we eat. I look over at Eli, who's chewing some marinated cabbage, and Jim, who catches my eye, again, and smiles. He's ordered something with bits of stir-fried chicken. Still, nobody's saying anything and I'm not the quiet type. I blurt the first stupid thing that comes to mind. "What's new?" What I say is simply idiotic but it's too late to take it back. And I've had three days of unrelenting stress and a big glass of wine. Why do I expect so much of myself?

Shit. I've got that bravado thing going again, that tough-girl, fake-it persona I invoke when I start to feel desperate. Part of the discomfort is due to the fact that it's been a long time since we've dined alone with Jim. For the last five years, we've been a foursome, Jim's girlfriend Ruth a lively conversationalist. I liked spending time with Ruth and we had a lot in common, from our high-stress jobs in marketing to quirky phobias to the fact that she'd married and divorced a man who was bipolar. Without Ruth, a friend to all, we were going to have to regroup.

Jim's not inspired by my "What's new?" and shrugs. "Not a hell of a lot. Ruth and I broke up last June, but I already told Eli about that."

I'm curious about this but can find no polite way to ask what happened. So I blurt a follow-up question. "Are you happy?" as if one thing leads to the other. For Jim, this question takes on special meaning.

"I'm no more, no less happy than I was," he answers, not so much squinting as turning his head, narrowing his eyes, seeing me anew. He later tells me the question is a boundary violation and that I'd veered into intimate territory. I never quite believe that and suspect that the breakup is simply a sensitive topic even six months later.

He gets back at me and I learn right away that Jim never restrains his pique. "It looks like you've been doing a lot more running." He's referring to my weight loss, a comment that makes me uncomfortable. It tells me that he's looking at me, seeing me, sparring with me. He's stepped out of bounds. These games are to him a devilish foreplay and he wastes little time smashing through all the defenses, yielding a certain type of lover with a certain love of danger.

"I run no more, no less than ever." I respond to his combativeness by parroting his earlier response.

"And what's new with you," he asks me. I note that he's angled his chair closer, to face me. I note, as well, that Eli is on the sidelines now, eating, barely paying attention. I worry about him, that he's feeling alone and left out.

"You okay," I ask Eli.

He nods yes and smiles.

"You don't mind?"

He shakes his head no.

I turn back to Jim, where the fun is. And it's right then that I sense something, some heat, some energy, some kind of flare-up. But it's nothing I can put my finger on.

"New with me?" I say. "Let's see." I think about Jim and Eli's friendship before answering that question the way I'd like to answer it. I know how much Eli values his connection to Jim and I don't want to put Jim in the awkward position of knowing too much about Eli and me, the couple.

I could tell Jim about the new photo department I've started up in creative services, the division I manage at the Peabody Essex Museum. I could tell him about my daughter's new job as manager of adult services at the Watertown Public Library. I could tell him about the novel I've just finished. But what I want to tell him is that I've asked Eli to move out. I've asked him every day for six months.

I look at Jim and betray Eli. "I'm in the middle of a midlife crisis, I guess."

I'm shocked by his response. He laughs. His laugh is loud, manly, and, always, I think, somewhat lewd. "Aren't you a little old for that?"

Now he definitely crosses a line. No one has ever called me old before and I don't like it at all. I tell myself, I'm fifty-eight. I am old. I still don't like it.

But then I see how he's edged in, moved closer. An actual boundary violation. That, I like. I like having him closer. His impertinent remark has invaded my space, sliced through all my protective layers. I couldn't find bluster and bravado at that moment if my life depended on it.

. . . .

Jim and his penchant for breaking me down. His pugilistic irreverence. He'd begun a process that would lead to a nakedness in me that only the most mature woman would dare allow. Whatever fantasies I'd conjured about Jim keeping me safe that night were totally absurd and completely sentimental. He'd ripped away my defenses and pushed me way out of my comfort zone. Had I ever felt that vulnerable, that unsafe?

Here, I said at the end of the dinner, take my email address. Who would have thought feeling unsafe would feel this good?

SWEET SURRENDER

CHAPTER 1

Sometimes when we make love, Jim grabs both of my hands and pulls them over my head. I love this. He holds my wrists so tight it hurts. He puts his other huge hand over my mouth, the mouth he has been kissing so long and so passionately that my lips have swollen like a sex organ. They are fat and wet and soft and blood red, something I know from having seen myself in the bathroom mirror after kissing him. Jim is strong—his biceps are round and hard and wrapped in a skin so smooth and white that I desperately want to bite down—but I haven't let myself do that. He's a presence wherever he is, certainly in bed, where, at six foot five, he is vast and powerful and prone to quick decisions. And though I am nearly six feet tall myself, I am helpless in his tight grip. Soon, I struggle. I am desperate for a breath.

He calls *us* a complete and total surprise. After our first night together, we sit down to breakfast at Moonstruck, the neighborhood diner. The tall leather-bound menus with page after page of omelets, salads, sandwiches, and more lie flat on the table between us. The coffee's been poured but sits, ignored, the steam now feeble tendrils. I'm as spent as that—sexually, physically, emotionally. It took so much to get to this place. I prop myself in the corner of the booth to keep from sliding onto the floor. It's a good feeling. If I were a cat, I'd purr.

He likes me like this—all melty, he calls it. He's done this to me and he takes the credit. I act out my satisfaction more than I articulate it verbally. I try but give up. There are no words for this. It's too primal. The closest I ever get is, "You own me. After what you've done to me, you own me." I hope he understands. I hope he's careful.

After a morning like we just had, it takes hours for the hormones to settle down, for the sex organs to shrink back to normal. Until they do, I'm not myself. I smile shyly. I'm this new, softer person.

How does a woman who's been taken over and who's allowed it, who's had so many things done to her with fingers and lips and penis, who has screamed out and been shocked by the sound of her own voice, how is this woman supposed to behave? I blink as if to call up comprehension, but finding none, drop my head. I worry whether or not my appreciation shows. I want him to know.

In the booth I sink into the cushions. I soften even more. Hispanic men with blue-black hair—thick and short, sharply cut angles, virile in the lift and body and texture—approach us. They wear crisp white shirts and black slacks and they proffer service in tandem. Water? More coffee? Food?

Yes, more water. My mouth is dry. I have no fluids left in me. Come back soon to give me more coffee. I'm sleepy and wish this booth were bed. But no more sinking. Maybe I'll have seven-grain toast. Maybe a poached egg. It should be well done.

I eye the dish of butter that one of the young men has put in front of me and my brain, functioning languidly, finds butter fascinating. I already know what's under those gold foil lids, the tiny dollops extruded by machinery into plastic containers the size of Chiclets gum. The drops of butter resemble flowers until they warm up, turn squishy, lose their edges, give up their details, their identity. They succumb to malleability, like me. Melty me. I am hopelessly drunk on sex and I smile, all my secrets right there in plain view. My lips, plumped up and blood red, look like the rutting mandrill. I can't avoid seeing myself. The walls in Moonstruck are lined with mirrors.

Jim, the watcher, is looking directly at me. There's nothing melty there, that's for sure. I'm starting to notice something, a hesitation going on between us. We're not poring over menus. We're not sugaring up the warm beverages. We're here. Landed. Suddenly cognizant.

Jim's got something to say, it seems. His face forms a question that he doesn't ask. "Well?" I say, a little worried. "What is it?"

He brightens and laughs. "What the hell? How did this happen, anyway?" He picks up the cup of coffee, finally, and asks, "What's Rae doing here in Chelsea?"

I don't like this question. I know where it's coming from. He doesn't want responsibility for *us*. He doesn't want to take any credit for this eventuality, for the conception of this thing. He is saying I started it and I don't think that's fair, but I keep it to myself. I've only known him in this new way for less than ten hours.

In one sense, I understand the surprise. Pinch me. I'm with Jim. He's been at me all morning, since our love affair didn't officially start till 3 or 4 AM. Jim's across from me now. He's the man I never really looked at, which might well mean he's the man I wanted most to look at. There are taboos about men like him, your significant other's old friend and special confidant.

There's a role some women inhabit when they need to be social but safely detached. A certain rigidity rides up the spine. A certain unladylike distance in the placement of the feet assures reliable grounding. A certain way you focus your eyes to look at people obscures many of the details you don't want to see. You impart a certain sharp quality to the tone of your voice—all business. A certain lift to the chin. Think Hillary Clinton—polite, geared up, a little abrupt.

With Jim in the old days, I looked away more than I looked. It's as if I set my inner aperture to wide-open. This setting yields more fuzziness than detail. An open aperture is used in low light, when seeing is a problem. It is imperative that things viewed this way remain perfectly still. They must remain *as is*. What you get in these circumstances is an impressionistic rendering.

Jim a surprise?

Perhaps it's true. It's certainly a good story for when we get found out. *It wasn't our fault. We were unsuspecting. It just happened.*

But there were moments of intent; small and hesitant negotiations that grew bolder as the expected resistance on both sides failed to materialize. Intent got us here, to this place in Moonstruck where we, for the first time, marvel at the fact of us.

I wonder, reaching for butter, how bad is this going to hurt?

. . . .

After our dinner in Chinatown I take it for granted that there is more to come. I have no idea what and it never occurs to me to speculate. Open to possibility, I move on with my life. I feel good.

I mention Jim for the first time in a journal entry I make on December 5. By this time my intentions are clear and Jim has become a secret I am keeping from myself. Nothing manifests, nothing assumes dimension till I record it and examine it in one of my sequential notebooks. You could call it a life log, though I don't call it anything. It's a pragmatic exercise lacking in profundity on any level. These are soundings taken in bed, late at night, on the cusp of sleep. They are, in part, fact-based notations made in interesting little booklets I've accumulated, always with an excellent pen. If I weren't so tired when I get to my notebook, it would be a very satisfying experience. I never burden myself with emotional rants for the simple reason that I don't have any desire to revisit the painful parts. My fact-based reporting begins with the date and temperature and a mention of anything dramatic, such as a deep snowfall or a news event. I often list the day's accomplishments and, if there's time before I fall asleep, I note what's uppermost in my thoughts. Often I work on a problem I'm having somewhere in my life. These solutions, which I work out step by step, are reliable, authentic, and doable.

By the night of December 5 a lot has been said between us and Jim has become a heavy thought surrounded by a huge static charge. Things are, by now, moving very quickly. Anxiety forces me out of my denial. I put Jim on a page this evening and make him real.

I find it odd, as I write, that I never questioned my intentions back in October and November. Instead I simply opened up and waited with uncharacteristic calm and absolutely no reflection. As I've often heard Buddhists say, especially with regard to meditation, we have monkey minds. Our thoughts dart and crisscross like monkeys swinging through the arboreal canopy. As a rule, I have double monkey mind. I've been called a worrier. What I am is an optimist who expects success for my hard efforts but who imagines the worst. I am, therefore, always on alert. I am also acutely appreciative of everything that comes my way.

But there has been no imagining the worst where Jim is concerned, just sexual fantasies, growing ever more frequent and intense as the date of our rendezvous nears.

When I got back to Rockport from that October weekend in New York City, I stepped right back into the frenzied budgeting process at work on top of the usual production deadlines. Eventually it occurred to me that I had not received an email from Jim, as expected, so in early November I emailed him one evening from home and asked if he'd tried to contact me at work using the address on my business card. He had. I checked with our IT department, who then authorized his email and retrieved the message, which had been diverted by a security wall of some kind. When it showed up, I forwarded it to my home address.

That evening I sipped wine and read how Jim spent a lot of time with his kids and that, since his breakup with Ruth, he felt that he was between social networks. His reporting of his social situation told me that he wanted to expand it, to possibly include me. I had to read between the lines to make this deduction. I thought of Eli, then, and how he'd feel if I, too, had Jim as a friend. Perhaps it wasn't a good idea but they spoke infrequently and saw each other only a couple of times a year. And I was always included in those get-togethers.

Fine, I conclude. I can do that. I'll be Jim's friend. I send a friendly email in response. Though I am very social, I write, my social life is limited because of the choices I've made. These are not choices I regret but I, too, could use a friend and confidant. Jim will be the first person I talk to about the *other* Eli, the one who suffers and who, occasionally, rages.

. . . .

Until Jim, I'd limited my email correspondence on my home computer. Home is where I write. I have just a few hours each morning, beginning at 5:30, to work on my novel. In the evenings I often make revisions. So it isn't until a weekend morning toward the end of November that I click on my home email icon and see: *I want to talk.* Jim had given me a day and an approximate time that I was to call, but I'd missed the date entirely. So I write back and say, *Tomorrow, 10 AM. I'll call.*

Now Jim haunts me. *I want to talk.* This is new. Everything changes with those four words. No man has ever spoken to me like this before. No one in my circle of friends and none of my former lovers even employed "I want" in their syntax. In my circles, interactions were more exploratory, more tentative, more time consuming and complicated. Here is a novel idea: *I want to talk.* It sounds so imperative, so direct, so childlike, so clear. Is Jim one of those people, not unlike Eli, who refuses to abide by convention? Who still has many of the great attributes from childhood that most of us are socialized out of? Or is Jim just a big bold alpha male?

I want to talk. How interesting.

About what?

With me?

How come?

Who cares? This is fun.

. . . .

Halfway through my run the following Sunday morning I stop. It's early December. Sixty-five degrees. I'm wearing shorts and a T-shirt and I head over to the wooden bench that overlooks Old Garden Beach on Rockport's shoreline. Normally I'd be dressed in polypropylene long underwear, wool socks, a hat and gloves, and a nylon or fleece jacket to block the wind that typically blows off the ocean in winter. How could this be December? I watch as, down in the water, a handful of men bob in a circle. They're novice divers, probably with vacations in the tropics coming up. They're taking instruction from a professional who's advising caution, yelling over the sound of the small waves slapping the sand behind them.

I stretch my legs across the length of the bench, feel the pull in my hamstrings, and look beyond the divers. Gorgeous. Baby-blue ocean and matching sky. It's usually slate gray this time of year, with contrasting whitecaps. It's so warm that my sweat has dried and my hair has puffed out like the Chia pet my young daughter gave me one year for Christmas. I slip my cell phone out of my shorts pocket and punch in Jim's number. It occurs to me that this will be the first time I speak with Jim alone, one-on-one.

The discussion is like a *Seinfeld* episode, about nothing. It's friendly and full of laughs. He calls me *sweetheart* but, I later realize, everybody's *sweetheart* to him, including his thirty-seven-year-old son.

Nonetheless I like Jim's bubbliness. He's easy to talk with and the jokes and laughs are second nature. I tell him all about Old Garden Beach, the pastel colors, the flatness of the ocean, the men squeezed into their wet suits, the oceanfront loop that is my usual run, how I left the house this morning with my little oval of a cell phone curled up in my hand. He listens as he eats his morning toast and drinks coffee. He was all ready for me. He had arranged his morning ritual to coincide with our chat. I call. He eats. We joke. We sustain our conversation without ever saying much. Yet this is really it for me—the true beginning of my love affair with Jim.

I stand up from the bench very reluctantly. I know that almost as soon as I run off from this little bubble of perfection, up the hill and away from Old Garden Beach, everything is going to change. Winter will come back. I will betray Eli. It ends up being far worse for Eli than even I can imagine.

For the moment, though, I'm happy. I resume my run and barely give Jim another thought that day.

．．．．．．．．．．．．

Did you know it would be like this? He asks me this question while making love to me for the first time.

Like this? I am trying to think but he is all over me. Like this? I can't figure out what he means. I resent that he is asking me to think. I wonder, why can he think? How is he so together right now?

He asks this question as he smiles, as he moves his body down, as he slides away until his head is between my legs. For a moment it is like he is leaving, like he is going under water, like those divers at

Old Garden Beach. But then he touches his tongue to my clitoris. He pushes his fingers, which ones I don't know, into my vagina.

Like this? I'm trying to understand the question because it feels important. Is he asking me if I appreciate his technique? Or does he mean did I think we'd make love literally for hours without sleep?

No, I say.

He reaches forward with a long arm and puts his wet fingers on my lips. I smell myself and taste what he's tasting. He doesn't move his fingers. He thinks I'm asking him to stop. I pull his hand away from my lips. I breathe. I try again to think. No, I say. No. I did not know about this. I did not expect anything like this.

He reinserts his fingers into my vagina and doesn't stop till I shove him off me. I do this after several orgasms, after I'm sure I couldn't possibly come again. Whenever I think like that he proves me wrong.

. . . .

Jim's a craftsman who used to make Tiffany-style stained-glass lamps. He's good with his hands, something he likes to remind me of: "You get the benefit of all this." He shows me his hands and I get embarrassed because, by then, I know their many talents and don't want to say how important his hands have become to me. But he never minds embarrassing me. Do you like my hands? he asks.

His hands are strong, like vice grips, and sometimes they scare me. His long body hung from his fingertips when he rock climbed. For years he relied on the muscles and dexterity in his fingers to build intricate works of stained glass. While harnessed and hanging from buildings he scraped, sanded, and rebuilt window openings. Those hands changed the diapers of his three babies, made love to only he knows how many women, and, now, they spread before me, an offering. He takes my hand in his and smiles. "I love you."

At fifty Jim had to make a change. He shut down his stained-glass studio and discarded everything. Started over. Now he owns and runs a restoration business in Manhattan. He hires and supervises small crews of skilled woodworkers.

He's tough. I like that. He uses language to establish his authority with the men. He says *Fuck that* when he's not pleased and *Fuckin' A* when he is. He tells me he yells. I've heard him. *Stop talking and listen to me.* Sometimes he apologizes. Other times, he digs in.

Uniquely, perhaps perversely uncensored in everything, he says *cunt* like I say *damn.* He passes the concierge at the desk in his apartment building in Chelsea and shouts his male greeting, "Hey, man. How's it going?" I adore these interactions and look forward to our walks through the building that takes up an entire city block in Chelsea. Actors, writers, artists of all kinds live here, but the real celebrities seem to be the lively staff. The men wait for him, want to talk with him. I can see it. People who smile as easily as they breathe are rare and wonderful. They light up your day.

At 5:30 AM, a concierge about to come on duty calls Jim. We are still in bed but we are awake. "Hey, can I have your parking space this morning?" Jim says yes, hops out of bed, showers, has his toast and coffee, and heads off to his woodworking shop in Brooklyn, where he'll meet his crew. As he pulls away in his Suburban, a concierge pulls in.

At Christmas Jim hands out new bills in holiday envelopes to the building staff, the people who open the doors, who search for his packages, who bring his dry cleaning to his apartment. They are the only

recipients of his holiday cheer because, he tells me, "I hate Christmas."
"Okay," I say and listen to the Boston Camerata's album *Sing We Noel*
on my iPod with ear buds.

Late one morning during my first visit to Jim, we set off to go uptown to the Metropolitan Museum of Art, where there's an exhibition
of Tiffany glass. We exit the apartment, take the elevator to the lobby,
then walk through the building. We pass one of the main concierge
stations. Three men, dressed in uniforms, stop their chatting as we
emerge from one of the hallways. Jim starts his spiel. "Hey guys, how's
it going?" They grin, just a tad mischievously. I am a new face. It's Sunday morning. We're a little the worse for wear. "Have a good day, man,"
Jim laughs as one of them nods.

My uterus clinches. My vagina actually drips. Good god, is there
no end to this? The sound of his voice, the rough greetings to the men,
the quick nod of the head, and I'm in want all over again.

He says to me on the phone one night when I bemoan my unrelenting desire, "You are turned on." And that, I realize, has become
my perpetual state of being, a state I inhabit for weeks, months . . .
forever?

Is it possible, I wonder, that at a certain point in one's maturity,
sex between two people is all they need from each other? They've got
their jobs, their social networks, their prestige, power, and status. Their
kids. Their homes. Their retirement funds. What's missing?

Eli and I stopped making love five years ago, when a number of
circumstances converged. He'd become a devout Buddhist. His psych
medications reduced his libido. His emphysema, until it became better
controlled, caused extreme shortness of breath during physical exer-
tion. It just wasn't worth the trouble.

Who else lives like I do? I have no idea. Sex among my friends never comes up. Books, food, movies, kids, work—yes. But sex is altogether missing from the conversation. Is it missing from all of our lives, or just mine?

I know that my capacity for physical pleasure is easily extinguished in times of stress or preoccupation. Even running, which buoys me, can be an enormous effort. Nine-tenths of the effort is spent making up my mind to run and then getting dressed and out the door. Running is the easy part. Step out the door and I'm in the groove, no matter how tired I am or how hard it feels. Once again my physicality rescues me. When I finish my forty-minute run I feel whole and happy. It's a feeling that stays with me all day.

Jim and I find ourselves shocked by our prowess. Our capacity for lovemaking seems boundless and it's not long before we start talking about it. If only we could tell other people what we've discovered, he says. The journalist in me agrees, but how would we do it? Just tell people, he says. I agree. We must not go on believing that age gives us license to turn our backs on our bodies. We have the capacity at age fifty, sixty, at seventy, to be potent lovers. "I'm lucky," I say to Jim. "So am I," he says.

Once, during dinner he says, "Everything is foreplay." He had been telling me stories and I'd been happily following along. We were having our second date, our second night together, and we were enjoying our first martini in what would become a mating ritual. Jim is a master. As my friend and fellow aficionado says, "That man makes a fine martini." So on our second evening alone together, we sip the delicious, icy gin, faintly scented with vermouth, and we practically swoon. He tells me stories and I respond with smiles, laughter, small jokes. It's delicious titillation.

"Everything," says Jim, spearing a fat green olive with a toothpick and holding it up to my lips, "is foreplay."

. . . .

The next morning, after two virtually sleepless nights of sex and talking and rolling around, and the powerful martini, I pull on my running clothes and jog along the Hudson River Parkway, which is just two blocks from Jim's Chelsea apartment. As I run, I can't take my eyes off the exquisite blue of the river. Suddenly up ahead, I catch sight of the Statue of Liberty. Everything is so beautiful.

I hum along, not at all tired or tiring. After a half hour, I reverse direction. I notice something different. My feet make no sound as they hit the pavement. I spring from foot to foot like I'm on a trampoline. And though it is cold and windy, my shoulders are relaxed and there's something looser, easier about my stride. When I get back to Jim, he makes me toast and coffee. It hurts a little to sit after so much sex after so many years of not having sex, but I relax on the couch and savor the food. My body is softer, more free, open. This is the new way I run, whether along the Hudson River in New York City or along the Atlantic Ocean.

ONE. TWO. THREE. JUMP.

CHAPTER 2

December 5, Tuesday

This past weekend I spoke with Jim on the phone and told him about Sarah and the trip we've been planning to New York City around the holidays. The timing is coincidental and it allows me to see Jim face-to-face, perhaps once or twice while we're there. He seemed very happy about the trip and said he'd drive us wherever we wanted.

Complications continue to arise, however, not the least of which is that the more I talk with and write to Jim, the more I realize I need to do this alone, sans encumbrances and distracting concerns.

I would love to travel with Sarah and I would love to explore New York with her. I can't seem to summon the energy for working through the problems we encounter having to do with childcare on her end, keeping expenses down, finding room, etc. Everything in me says: Keep it simple.

At the heart of all this confusion is Jim. I want a clear path. Nothing in the way. Opportunity for me to see, experience, react. Haven't said any of this part to him, naturally. I need to be honest with myself about what I want and I'm not there yet.

After a lot of soul-searching I tell Sarah I want to wait till April. Then I call Jim and ask if I can come to see just him. Even that is a problem because of the difficulty I've had finding hotel rooms. The attempts to plan a trip to New York City with Sarah were thwarted by a dozen obstacles, most significantly the cost and lack of affordable hotel rooms during and right after the holiday season. There are still parts of the trip I would love to salvage, such as an opening at an art gallery on Fifth Avenue and the visits I'd lined up with two museum colleagues relocated to museums in Manhattan.

All the things that feed into the burgeoning connection with Jim—phone calls, emails, nighttime sexual fantasies, stomach knots that ward off any desire for food, and the big one . . . sexual desire— pitch into high gear when he agrees. What was I thinking? You bury your sexuality for years? I admonish myself. Well then, you'd better brace yourself. Someone can pass by, skirt the periphery of your tidy little world, and boom, he or she has triggered an explosive sexual reawakening. I had not taken responsibility for myself in important ways. People were going to suffer the consequences.

December is insane, though, of course, I have no idea how much worse things will get before the month is out. Things telescope. A lot happens in a day. Soon I know I will be staying with Jim. Soon the tone of the emails shifts from that feisty banter we had going to something a little more sobering. Jim calls me one day and puts it right out there. "Are you freaked out?" Holy shit—there's another one of his already infamous boundary violations. But it feels sexy, bold, provocative.

I'm smitten. I admire him for his honesty at bringing this shift in our relationship into the open and for his frank curiosity. It's an enormous turn-on to be approached in this candid and probing way.

Freaked out? "It's a disruption to the status quo," I say as if it's all just a minor inconvenience. I hear myself sound like the sociology major I was in college. *Freaked out?* As the date of my trip to New York City nears, I detect a small tremble throughout my body and nothing I do can stop it. In fact it grows from tremble to quake and, like an eye twitch or endless hiccups, I have this new, very visible problem to contend with. Utensils shake in my hands. My voice cracks. In bed my arms and legs seem to shake the wrought-iron frame and I wonder if Eli picks up on any of it. I am, of course, very frightened but never once consider not making this trip.

But I do tell Jim in an email on December 10, as my visit fast approaches, that I am frightened. I spend a long time considering this admission. It's another of the big risks I seem compelled to take. I'm keenly aware of the prejudices toward women and expression of feelings. By bringing fear into the discussion, I reveal that I'm typically female, emotional, in need of comfort. At least that's how many men would perceive it. Such unflattering notions are admittedly counter to my own perception of myself, which is fed by my leadership role at the museum and a desire to be seen differently precisely because I am emotionally expressive. Years before, a valued counselor coached me on my use of language at work. We tweaked my business lexicon, culling words that betrayed emotional content.

In the end I decide I will always be honest with Jim, that I will present as true a version of myself as I can. So I send off the email.

Hi Jim,

I'm guessing from that missed call that you checked to see if I got my Treo 700w. It didn't happen. Lots of other things happened, all of them nice, fun

Saturday-type things, and I never made it to a smart phone store. Not to mention, my capacity for the new and the novel is already being seriously tapped, as you know. . . .

I hope all is well. I like it that I'll come to your place but I am scared to death.

—Rae

Me, too, but in a good way. I grew up in S. CA and went bodysurfing when I was a kid and most times when I'd get close to the ocean I'd get this feeling in the pit of my stomach and I thought for the longest time that it was fear but later on I realized that it was primal excitement and that is kin to fear. I loved the sea and roiling around in it. You'll love this sea and roiling around in it also.

Talk to you soon.

—Jim

With this email response, so beautiful and sexy, and so linked to my own experiences growing up in the beach town of Santa Barbara, Jim sews it up. He's unthreatened, undaunted, strong and masculine, creative. Or so I believe. Mostly he's sexy and he's helping me get ready.

The tremor does not abate. How could it? It is pure energy. I will put my hands on Jim and begin to experience some release from all of this. In the meantime, though, it feels close to unendurable.

• • • • • • • • • • • •

All the while I work every morning on my third novel, a story about a man and a woman in their forties involved in a complicated love affair. It's character driven but the characters grope about in the ugly morass of mental illness. Those affected by mental illness understand the horrors and frustrations. These are closet diseases, and medieval attitudes still influence the treatment—and the appalling lack of it. My novel, *Earth to Ben,* is a work inspired by love and helplessness because of Eli and those in my family who have suffered and died from mental illness. My job as a writer has always been to call out the injustices as evocatively as I can in hopes that a spirit of change might be incited. I know these are lofty goals but they are also tireless motivators.

I send Jim excerpts from a chapter in which Ben seduces Eva. Writing these scenes was a lot of fun. Two proud people, their years imprinted inside and out, take off their clothes and make love to each other. I imagined that it took a lot of courage to get through that first night. Suddenly I was facing something very similar.

Jim calls me. "I can't believe you sent this to me. You surprise me."

"Why?"

He doesn't explain. How could he? He would be giving away certain impressions he has of me, impressions that may not be accurate or that may hurt my feelings.

Instead he says, referring to the bedroom scenes, "It's so true." I know then that he, too, is anxious about what's coming.

Jim plans to roil. Fine. By emailing him the excerpt from *Earth to Ben,* I've shown him that I can meet him halfway.

• • • • • • • • • • • •

I walk into Jim's bedroom late one evening to find him waiting for me. Small white votive candles flicker on every surface. The bedroom, with its deep blue sheets and pillowcases, is dark except for these spots of soft light. I am delighted.

The candles illuminate nothing, cannot penetrate the dark corners of the man's cluttered bedroom. Then, Jim and I take off our clothes and it's as if the light comes alive. It finds our naked bodies. Our skin glows, golden and beautiful. I am almost twenty years older than Eva and Jim is nearly thirty years older than Ben. Yet we are freed by the light. We wrestle and fuck like we are teenagers. *I like this,* says Jim. A few of the candles burn down before we are finished.

I want to make a video of us making love, Jim tells me over the phone one night. I want to do this, he reiterates. Okay, I say, I'll think about it.

Shit. What have I gotten myself into?

That week at my hairdresser's I pick up a copy of *Cosmopolitan* magazine. I turn to a story on how to keep your sex life alive. A month ago I didn't even have a sex life. I look around to see if Jeffrie is watching me. All clear. I get to tip number 3 and laugh out loud: *Make videos and then watch them together.* Where have I been?

Celibate. I've been celibate. Writing about Eva and Ben's sex life is not the same as having one, any more than masturbating is like fucking the man you can't stop thinking about.

I call Jim that night and say, okay, I'll do this, but we can't make it look cheap and pornographic. We have to do it right. I hang up and make a plan. I'll script it. I'll wear black lacy underwear and peel it off to my best advantage. Naturally we'll shoot by candlelight.

But what am I thinking? This seems way out of my league, more Eva than Rae. There are really only two things I must have for a sex video: Jim and a shaker of martinis.

I imagine dialogue from our "movie."

Him: "I want to do this."

Her: "I want a martini."

. . . .

Just before Passover the little market on the corner of Jim's block puts the votive candles on sale for ninety-nine cents each. They are not, in fact, votive candles but Memorial "Yahrzeit" Lights and each one burns for twenty-four hours. I show Jim and he and I buy two boxes and haul them home. We store what we don't need under the sink. We laugh at the excess, at our optimism. We're set for life.

. . . .

A friend and I meet for a long-awaited lunch at Passage to India in early December. She knows I'm taking a few days off soon and I've acknowledged that I'm heading to New York to meet a new friend. I've decided to say nothing more about it.

Monique is beautiful, smart, exotic, and French. She orders wine, something I never do on lunch hour. But nothing right now is normal. I can't sleep. I can't eat. I can't relax. Enjoying a glass of red wine with Monique as we inhale the fragrances of cumin and garlic and coriander seems precisely what I should be doing at this moment. I look out the window and see snowflakes drifting to the sidewalk.

Our wine arrives. Monique's is something heady, more purple than red, more black than purple. Like mine, it's served in an overly long-stemmed glass with a deep bowl, something you want to hold with two hands to steady it as you raise the bowl up. It's chalicelike, amid this infusion of pungent aromas, though Monique grasps gracefully just where the stem joins the bowl. I think this is the epitome of elegance. She has soft dark lips and wears no lipstick or makeup. Her lips seem to twitch, utterly prehensile. They eagerly reach for and lightly grasp the edge of the thin rim. I cannot stop watching. Her eyes drop, long black lashes rest like lacy fringe on her exquisite cheekbones. Her top lip lifts almost imperceptibly and the dark liquid slides into her mouth. She sighs as she sets the glass back on the table. *Mmmmmm.*

Monique has worked in broadcasting. She speaks in a low, breathy voice, even to me, and appears to consider it key among her arsenal of devastating skills. My trembling is nonstop. She gives me chills, on top of it. She has cultivated a sensuality that looks languid, wild, in wait.

Yet this sensuality, despite the nuances and affectations, renders her terribly open, fragile, vulnerable. I find myself concerned for her well-being, at times. Yet she has a stubbornness that's childlike, innocent, and affecting. All must see this; many accede. In this way she persists beautifully.

A leonine mass of unruly black hair frames her amazing face, which stares frankly at me, an unblemished expanse of luminous white skin. Has she never been touched by sun? At this moment, though, with winter hovering and worldly concerns dispatched to the far reaches of the universe, she's a living, breathing question mark, insatiably curious about my love affair in the making. I resist her inquiries. She probes but offers little of a self-revelatory nature in return.

I sip wine, as well, even though there are meetings to go back to and even though the wine stains our lips an obscene, telltale shade of purple. Everything about this moment feels sexual—the steamy windows, the tinted lips, the Indian aromatics, the sideways glances of the proper, petite waiters, the tight clusters of traveled museum colleagues at nearby tables savoring the spiced foods, judging authenticity. I take small sips of wine and feel its effects immediately. I'm grateful for the opportunity to let down a bit physically. My all-consuming obsession—probable sex with Jim—interferes with eating and sleeping and reading. Work, intense and demanding, is the one thing that takes me out of myself.

A small Indian man dressed in a starched white shirt and black slacks serves our food in a detached and formal fashion. He's erect and polite and does not make eye contact. Monique, so openly hungry—for all the sensual pleasures in life, it appears, and so self-indulgent, has bypassed the less expensive lunch menu and ordered three entrées from the dinner menu. She spoons a little of each thing onto her plate. She asks for a second glass of wine when my order is placed before me. It's dal, pungent and hot, perched over a tiny candle. I spoon a bit onto my plate, along with long-grained, fluffy basmati rice embedded with caraway and coriander. I am having one of my favorite dishes but I cannot imagine chewing or swallowing, I'm so far gone. I want Jim, not food.

"You're not hungry?" she asks.

"I haven't had much of an appetite," I say.

"Why not?"

"I don't know." I sip wine to strangle any urge I might have to talk, to let it all out.

People enjoy Monique's company. To some, she seems flirtatious and wide-eyed, even in business, even among women. She's curvy, petite, and seems to me to be very French, with her penchant for wines—especially champagne, and cheeses, and dining out, and, now, her appetite for details of the affair.

She's had two glasses of wine in less than an hour, and she's asked our waiter to package up her leftovers. She places the linen napkin on the table and speaks frankly. "There's nothing so powerful as the state of want," she says. I'm surprised. And awed. "I envy you." She whispers the word *want,* draws out the vowel, sharply articulates the "t" and tips her water glass in my direction. "Want is torturous. And delicious."

············

Late that night, while sitting outside on my granite front steps, I tell Jim about my lunch. "I like her but I'm wary," I say. "She wants to know more and yet she has made some judgments. I sense this problem she's having with me. She says very little about her own life, prods me about mine, and, yet, she avoids me. It can't be good for me. And anyway, what is there to say?"

There is nothing to say because nothing has happened. There is a date: December 14. On December 14, I'm going to take Amtrak to NYC and visit Jim.

"My better judgment tells me to steer clear and keep my mouth shut."

"It's already too late for that," Jim says. "Believe me, everybody's talking."

SECOND THOUGHTS

CHAPTER 3

Every once in a while I slide off into *pause* mode. Everything stops, as if the body has decided to call a time-out. This happens on a Monday night in December, when I begin to feel that what I'm about to do—board an Amtrak train to see Jim in Manhattan, while leaving Eli alone and perplexed—may be too much.

I return from my writers group and look over comments made to an essay I'd written and read aloud. I page through everyone's annotated copies, go to my computer, and make the few changes we discussed, all of which make sense. By then, it's almost midnight and my eyes burn. I drop into my reading chair, too buzzed from the long day to feel tired, too spent to do anything constructive. That's when the full weight of the inertia sets in.

Everything seems so quiet at this hour, at this place, at this juncture. It's as if I, in this stupor, am a reflection of my circumstances and nothing more. Rockport in December at midnight is surreal, the very embodiment of a desertion of spirit. After the first frost, after the heat starts pumping, people go inside, lock down the storm windows, and settle in for three or four long, lonely months. The camaraderie we grow into over the summer, as we mow the lawn, pull weeds, water the garden, stroll across the street to the beach for a late afternoon swim, all falls away. In winter we are on our own.

When we emerge in 2007, things will be different. Two neighbors who come for the summers have heart attacks and another has multiple bypass surgery. A friend's cancer returns. A man throws out his back and can barely hobble from his car to his front porch. And Eli, whose struggles never seem to end, is taken away one night in late December, never to call this his home again. Neighbors watch the blinking lights of the cruisers, the stretcher being hoisted up and into the back of the ambulance, the police officer pulling closed my front door. Neighbors watch all this from their windows and wonder.

In my neighborhood, populated by Baby Boomers and the elderly, I hold my breath throughout the winter. Crocuses break the surface of the earth in late February or early March. In April or May, familiar cars pull up and the summer neighbors trickle back, thinner, older, stooped, more frail. We get used to each other all over again.

Tonight Rockport has a hollow, desolate feel. No one's allowed to park their cars on the streets at night after November 15. I feel abandoned as I look out onto emptiness. We are nudged inside and into hibernation. I sit in my chair and listen. All I hear are the wind and the waves and the echoes of waves.

I am in limbo, waiting for Jim, waiting for December 14, waiting for the waiting to be over with. This is *pause* mode. I sit and listen.

Eli heads upstairs to meditate. The two cats, Boo and Lila, follow, the sounds of their paws on the stairs to the attic rooms giving up their identities. Boo is lighter on his feet than Lila, but together they sound like a herd of horses racing upstairs. When Eli sits, they always settle down beside him.

At first I do not wonder about anything, not the fate of my life with Eli, my cats, my job, my beloved oceanfront home in this sweet little community that I think of as my safe place. In *pause* mode, I'm squarely in the moment. Nor is my love affair with Jim a question for me, at least not yet. He feels exactly right.

But why did it have to take this long? That is the question, though I'm too caught up in the moment to rue all the hardships and heartbreaks that came before.

I don't belabor what is—that it's taken fifty-eight years to get here. This is hardly the time for regrets. I have grown. My courage is more readily accessible, which means I can make wiser decisions. I'm fifty-eight but my range of motion, metaphorically speaking, has never been better. I reach high for this man.

Soon. Soon. Soon I will have my arms around him.

This is all that matters now as I pause between work and writing and sleep, between what has come before and what will be.

To some of my friends, I'm Pauline. In one man's thinking, I don't have a life, I have perils. He gives me the key to his apartment in case I must flee. He feels it isn't safe to be around Eli. I take the key, grateful. Once I am forced to use it.

A new, slower, richer, deeper life is coming. I don't want to blame any of the long struggle on my mother, whose mantra—"I wish you were never born"—stymied my self-worth. I hesitate to even think of her in this context, since her extreme behavior distracts from this love story. But it's important to acknowledge that many of us have to bushwhack our own way in life and in love. And I don't want to give too much credence to the violence in my household that so often sent me out my bedroom window late at night and into the bushes, where I cowered till dawn. Fear is still my first response to almost anything, bad or good, and I'm afraid now. That's okay, says Mitch, the man I visit when I need to talk something through. You invoke courage when necessity surpasses fear. You are courageous, he says. You are going to try this experiment. You are choosing yourself.

He's right. I'm doing it.

It's often hard to accept who we are. Mitch once told me I was a miracle. What? Isn't that better left unsaid? Yet the notion puts my life in context. It lays out the situation. I have to own that my most hard-won accomplishment is my survival. For most of my friends, survival is a given, a fact of their existence, their starting place. I am worlds apart. I am always about survival.

If you live believing you're endangered, your capacity for gratitude is immense. Every second is a second of life you weren't counting on, a second that you may not feel you deserve.

Once, early on, Jim calls me to say hi and check in. Just as we're about to hang up, I tell him, "Thanks for calling."

He says, "Don't do that!"

"Do what?" Appreciate the effort? Be happy that someone loves me?

"Don't say *thank you*." He's angry.

I decide to ignore this about him. I'm appreciative of the effort and the intent, and I like to express my gratitude. There are people like me. I've heard them in markets, at the theater, in doctors' offices. They say, "Thank you so much," but what they're really saying is "Your efforts on my behalf mean more to me than I can possibly express."

Gratitude for small considerations such as phone calls implies weakness. Jim wants me to expect consideration and maybe, even, demand it. He likes it best when I'm mean or tough or arbitrary and he jokingly associates it with my colorful Mexican father and our lively heritage. He even has a name for that feisty part of me: Spic Bitch.

"Thank you," I say, after he opens a door for me.

"Cut that out," he says.

"Fuck you," I say. I figured out I can be both—grateful and a bitch.

. . . .

I was seventeen when I ran away for good. I took two record albums—Dave Brubeck and the Mamas and the Papas—a book-length poem and a novel I'd written, and a small field guide to North American butterflies. These were touchstones, items that connected me with myself, with my joy. I went from Santa Barbara to Florida and hid from my mother. "Don't ever think you can run away from me. I'll track you down." But she did not.

My gratitude explodes when I find Jim. There are more thankyous in me than grains of sand on Front Beach. I like everything about this man. A surprise is in store for me, however. It's not long before I realize that, in fact, I don't have to work that hard to reach for him.

Jim calls me three times a day. He knows just what to do. I'm relaxed about his goodness and commitment from the start. Early on he says to friends of mine in my presence and possibly for my benefit, "I'm true blue."

In December, Jim and I are relative strangers to each other. But he's responsible to this experiment. He feeds it what's necessary for the best possible outcome, whatever that may be. He works hard at this, but like so many of the most gifted, he makes it look easy.

As I so often do in my meditations, I leave the moment and roam everywhere. I catch myself and go back to my breath, to the silence, to the inventory of my blessings. I realize that I love Rockport when it's quiet like this. I love the emptiness. I love the openness. These are the attributes I try to absorb as I gather the energy to stand up, switch off the rest of the lights, climb the stairs to my attic bedroom, persist in the plan to wheel my suitcase through the corridors of South Station and through Penn Station, where Jim will be waiting.

As I ascend to the third floor, the temperature drops a good twenty degrees. The top floor is unheated and uninsulated, and the cold presses in from all directions. I undress quickly, shivering, and wrestle the heavy down comforter up to my ears. In just a few minutes, I'm completely warmed. I can count on this, just as I can count on Lila, who leaves Eli when she hears me, and comes into my bed. She crawls under the covers and presses her little body against mine. I fall asleep to the soft vibration of her purr.

. . . .

Lust at fifty-eight isn't much different from lust at seventeen. That's unfortunate, because a giddy fifty-eight-year-old isn't pretty, especially to her twentysomething assistant, who visibly cringes whenever Jim calls my work phone and I giggle at his jokes. I know I should get a grip, but it's hard. I'm utterly happy. Impossibly smitten.

I romanticize the simpatico I feel with Jim. When we're on the phone together, my body hums, his voice ringing through me like harmonics. Music is what I crave, in fact, because it corresponds with my energy. I wear out my iPod and have to get another one. I have close to two thousand songs and create over one hundred new playlists in just the first three months of our affair: After the Rain, First Crocus, Holiday Tree Up in the Square, Hudson River Run, Run Fast, Houston Slog, Marathon in the Morning, Early Morning Train Home. These are heart-bending times and being fifty-eight doesn't seem to make it any less inelegant. Give me rock 'n' roll. The louder, the better. My bright young assistant gives me CDs with eighty-six songs she knows I've never heard—techno, classical, Japanese folk, alternative. She wants to expand my horizons, show me the world doesn't stop with Led Zeppelin, that lovers can swoon just as passionately over Devendra Banhart as Freddie Mercury.

Every day feels like Thanksgiving, my favorite holiday. I think of the bounty on that one day, the permission we're given to do what I do best—to express our appreciation for all that we have, the carefully cultivated appetites to accommodate the eating rituals. Jim is the Thanksgiving dinner of my life, the bounty I am so ready to gorge on and give thanks for. This is how it is for me. Every minute. Thank you, thank you universe, for the possibility of Jim.

. . . .

As my trip to New York approaches, I try to avoid thinking about the lies. Little about my life is righteous right now, despite whatever high-minded notions I might have at the beginning about being honest, telling Jim the truth, not resorting to makeup, being naked figuratively and literally. This is illicit, after all. There are the lies you tell others. There are the lies you tell yourself.

A lie is already embedded in the early pages of this accounting.

It's not true that I never noticed Jim *in that way*. We ate and drank together on several occasions, sometimes just Eli, Jim, and I. Once he came to my home for Thanksgiving and slept in a room on the second floor directly above my bed. I remember going up one morning to see what his nest might look like. Nothing! There was no trace of him, not an item out of place or left behind to indicate that he'd even been there.

How could I not notice him, someone taller and broader and bigger than I, someone so full of opinions and emotion and passion? I say I didn't see him only because I couldn't have him or even approach him. He was verboten, which is not the same as invisible.

Once Eli and I borrowed Jim's apartment so I could attend a conference for authors and journalists in Manhattan. To accommodate us, Jim offered to stay with his girlfriend Ruth in her Manhattan apartment.

Jim opens the door for us when we arrive. We pour in with all our bags and our load of untamed hyperness. We came by Amtrak. Eli had some very bad moments in the subway at Penn Station because he couldn't get the hang of running his MetroCard through the slot at the turnstile. When a man took it from him and slid the card, Eli exploded in a rage. He felt inadequate and lashed out. Then, of course, he had to go find the man and apologize. The fact that the man was an African American MTA worker made the guilt that much worse for Eli.

Thus our chaotic arrival at Jim's apartment. Jim's all business, having no doubt sensed something. He says hello, gives us a tour, grabs his duffel bag, and leaves, literally shutting the door on Eli's percolating agitation.

That night while lying with Eli in Jim's bed, I cannot sleep. Here I am—in Jim's apartment. Who is this man I have dinner with twice a year?

I squint into the darkness to see a row of extra-large starched shirts hanging on a long rod underneath long, horizontal bookshelves. There are two very pretty stained-glass lampshades Jim made earlier in his career, one overhead and one at his bedside. One is a gorgeous jumble of pink, purple, and blue pansies. Another looks like clusters of grapes. It's asymmetrical, with uneven edges, and I admire the interesting lines and the artistry. Lots of books line the two wall-to-wall bookshelves. His grandfather owned and ran a small Midwestern newspaper and I believe I can see that Jim is somehow a product of that inquisitive, observant, prodding mind-set. The authors he reads are of like kind, as well—Alice Miller, Noam Chomsky, Mollie Ivins, Bertrand Russell, Alan Dershowitz, Malcolm X. There's a television across the room and a small stereo system.

I treat Jim as if he's of no interest to me and I'm of no interest to him—two cardboard cutouts that go through the motions over mediocre Thai food ordered in at Ruth's place. I never want to open myself to him but it happens anyway, despite my resolve, as I lie in his bed, take note of the artifacts that describe his interests and passions. I am in the thick of Jim.

There's a small bottle on one shelf—Orange Motion. I get up and smell. Yummy, like an orange creamsicle. The bottle is greasy. I realize it's probably to use while masturbating. Or is it for Ruth? Does she come here? Doubtful, I think. I suspect the place is too disorganized for her. I squeeze some Orange Motion onto my fingers before I put the bottle back on the shelf. I've never used a lubricant before. It feels warm and silky and it tastes like a creamsicle.

Jim is becoming more action figure than paper doll, more three- than two-dimensional as I poke around. I find myself remembering little things about him, like the time he went to a Bradshaw workshop in Boston. He was overcome at lunch as he told Eli and me about his cathartic morning. Another time he called me late one night in my motel room to tell me that he'd just heard from Eli and that Eli was threatening suicide. And over the years, Eli would fill me in on Jim's status: married, divorced, dating. I begin to feel his drive and sense his energy. I begin to note the scope and scale of his world.

I get back in bed and watch Eli as I do so. He's sound asleep on his back just inches away from where I lie. Something's changed in my perception of Jim. I decide to make a little room for him, allow him in a bit.

To begin with, instead of the usual stiff hug and peck on the cheek when he opens the door to Ruth's apartment at dinner tomorrow night, I'll just reach for him, lay my hands lightly on his biceps, pause as I angle my face up to his, stand on my toes, kiss his cheek close to his lips. I'll hold right there, just a second or two longer than he expects, than is common practice.

The first payoff in this micro-fantasy is the look I see on his face. His hazel eyes widen. His smile drops off. Our faces are just inches apart when he's caught and silenced in that paralytic half-a-moment of surprise. He likes surprises. I hover on tiptoes just one-tenth of a second more. It has to feel ambiguous. Right then Jim pauses to consider the new world of possibilities. His eyes smile again and I step back, out of range.

My body is hot. A hot flash maybe. Even so, getting hot and sweating in bed is Pavlovian, a total turn-on. I can feel my heart beating deep in my vagina. With Eli lying right beside me, this could be a sad feeling. I won't reach for him because that part of our life is behind us. But I like this feeling and know it leads to the very best, most intense orgasms. It's a shame to waste it.

My fingers, wet with the scented oil, slip between my legs. I bend my knees. I think of Jim lying there instead of Eli, watching this. I am suddenly so sure he'd like to watch. I don't intend this, but I have an orgasm almost immediately. I can feel contractions all the way up into my uterus. Caught by surprise, I'm unprepared and disoriented. Am I moving too much? Am I making noise? It's like I'm inside a drum. My heartbeat pounds hard in my ears, in my cheeks, in my vagina. I can't hear a thing. Please god, I pray, don't let me cry out.

Did I just do that? Have an orgasm with Jim's Orange Motion in Jim's bed? I giggle and Eli grunts, "What's so funny?"

"Nothing," I say. "You must be dreaming."

The second payoff, the best of all payoffs, is the faint odor of musk and citrus that I leave behind for Jim. I want this, want him to know me this way and this way only: By how I smell in the night in the dark between his sheets. The thought of it, of him undressing and slipping into bed, sniffing the sheets, wondering about me, is almost more than I can stand.

Only in my fantasies about Jim do I have the upper hand like this.

* * * * * * * * * * * *

I've rehearsed this moment a million times in my mind, it seems. It's finally here. At 1:20 PM on December 14, I interrupt the meeting and remind the eleven men and two women gathered around the table in the large conference room that I must leave. People nod politely and go back to the discussion, and I slip out. Finally finally finally I am on my way to Jim.

It goes as planned and yet it doesn't. The meeting, deemed by me and the head of IT services to be very important to the museum, heats up the minute my boss enters the room. He's twenty minutes late and I'd sent people everywhere to find him. He sits and listens for less than a minute before he begins criticizing the ideas he thinks he's hearing.

We're discussing large-capacity data storage and before I know it, he turns and takes aim at me. I argue back because I have to. This issue is important but the combativeness must be a drag for the techies and deputy directors at the table. Finally one of the deputy directors has mercy on me and puts a stop to my boss by saying, "I agree with Rae." By then, though, my white blouse and black slacks are drenched in sweat for the first of what will be several times before the day is out.

Eventually my boss catches on and argues brilliantly for exactly what we advocate—a safe, backed-up way to store all our digital materials, in particular the thousands of photographs of works of art, considered works of art in their own right. Things settle down and we dig into the complicated details.

My boss is aware of my planned leave-taking. I stand, walk over to get my suitcase, put on my suit jacket, and head for the door. Then my boss stands and approaches. He hugs me and wishes me a good trip in front of everyone. I'm dumbstruck but play along. It's staged drama but for him there's sincerity in his well wishes. I'm his nemesis. My presence galls him. Once he screamed that I was the biggest problem he had at PEM. Since he has no grounds on which to fire me, he'd like nothing better than for me to ditch Eli, fall in love, get married, and move away.

I thank him, he holds the door for me, and I pass through the museum office center reception area. I hear my boss resume talking as the conference room doors close behind me and I walk away from that meeting and from that museum.

Outside I encounter a gloriously sunny afternoon. It's seventy-six degrees—unheard of in mid-December in New England. I traverse the brick-lined pedestrian walkway, the wheels of the suitcase clacking behind me. It's happy noise. At Washington Street in downtown Salem, I turn right onto smooth sidewalks. Holiday banners and festive windows are simply surreal in this heat wave.

Five minutes later I descend two flights of stairs to the Salem commuter rail train station, where I wait for the train that takes me to North Station. The trip is like an obstacle course where it's not just your body and your psychology but your luggage that you have to wield from one challenge to the next, from hoisting bags up and down endless flights of urine-soaked subway stairs, dragging stuff along cobblestone streets, timing the various train trips so you make it to the finish line. At any juncture along the way, the ambivalent person could easily turn and go home.

But I keep on, lust on overdrive. No idea, really, where I'm going. Or even if I'm going to something rather than away from something.

Sometimes we close our eyes and let faith take over and this is what I think I've done. Faith in Jim. Or is it faith in the new? Faith in change?

From the inhospitable North Station, where commuter comforts are few and filthy, I take the Orange and then the Red Line to South

Station in Boston. There I get my ticket from one of the automatic kiosks, buy a *New York Times,* a cup of coffee, and some "chocolate orgasm" brownies from Rosie's Bakery kiosk for Jim. Even if he doesn't like brownies he should appreciate the renowned confection for its name. If the sex falls flat I can always hand him a brownie and say "You can't say I didn't give you an orgasm."

Finally it's time to board the Acela to Penn Station. If all goes as planned, I'll see Jim around six that evening.

For the next five hours I torture myself with one idea: You can still turn back.

. . . .

South Station, Back Bay, Route 128. At the Providence stop we have to wait a few minutes because we're a bit ahead of schedule. I leave my seat and walk into the vestibule where I've stored my suitcase. What was I thinking? I can't do this. I can't take all my clothes off for a man I hardly know, a man who happens to be the good friend of my significant other for the last eighteen years. Shit. What if I don't like the way he kisses? What if he has herpes, like so many of my friends who took full advantage of the sexual revolution? What if he needs Viagra? He's sixty-seven after all. Does that mean hours of boring fucking to get the most out of the pricey hard-on? Shit. Shit. Shit.

You'll love this sea and roiling around in it also.

Of course.

I step out onto the platform and breathe in fresh air. Slowly, in and out. Count ten breaths and start again.

Better.

I look around and notice that I'm feeling more myself, more grounded. It's not that the second thoughts aren't there; they're just more acceptable. Why shouldn't I have second thoughts? Second thoughts are choices disguised as anxiety. And women of my generation recognize the value of choices. We can choose our men. And we can choose to opt out. It's up to us. To me.

All I have to do, I tell myself, is reach inside, grab my stuff, and walk into the Providence train station. An Amtrak train heading north will come by before too long and I can just end this ridiculous drama. I have refrained from ageist thinking but I succumb, finally, as a last-ditch effort to save myself from what will surely create tremendous emotional havoc for me, not to mention Jim. I give myself permission to say the words: I'm too damn old for this.

The conductor approaches me. "You'd better take your seat now."

I look at him and nod. As I step back onto the vestibule he yells "All aboard" and follows me in. Behind us the automatic door slides closed and locks.

Next stop: New Haven in an hour and a half. No problem. I can always duck out there.

. . . .

The Acela eases out of the station with the gentle clip-clop of a horse-drawn carriage. I look out at the faces of the people left behind on the platform. Their eyes fix on nothing, in that posture of waiting we all know so well. A man in a suit appears relaxed. He rests his briefcase on the ground and reaches into his vest pocket. I expect to see a cell phone but what he pulls out is a folded handkerchief. He sneezes. A woman sits down on her suitcase, legs spread for balance, and there's enough time for all of us on this side of the Quiet Car to look up her skirt, note the pink panties, develop ideas about her immodesty. Another man drains a bottle of water and tosses it effortlessly into a trash barrel across the platform. Despite their small, inconsequential creature-comfort adjustments, these travelers are detached, disengaged from the ear-splitting whine of the engines, the stench of diesel, the snaking train dragging away its booty. Faces on my side of the glass look back at them, needing to read every twitch, every shift, every bored blink. They give us nothing. Expressionless. It's so hard to read a traveler's face. They wear flat, protective masks that conceal a load of vulnerabilities: disorientation, hunger, thirst, sleepiness, perhaps some extended family crisis that rushes them from the dinner table to a city to the west. Humans hide so much. What will I see in Jim's face when I first catch sight of him at Penn Station? What will he see in mine? Will we find intimacy or will we just fuck?

It could go either way, of course. What I'm about to discover is that there are alternatives to the anticipated scenario that I couldn't have imagined.

The faces on the long Providence platform blur as we pick up speed. What I see now is one face, an amalgamation of inscrutability. A Buddha gazes back at me, serene and motionless. I don't know what to think.

We lurch. There is a cowboy driving this train. He wants to play and we fly past marshes and sandy beaches and abandoned osprey nests and the shock of blooming forsythia in this aberrant December heat wave. He's got us at full tilt now, 150 miles an hour—full throttle!—and I am scared by the unexpected acceleration of my journey. I'm not ready! I lie back into my seat and feel myself plummeting, out of control. Jim says once, when I lament the risks in this love affair: "Enjoy the free fall."

But I have everything to lose.

. . . .

The night before I leave for this trip, I watch scenes from an old episode of *Boston Legal* in which Brad turns to Denise for kissing lessons. The whole thing's absurd but I don't care. I hardly pay attention because I'm drinking a glass of wine, paging through the latest issue of *The New Yorker*—which notes a Tiffany exhibition at the Metropolitan Museum of Art that I will see with Jim sometime during our weekend together— and occasionally petting Lila, who burrows into my lap to stay warm.

Eli is away at his meditation group, I've finished packing, and I just want to zone out. I don't watch television but I rent DVDs, which I save for weekends. But this night is special so I pop in the disk and relax.

The episode is from late in the second season and, of course, I have no idea that I'm going to see two people conduct kissing lessons. The young, blond lawyers embrace and Denise begins her tutorial. Make contact with this middle part of her tongue, she instructs Brad. It's the most sensitive part.

Really?

Well, how would I know? It's been years. And anyway, who parses the mechanics of the kiss?

Denise does, in a version of kiss-and-tell.

Kiss. Discuss. Kiss. Discuss.

I perk up, dump the cat, toss the magazine, gulp the wine. I study Denise. She's into it. This could be me, tomorrow night. Wow. This is hot. This is wet and erotic and real.

I replay the scene and think, I want some of that.

. . . .

So much, if not all, of my anticipation about Jim comes to bear on that perfect second when the kiss begins. I imagine this scene a million times in a million different ways. How much time do I waste on a recurring daydream having to do with the dynamics of lips aligning in slow motion? I justify my sexual fantasies with fact: Men think about sex at least once every two minutes. Or at least that's what I was told in the sixth grade in a filmstrip that our teacher, Miss Hanson, played for us in that momentous lesson when the words *penis, menstruation,* and *vagina* were officially inserted into our lexicon.

So that's what those notes sent home to parents in sealed envelopes were all about.

The film scared the hell out of us girls and introduced us to a shocking world that tipped some heretofore perfect balance. Life had turned irrevocably unfair. Girls have periods. Boys have. . . . What do boys have? We girls raised our hands and implored—What do boys have for god's sake—already sensing the conspiracy, the injustice of biblical proportions.

A nurse was there and to appease our mounting agitation, she smiled and said: Wet dreams. Boys have burdensome, messy, uncontrollable wet dreams. And they fantasize. A lot. Every two minutes to be exact.

We, on the other hand, bleed. And it hurts.

That was before Alex Comfort clued us in to *The Joy of Sex*. Women, come to find out, want it, too. But they like something called foreplay and that includes fantasy, exotic oils, candles, and lots of kissing. They want to note the feel of lips touching lips. They want to bookmark that hungry look in his eyes as it starts to happen. They want to register the sensation of middle tongue against middle tongue, push and suck, push and push back.

They want to turn to the premature ejaculator and announce: Now it's my turn.

For those boys/men, it's about how to get that penis lodged in good and tight with a minimum of fuss. For me, it's about how the start of a kiss is the end of thinking.

* * * * * * * * * * * *

One night, after much lovemaking, Jim kisses me. It's a postcoital moment and I appreciate that he takes the time for this. I'm on my back, spent, and semiconscious. He's on his side, propped up on one elbow, saying something. As always, I want to tell him thank you, how wonderful it all was, you are the one, the master, the man, on and on. And as always, nothing much comes out but sounds of swooning, little sighs and half-smiles because I'm still back there, on the orgasm. For as long as I can, I relive the way it all happened. Him making it happen. It took time. Was nothing sudden. I felt it coming for minutes—a slow slow building up of want and pressure and anxiety and something else about him and that scary insistence he has—a boring down as he does this to me.

He reads me so well. He's in my skin, somehow, right there with me, riding the contractions in my vagina as if it's that roiling sea. And more. It's as if it's his vagina, his breasts, his clitoris. I sometimes wonder about this. I wonder, did he spend inordinate amounts of time role-playing his mother or his kindergarten girlfriend? Where does he get this real time sense of me, of what my vagina wants next?

In lovemaking, I often develop this profound curiosity. His mouth and tongue are doing something to my clitoris. What? What is he doing that feels this good? I put my hands on his head, his mouth, I shove my fingers up alongside his tongue, feel his lips move from my clitoris to my fingers. I want to know but he quits with my hand, shoves it away, and fastens his mouth back on my clitoris. His fingers are in my vagina, now, pushing out, making me feel like I'm going to explode. It's almost unbearable, a mix of fear and anticipation and intolerable pressure from deep inside.

My orgasm goes on and on, with shock waves afterward. A day later and I'm still there, living it. Can't take my hands off him still. He's done, though. Finished with me. "Fuck addled" is what he says I am and he laughs.

That night, after we finish making love, he rests on his elbow and he watches me. He's proud of himself, I realize. "You want to see how I do it?" he asks. I nod and get another kind of kiss. He puts his lips on mine, sticks the hardened tip of his tongue against mine, pushes in and out. He sucks on my upper lip. I move my vagina tight against his thigh and suddenly I'm coming all over again.

· · · · · · · · · · · ·

A beautiful young woman with gorgeous red stiletto heels and a luscious black silk suit returns to her seat from the club car. She's just across the aisle from me. I nod and smile. She sets a small cardboard box containing a bag of pretzels and a half-liter of red wine on the tray table beside her. She sips the wine as she examines spreadsheets on her laptop. I want wine, too.

. . . .

My phone is on vibrate and I feel it buzzing in my pocket. I check the number and see that it's my friend Mary, who I plan to see on this four-day weekend. I walk out of the Quiet Car, back into the vestibule, and answer. She tells me her husband of ten years has just walked out. Just then. And for good. He said he had never wanted this marriage with her, that their life together was a farce, that he never wanted to see or speak with her again. Do not call. Do not email. Do not try to contact me. I want a divorce.

This is not happening, I think in a panic. Mary and Peter, just thirty years old, have a perfect marriage. They are both beautiful, young, talented. He's a poet and an actor. She's an artist, a curator, and a teacher at the New School. They live interesting lives in Greenwich Village. They took big risks to move to New York City from Boston, to explore and to reach as high as they could, as far as they could. They had no idea for what.

I am too shocked to console. She is too hurt to notice. She talks for an hour. Good god. I don't want to know this about men, about the ways love can hurt people, about endings as brutal as this. I just want to be happy today. I want to stay blind and ignorant and in the dark as I blast my way south. God save Mary. God help me.

NO SHOW

....

CHAPTER 4

This is free fall. It's where people like me, people with a penchant for control, never choose to go. In free fall, you cleave to the moment. There are no expectations to live up to, no ideas about the future to dictate next moves, no to-do list to give the days and nights to come a structure. Question: Are there days and nights to come? I have absolutely no understanding of what's next. I have to just be. I am not the type.

Free fall goes like this: Jim's not here. It takes me fifteen or twenty minutes to get it. He hasn't come to Penn Station to pick me up as he said he would. He's nowhere.

I'm being stood up. In the heart of New York City an abandoned older woman stands befuddled, clutching the handle of a beat-up suitcase, carrying little more than pocket change and, what's absolutely horrifying, this older woman, her thinking muddled by weeks of sexual fantasizing—has no place to sleep. I'm feeling homeless, lost, frozen in place.

I'm sure he said he'd meet me outside Penn Station at the corner of 31st Street and 8th Avenue so that's where I wait, borrowed luggage at my side, a mute cell phone asleep in my hip pocket.

I assess the situation. I'm at the southwest entrance to Penn Station. It's a concrete expanse reaching from the bank of doors behind me out into the busy intersection. It's made to resemble a plaza with a few small evergreens in concrete pots that double as barriers to vehicles bearing bombs.

Where is he?

It feels like an island. And here I am, stranded. This can't be happening.

Cars, primarily yellow cabs, spin around me clockwise, speeding east to west and south to north. There are buses, too, and rows of double-parked vans. It's a din. Honking horns, buses shifting gears, delivery trucks braking noisily, people shouting. To my immediate left a staircase descends from the sidewalk to the subway below. Hordes of people, just getting off work, periodically spill out, adding to the confusion.

I look around. Maybe Jim's coming up from the subway. From behind me at Penn Station. From one of those parked cars to the right. From a cab to my left. Maybe he's on foot, walking to meet me. But from which direction?

And why hasn't he called?

I can't hear beyond the din. Would I even know if my cell phone rang? I can't find a method to systematically track individual cars and their drivers in this glut of cranky traffic. This is a problem because I don't know what kind of car he drives or where he lives in relation to Penn Station.

Damn. Who can breathe this air? It's a noxious stench: hot, metallic exhaust; ripe urine; body odor that smells more like rotting rodents than anything human. Even the rats must get lung cancer here. And from every direction people bump against me as they rush in and out of the station. There's no logical place to stand and I start to think I'm not meant to be here at all. Free fall is disorienting. It's the tearing away of everything you know. I'm upside down. Or not. I'm nauseated. I'm excited.

I do this thing called Stop Thought. You just stop thinking. I will my usual host of fears—little terrorist anxieties forever gnawing away at my resolve—to back off, to stay the fuck away. This is the tug of war I've been at now for weeks. I win simply by persisting.

Of course I could call Jim but of course I don't. It's not an option. Either he calls me in the next fifteen minutes or I go away forever.

I sidle up to my new best friend, one of the concrete planters, and let myself lean back and relax. The good news is that I'm finally here. I'm on a busy street corner in downtown Manhattan. I could be having a love affair or I could just be here on this corner, waiting for the next thing to happen. I'd intended to meet with friends, go to a gallery opening, see an exhibition at the Met, but I made no firm plans. No matter what, the weekend will be new and different because, for the first time in two decades, I am entirely on my own and I haven't a clue what will happen next.

Men and women pour out of Penn Station, briefcases and suit jackets in tow. Everybody is smiling. The warm weather is an unexpected gift. We're in the midst of the holiday season. Christmas trees are for sale on street corners and the warm weather has uncorked the balsam perfume, which rides atop that nasty funk. Young men weave in and out of traffic on their Pedi cabs and bicycles.

For a while, the stream of people preoccupies me. A woman thinks I'm from the city and wants to know the cross streets. I can't help, but we end up chatting about this surprise of a night. If she only knew.

Someone else offers me a free bottle of Vitamin Water, which I take and drink. There are free newspapers, too. Another man has a flier for me, something about eyebrow threading. I don't want this.

I get into watching a couple of police officers over by some concrete barriers on 31st Street. They're very animated. They chat and laugh and occasionally glance around as if looking for someone, perhaps their boss. They look like a waste of taxpayer money, so I approach them and ask, "Is this the west corner of Penn Station?" knowing full well that it is. They nod simultaneous yeses and turn right back to each other and their conversation.

Oh well. Just five more minutes before I go away forever, whatever that means. I cannot exist in a to-do-less state. I cannot just be, like a fetus in utero, where the only job is to grow lungs cell by cell and make hair, in my case, lots of it, and put on weight. My to-do item for now is to start action, to unfreeze, to summon the courage to leave. I do a stop thought on the fetus. No way will I get into any hackneyed birth metaphors. Free fall is bad enough.

My cell phone rings but it's only Eli sounding lonely. Just fuck off, I think. I give him my flat voice and say I'll call him later. Aye, poor man; but I can't think about him right now.

The clock has ticked down. Jim has less than two minutes left when he calls. I'm glad I don't answer with my flat voice because he has bad news. He's in the ER at some hospital with his son, who has an acute migraine. They're calling it a migraine but nothing they try works. The pain is so bad that he's hallucinating. I wonder, is he having a stroke?

Jim cannot leave his son, of course, so I must get to the apartment alone. He tells me he knows I can do this. He's left a key for me at the concierge station and he's told them to assist me in any way I need. He'll call me later. Goodbye.

I just stand there, incredulous. I think maybe I should go back down and catch the next train home. That would work best for Jim, who has his hands full. But he calls thirty seconds later to tell me everything is going to be okay.

I've had enough of Penn Station, though it takes me a while to do the simplest thing—hail a cab. Just hilarious. But the fact is, I don't know how. I watch others, get up the courage, and go ask for a ride. There are plenty at this time and place. I simply walk over, get in, and give the driver Jim's address.

The traffic isn't moving. The driver tells me he has to turn around and I say never mind then. Go ahead to 5th Avenue. I'll stop by my sister-in-law Susan's gallery opening, one of the main reasons I'd picked this day to come to Manhattan. I'll figure out what to do with my suitcase once I'm at the gallery.

We head uptown, which is overaccessorized for the holiday shoppers. This is fun! My apprehension lifts. Joyful associations from childhood, like certain aromas that take you back, trigger this welcome change of attitude. Oh my god, I say over and over to the cheery cabdriver, who's regaling me with stories of his cab misadventures. Everything is fantastic, like I'm inside a snow globe full of glitter. The whole place sparkles—the white lights, the holiday trees, the storefronts, people's smiles. It's just a few days before Christmas and when he swings around and drops me at 5th Avenue, I hop out and join the mob. In this moment, there's no war, no Darfur, no friend back home with breast cancer that has spread to her bones and lungs. No Eli telling me as I leave the house that he wishes he could come, too.

So what if Jim stands me up?

When I arrive at the gallery, a young woman immediately welcomes me and disappears with my jacket and my suitcase. Another woman steps up and asks if I'd like a glass of wine. We squeeze through three large and crowded gallery rooms, surrounded on all sides by Susan's works of art. The party's been going on for some time, it's clear by the ramped-up volume. In the small back workroom we finally come to, I see a banged-up worktable covered with open bottles of wine. What the hell? I push through a bunch of people, find a bottle with some wine left in it, fill a plastic glass with something white, and cocoon myself in the fog of inebriation. It happens instantly.

Just like on the street below, the gallery is packed with handsome people. As I walk around, I fixate on their stylish haircuts and gorgeous shoes. Where do you go to get these things? How much do you pay? In New England we wear Merrells, debate the merits of the various pull-on ice cleats, and compare hat hair, achieved with the regular use of wind-block polar fleece beanies and berets. We have Malden Mills and Polartec. New York has Tim Gunn and *Vogue* and fashion shows.

Though I know Susan's art well, this exhibition of large canvases catches me by surprise. It's affecting and I grow excited as I move from piece to piece. Many art museums including the Met have purchased her work. While I was at the Museum of Fine Arts in Boston, she was invited to judge the annual alumni and student art exhibition. Afterward, we had dinner in Boston and she spoke of her husband, Eli's younger brother, and Eli, and how alike they are. This surprises me since Eli is bipolar and his brother has often taken great issue with Eli and his behavior.

I get high from Susan's art. It's part alcohol, part Jim, part me feeling free and alive, but mostly I'm captivated by the art, filled up with Susan and what she creates. I vow to examine each piece before I leave because, suddenly, this art is all that matters right now.

Wow. Over and over. Wow. Art beheld afresh, outside of the somber museum setting, taken with wine, shared with family.

Almost the entire show is made up of self-portraits; many are nudes. Susan's body is never quite the same in any painting, all of which are disturbing in the way they skew reality. Shadows are imperceptibly misplaced. One arm is just slightly longer than the other. Facial muscles stretch the mouth into a grimace that suggests pain. A right hand twists into a claw. Eyes seem to focus on things you hope you never see.

I look around. People sip wine from plastic cups and chat with each other. If the art is troubling, they don't show it. I turn and watch Susan for a few minutes. She's cropped her hair close to her head and put on a short black dress. She's transformed herself from flannel-clad painter atop a six-foot scaffold to a bit of a belle. Is she on speed? She's so giddy, so talkative. As Jim would say, she's turned on. For good reason. People are jammed into this space, taking her work very seriously.

She takes hold of a man's arm and they begin to chat. He says something that must be very funny because she opens her mouth, tilts her head slightly upward, and lets out a loud laugh. The word *guffaw* comes to mind and I conclude that this is hard, hard work. When she twists her head around to greet another guest, I catch sight of the long thick scar that crosses the nape of her neck and disappears down her back. The line marks the place where the surgeons parted skin and muscle, moved a shoulder out of the way, and extracted a large tumor at the base of her brain sixteen months ago. This five-year retrospective of odd emaciated bodies culminates here, at the place where Susan's own methods of stitching bodies and psyches display themselves on life-size canvases.

Susan sees me and comes over to say hello. Leonard and Eli's common attributes is a theme she reprises with fervor again tonight. She draws me into the back room, where she balances on a pile of boxed catalogs. She wants to talk about Leonard, his brother Eli, and their mother. I look behind her at the people lined up, waiting to congratulate her, and realize that this night, like so many she's done like it, must seem very surreal to her. She's desperate for grounding.

Jim calls every fifteen or twenty minutes. I step into the corridor to talk because many of Eli's relatives are at this show, including his mother. Jim tells me his son is no better. They've given him morphine and even that hasn't helped. I tell Jim where I am and he says he's happy that I'm having a good time. He sounds strong and positive and centered. Once again I begin to believe in the idea of Jim.

I spend time with Eli's relatives before I say goodbye and retrieve my suitcase. Eli's cousin asks me if I'd like to spend the night at her home in the Village. She seems confused by my leaving, by the absence of Eli. I say no thank you, I've got plans. I am very fond of these people. And I already know they will never want to see me again after this night. Some will hate me. I look at all of them, happy, laughing, gathering around Eli's mother as the night comes to a close. The opening was well attended. It has been a success on that level. I want to hold on to this.

When I finally leave, I begin to face facts. I must go to Jim's apartment on my own, get the concierge to let me in, and wait for a man I barely know, have never kissed like Denise and Brad do on *Boston*

Legal, and who I must lie beside undressed without the advantage of talk or wine or foreplay. I begin to forget what Jim looks like. He is transformed by my new anxieties, a stranger.

Across from where Jim lives is a diner called Moonstruck. I walk in still dragging my suitcase behind me and take a seat. Jim's probably called me five or six times by now and he knows I'm here, getting something to eat. I want wine and order a cup of pea soup since I haven't eaten in what seems like days.

A man brings wine and water right away. I reach for the glass like it's a lifeline and consider the possibility that I'm drinking too much. So what? I look up and there's Jim, standing at the door.

We're more than friends even if we're strangers. We're would-be lovers who've talked about sex and written about sex in our emails. It's okay to give me a passionate kiss but he doesn't. It's small, discreet, on the fence. I'm disappointed because I still don't know, without the kiss, whether I belong here or whether I've made a horrible mistake.

He walks me back to the apartment, brings me into his bedroom, shows me where everything is, and then leaves. His son is still in great pain and no one knows what's wrong. Of course he has to return to the hospital. Of course I'll be just fine. . . .

• • • • • • • • • • • •

Early one Wednesday evening in the spring I arrive at Jim's apartment. We've been lovers for four months and there are already some rituals we've established around our coming together again after our usual two- or three-week separation. These rituals involve food and drink and talking and laughing and, eventually, sex.

So we sit on his bed, still dressed and nervous and ill at ease. We toast, in this case it's a French beaujolais we purchased together minutes before, and we nibble on cheese and crackers. On this night, the ritual is protracted. I can't allow Jim to come near me quite yet. Eli is due out of surgery anytime and I'm expecting a call from the hospital. I must be present, so to speak, for the news in case it's bad—as it has been for the last four months.

It's midweek and I've come into Manhattan from Long Island, where I'd been on a press check with one of my graphic designers, a man who's aware of this affair but has had the good sense to refrain from speaking of it. The printer's rep, who seems to know as well, generously offers to have his driver deliver me to Chelsea after the press check. Instead of asking how the hell he knew I'd like to be in Chelsea for the night rather than some plastic-appointed motel room on Long Island, I graciously accept. This midweek tryst is an unplanned, unexpected treat.

Jim and I finish the bottle of wine and, since I'm still waiting for the phone call, we go down to the corner wine shop for another. I'm too embarrassed to enter the liquor store a second time, especially since I'm showing the effects of precisely what they're selling. How absurd is that, I ask myself? But we're in mid-foreplay. I'm giddy and turned on and cannot face the clerk at the counter. Jim, the gracious man, goes in alone. I fidget and titter on the sidewalk like one of the ubiquitous swallows underfoot.

We return to the bedroom, sit, drink a little more wine, talk. Things have slowed, moved down somehow, deeper. I cannot resist him for much longer and experience a stab of panic. I noticed he's clearing things like newspapers and the cheese and crackers off the bed. Nothing's been decided, really; he just starts clearing away the impediments till they're all gone and there's nothing between us. I edge closer and closer till we're inches apart, sitting up, knees touching.

Are you going to kiss me? he asks. The remark seems impertinent. To me he's saying, *It's time, isn't it?*

No, I cannot kiss you. You know that. The phone call.

I don't want to stop. I want no interruptions. He smiles. What choice is there, really? Something pulls me forward and I kiss him. He opens his mouth wide and there I go.

He goes for me like I am prey. I am half-conscious with want. I'm on my back, naked from the waist down. How? He is between my legs, touching me, and I can barely endure the exquisite pleasure. His touching is exactly right, exactly urgent, exactly exactly exactly. I am positioned so that my vagina is illuminated by the Tiffany lamp as if I'm on an examining table. I open my eyes and see that he is watching everything he does to me. The phone rings. The sadist, who has planned it this way, withdraws his fingers.

I try to talk. I try to breathe. I try but have to hang up on Eli. For a moment, I actually hate Jim. Hate the both of them.

· · · · · · · · · · · ·

When Jim finally comes home from the hospital that first night—two or three in the morning—it's with his six-foot-five son who's so drugged he practically has to be carried. I intuit all this by the sounds I hear in the other rooms. Jim puts his son to bed on the couch then disappears into the hallway again, then into the elevator, down the ten floors to the lobby, out to his car, and around the block again and again till he finds parking. Five or ten minutes later he comes back. I am un-dressed, in a nightshirt, reading in the middle of his bed. I haven't lain down at all but stayed upright, mid-bed, reading a book, making notes for a book review, perfectly composed and surprisingly relaxed.

Jim is now a complete stranger. There's nothing about him I rec-ognize at this point. He's tired but not particularly stressed and now he's all about the business of undressing. It's the farthest thing from erotic I would have imagined. He pulls off his shirt, pulls down his pants, and approaches the bed wearing a T-shirt and underwear. He takes my book from me and we both get under the covers. Jim turns off the light.

I tell myself to focus, to jettison expectations, to hold still. I think I'm going to faint. I breathe and count, in and out. I'm at three when Jim starts talking.

He tells me his son is still miserable but very drugged. He'll have to take another dose of something in the morning but for now, ev-erything's okay. It's most certainly a migraine, something his son gets, though rarely. When it started he didn't have his medicine with him so it exploded into this.

Jim lets out a long, quiet breath as he stretches out. I let that sound guide me to his state of mind. Exhausted. Concerned. Puzzled, perhaps. There's nothing about me there that I could hear. He wants to try and relax. He wants sleep. He probably wishes it would all just go away.

As if to prove my powers of deduction, he rolls over so that I face his back. As he does this, he says something about his son being in the other room. In these close quarters, with the emergency now reduced to a gentle simmer, Jim has found a way to take leave of me.

I lie, flat out on the bed, wide-awake, and stare at the ceiling, which is not nearly as comforting as holding on to a book. There is, in this moment, no comfort to be found. All this anticipation. All this waiting. And here I am, as alone as I've ever felt in my entire life.

I haven't slept in days and though it's 3:00 or 4:00 AM now, I'm wired and my head's spinning. In the dark, in this state of bewilderment and disorientation, my senses play tricks on me. What I perceive as a man—did Jim get up?—at the foot of the bed is shadow play. What once felt like excitement now feels like a fever-dream. What I thought were a couple of votive candles flickering on an apartment windowsill across the courtyard now look like the haunted eyes in one of Susan's paintings. This whole thing feels like one of Susan's paintings. I look at my hands to be sure I haven't grown claws.

Jim settles himself into his pillows.

Shit. What in god's name have I gone and done now?

"ROILING IN THIS SEA"

CHAPTER 5

Is he asleep, I wonder? I lie beside him, making a conscious effort to hold all the parts of myself still. I listen to Jim's breath, in and out, slow and steady. What a man. This guy can rise above just about anything. In and out. In and out. It starts to get to me, like strobe lights or a dripping faucet in the middle of the night. But what else am I supposed to do here? What else is there to do?

Panic. Go ahead. Do that. Make a fuss. Melt down. Freak out. I've been the picture of self-control way too long. Fifty-eight years, to be precise, of always doing what I was told, doing what was expected of me.

Now I'm supposed to roll over. Fall asleep. Forget that the man I've fantasized about for weeks is mostly naked next to me. Forget every effort and every lie it took for me to get here. Well, fuck you. I'm not tired. I jiggle a foot. This feels like the height of hostility.

I turn my head and look at his back. A flat hard cold impenetrable wall. A billboard that says: I need my space. Fuck you back.

Calm down. Someday this will be funny.

What's funny about a sixty-seven-year-old father, after a long day at work, being called upon to rush his hallucinating, adult son from emergency clinic to emergency clinic? The boy needed medication. He needed health insurance. He needed a primary care physician who could advise them what to do. Lacking these resources, the father, moaning writhing son in tow, must drive through the streets of Manhattan in the dark of night, searching for help and relief.

I look at Jim again. He's kind of fetal, his head tipped in the direction of his knees. No surprise. The poor man. He's had the day and night from hell. That's what I'm thinking as I reach over at 3:00 AM or so and lightly touch his back with the tips of my fingers. Poor man. The day and night from hell.

I never ask him about those minutes when he withdrew. I never say, "What exactly were you thinking right then, you jerk?" I never demand an answer because I don't need to know everything. I do know that he spent twenty-five years meditating with the Gurdjieff Work, that he has a remarkable facility to do just what he feels like doing, that he is extraordinarily able to slip into the moment and leave it at that. He's free in ways I can't imagine.

Someday this better be funny.

I realize I've touched him and pull my hand quickly away. Jim says something while still curled up, while still self-protective and still self-contained. It sounds like "What the hell," but I'm not sure and don't want to know what that means either. After the mumbled words he rolls over to where I lie on my back and he kisses me and doesn't stop for hours.

• • • • • • • • • • • •

In my journal a few days later, I rhapsodize about Jim's physicality. He weighs one hundred pounds more than I do and his broad Michael Phelps–like shoulders, which I appreciate for the way, for instance, that they announce his presence as he crosses a street toward me or approaches me in a roomful of people, are rungs on which to cleave as we wrestle in the night. I like this, for all the erotic ideas a big and powerful male conjures up for me. Subjugate me! Dominate me! Show me my place. My hardwired feminist brain is shocked. I should be ashamed of myself. Shouldn't I?

Jim's new and different. My lovers have been cerebral—artists, musicians, a poet. This bevy of creative stock I understand—clever, self-absorbed, driven, neurotic men for whom values associated with masculinity evoke snickers. These men are familiar. They are smaller in stature, prone to torment, not quite accessible in their clouds of cigarette smoke and boozy hand-wringing over audience turn-out, rejection letters, critical reviews of their work.

What's happening to me? I'm desperate for macho.

Even though I have strong solid bones, Jim is a crushing force when we fuck. This alone is a turn-on. He can fuck easy and he can fuck hard, but he's a bull all the same. As a child, while in the car with my mother on a long drive to a remote beach in Southern California, we pass some rugged grazing land. Staring out the window I catch sight of a massive shape hurtling up a hill between a couple of oak trees. An enormous bull has mounted a cow that reacts violently, erratically. She races, seemingly directionless, while the bull humps from the rear, his back two legs running and bucking, his pelvis pumping vigorously, his dark rounded torso freakish and mountainlike on top of hers. They zigzag up and over the crest of the hill kicking up storms of dust and divots of tough, rocky sod in their frenzy. This is not a forgettable sight and over the years it works on me, burrows its way into my ideas about sex. In terms of bulls, I know whereof I speak.

Now it appears I'm drawn to this big reckless man as I, in defiance of everything that came before, run roughshod over everything I've so carefully arranged in my life.

. . . .

On that first night we don't sleep. Jim is remarkable on that score because of what he's just been through, though I'm pulling off quite a feat myself. After all, when is the last time I slept more than a few minutes at a time? Or ate more than a few nibbles of something nutritious? And there's that other part—our combined ages of 125 hard-lived years, a respectable fraction of that time engaged in acts of sex. And here we go again.

Somewhere at the start of that epic weekend (I later confide in my friend Lisa, the only one I speak to about the details of this love affair, "I don't think we ever tried to sleep. Why are we still alive?"), I inform Jim that it has been perhaps five years since I've had sex with Eli or any man.

There are plenty of reasons for this and we've been together eighteen years and time, it is said, erodes desire. Yet my last sexual experience with Eli, though I don't remember it precisely, was certainly erotic and passionate because that's the way it was.

No. I stopped having sex with Eli because I had merged with him. In some fundamental way we were not separate people. It was as if I could feel the shape of his heart, taste his sadness. The intimacy had grown acute. Lovemaking like this was impossible. If I were to make love with a man again, it would have to be different. It would have to be more like play, like roiling in the waves.

. . . .

Jim lie beside me in bed and quietly takes in my sad story about absence of sex. Perhaps gloating a bit or perhaps just embarrassed for me or perhaps he is truly sorry he can't commiserate, because that's the way it sounds when he finally responds, "I'm sorry. It hasn't been that long for me."

Despite his love of simple, uncomplicated fucking, we don't do that once during the first three days and nights we spend together. Whatever pleasure he takes from our first weekend together has to do with pleasing me.

I learn that Jim doesn't stop until some unspoken signal passes between us, some chemical gently begins to recede, some electrical stimuli softens, dulls, departs. Until then, his stamina and vigor are matched by a surreal sensitivity to the erotic parts of our lovemaking. It's as if my body is telling him, "Do this next. Then this. This is what will feel good now." He does precisely that and my orgasm catches me completely by surprise. It's so powerful a force that I have to shove his hands and mouth away and I instinctively pull my knees into my chest where I clasp the roiling, rolling contractions, squeeze my thighs, channel the tempest up, deeper, higher, triggering a cascade. On and on. I am anaerobic because I forget to breathe or maybe the breath is knocked out of me. There are no words or ideas or thoughts. Just these waves of mindless ecstasy. I am all body. Delicious abandon. I ride this for what seems like an eternity. When at last awareness comes back to me, I am gasping for breath.

. . . .

"Did you know it would be like this?" he asks me at the end of our first weekend together. We're spent, stretched out on our backs on his big bed, not touching, limp and wet and breathing in all the smells of each other. It's almost time for me to get up, shower, and go to Penn Station where I must catch the early train to Boston but I don't think about that until the last possible second. This, I come to see, is my usual way in the year of coming and going that is to follow.

"No," I say. "I didn't know anything." I don't tell him that my fantasies, for some reason, never make it past kissing. But I don't congratulate him. I don't tell him, "Good job." I don't say anything but "No" because I'm not quite sure what he means by "like this" and because I want sex, not seduction, and not a tour de force.

"Like this" at that very second is far more complicated than he can possibly imagine. "Like this" means that I have no feeling left in my body other than soreness. "Like this" means that I am sleepless and wired and hungry and fifty-eight years of age and I have to ride on Amtrak for 4.25 hours, take a couple of subway trains in Boston, wait at least an hour for a commuter train to take me north to Salem, where I'll magically revive, pop into work with that same worn suitcase in tow, and stay late, as always. "Like this" means I roil adulterously with no remorse and now have to summon duplicity and lie once again to Eli. "Like this" is what I must walk away from in mere minutes without knowing if I'll ever be "like this" again.

. . . .

We don't sleep but we do leave the apartment a couple of times. His son wakes the next morning feeling much improved. I meet him and like him. Despite his ordeal, he's calm and relaxed. He even makes a few jokes. He has the same deep voice and friendly smile as his dad. The three of us use up a lot of space in that small Chelsea apartment. Joshua, born to a Jewish mother thirty-seven years earlier, touches me instantly with his sweetness and clever humor. He collects his things and heads off for a weekend with friends as if the night before never happened. Later I will wonder about that horrid headache. I make associations between the brutality of the pain and the hard changes to come. Joshua, who lives with Jim, will eventually have to find his own place in Manhattan.

His adult children are gracious. We will find common ground in time. I see that there's civility and respect on both sides, regardless of Jim's past history. I don't know what's come before and view myself as part of a continuum. There's life before me and life after me. Jim's kids have a time-tested understanding of their father as the handsome, freewheeling, accessible bachelor. I'm not really an easy fit into that scenario; my decision is to simply be, and to do my best to be myself. I hope that little by little we can all find connections with each other that, however large or small, are positive. Kids are kids, no matter how old. We can all use a little extra love and support.

. . . .

On Sunday Jim and I climb out of the bed and shower and dress up. We are going on an outing. We are going to the Metropolitan Museum of Art. And we are going to see an exhibition of Tiffany glass. It is a perfect choice because I am a museum person, I am drawn into art of all kinds, and Jim is not only a stained-glass artisan but he created stained-glass lamp designs and ran a factory with twenty artisans who made the lamps he designed.

What is not perfect is that stunning transition from horizontal in bed to vertical in public. We are the epitome of new. He knows more about my labia than he does about my coffee preferences.

We leave his apartment smelling like soap, call for the elevator, and step inside. The doors pull shut and I look at him. We smile and I am shocked to feel that want and passion rising up all over again. How can this be? I tell him, "All it takes is for me to look at you." He says, "You've got it bad," and I worry that perhaps I'm tottering, alone, on a very fragile limb. But he steps toward me and pulls me against him. It's sexual and playful. It's a silly game but it works for me because it gives continuity. "Bump bump bump," he laughs. Later in the day when we're standing on a corner, awaiting a bus, he does it again, discreetly. He sidles up to me till his hip touches mine and he bends and whispers, "Bump bump bump." It's a relief to acknowledge what we're really doing there. These alien forays into civilization are probably necessary but I long for the darkness of the bedroom, the clutch of passion, the moans of abandon. I see that Jim is meant to take me away. I want, need to be taken away.

We walk around the gorgeous, light-struck, shimmering Tiffany exhibition independently of each other. I want to do this part alone but I go find him whenever I want to show him something I like. He, in turn, points out something he's looking at. He lets this be about beauty and art, never bringing up his own knowledge of Tiffany glass works, some of which he owns. He never explains anything. He rarely reads the labels. He just stands back and looks.

In an hour or so we move on to an abutting show of paintings by a group of German artists. These works are hard and angular and provocative. The men's faces in some of the portraits are contorted with stuffed, complicated emotions, made heavier still by the artists' dim light and thick shadows and the dark palettes. These works are in extreme contrast to the gorgeous lavender and yellow and green stained glass refracting light in the galleries nearby.

Four or five paintings into it, the enormity of what's happening hits me. I think, *Holy shit, I'm here in Manhattan. I'm with Jim. I made it.* I notice, however, that there's no big drum roll going off in my head. No *Pinch me, I must be dreaming* sense of the surreal. It's nothing like that. It's simply normal. There's no sense of hard-won victory or triumphant bravado telling me, *Hey, this is where I should be* or *This is where I belong.* Instead this accounting I'm taking leads me to realize that I'm simply here, in the Met, looking at art and my lover is here, also, looking at art, somewhere in one of these galleries, though I can't spot him at this time. I take a breath. I am in this moment, not savoring it or celebrating it or ruing it. I don't jump ahead. There's nothing I dare to worry about. I have so little time so I stay right here, living it as deeply and as completely as I am able on no sleep and no food, and it feels natural. I am having a moment of acceptance. I am at peace.

I find that I have stepped back, out of the three-deep, clockwise queue of people shuffling from canvas to canvas. I know the look, am familiar with the somber, intent pall that suffuses everything in this room. I work in a museum. I market this kind of magical state of mind, this spiritual absorption. I write copy that's meant to trigger in our museum-going population a compelling desire to get in the car and head for a one-on-one connection with a work of art. I know the contained euphoria going off behind the inscrutable faces as people allow themselves to be taken over, transported by art, as they begin to make associations between this and other works, between the art and their own experiences. It feels worshipful. Sacrosanct. Holy. Don't be deceived. It's orgasm of another sort.

I scan the tops of heads, looking for Jim because I notice I feel a little dizzy and dehydrated and shaky. I can run along the back shore of Rockport for forty-five minutes or look at art for two hours. Each feels like a marathon as I near the end of my endurance quotient. I love these German works but I now want to leave. Jim approaches, as if on cue, and asks how I am, would I be interested in lunch and a glass of wine.

I think about Jim's idea of foreplay as we eat. It's certainly erotic. We're sitting close to each other on stools in a small, attractive basement restaurant near the Met. From our seats we can look out at the sidewalk, just below level with our line of vision. I see many more pairs of great shoes, boots, bare-legged runners because it's still in the sixties, children's carriages, dogs sniffing their way around the block while their owners yank at the leashes to hurry them on.

Jim reaches for my glass of sauvignon blanc and takes a sip. "Mm-mmm," he says. He spears a moist flake of citrusy salmon from my plate with his fork. "Good." His voice rumbles. He tries the rice. He slides some of his hot cheesy omelet onto my bread plate for me to try. This intimate exchange of soft warm foods, conducted by Jim, is tantamount to sex and I am growing desperate to get out of there. I fold my napkin, place it beside my plate, and wait for Jim to finish. Hurry up. I did not come to New York City for the food.

Once, a few months into the love affair, my boss asks me what restaurants Jim and I like. My boss loves Manhattan and fine dining. Before I think, I blurt out, "Restaurants? We never go to restaurants." He seems puzzled. I say, "There's no time for that. Maybe later." I walk away, feeling like an idiot for revealing so much. On the other hand, what do I care what he thinks? If only he could be so lucky as to disdain food in favor of love.

....

Shortly after my first weekend alone with Jim, I call Mitch, the therapist I visit as needed. I want to tell him about this love affair. And though it is *illicit,* I'm surprised to find I am untouched by guilt. I've been pulling away from Eli for six months, months before Jim enters my life. Before Jim, I've made a point of saying, every day, "Eli, you agreed to move out. Have you started looking for a place yet?" The fact that he isn't budging complicates things but doesn't change what is happening to me. I speak openly about my need to separate, to write in peace, to find some serenity before it's too late. I even tell him about my desire to date again. It is impossible to overstate the desperation with which I crave serenity. Bipolar disease is a serious form of mental illness. We manage it, but it brutalizes the both of us, all the same. By saying these things aloud, by seeing Eli hear them, everything begins to change for me. In late summer I tell my good friend Lynn I am separating from Eli. I begin to set myself free. Eli is uncomprehending.

I owe it to Eli to be forthright and to treat him with respect. And I do not. I conduct this love affair secretly. Eli is none the wiser.

I sit on Mitch's soft couch and we chat for a while about my job, my boss, about how Eli's doing, about my daughter.

Mitch eats sardines as we talk and I sip coffee from a travel mug. I haven't been to see him since my mother committed suicide a year earlier but nothing seems to have changed about Mitch. He grasps the problem, no matter how hard I think it is, and he comes up with sensible strategies. I like this kind of therapy. It feels like problem solving. I also like that Mitch brings Plato into the discussion. He cites Buddhist tenets. He shares his rabbi's teachings.

"So," he says, "tell me about you and Jim."

This catches me by surprise, for some reason. I switch my attention to the sardines, which he puts on crackers just as I do, though I like a little mustard and salt. If there's ever a need to remember Mitch is human, this sardine-eating moment is it. I catch a whiff of the sardines as he wolfs them down and I remember my grandfather, whom I watched eat sardines on saltines for lunch on Saturdays. He ate at a Formica kitchen table, drank strong black coffee he made himself by boiling grounds in a saucepan with eggshells. I sat across from him and watched and I babbled on and on. Rare happy times in youth.

I remember, too, other therapists' offices and other less palatable food smells. Lots of therapists eat in their offices and their offices smell like raw onion, pepperoni pizza, and my least favorite, Italian subs with hot peppers turned rancid and rank by the ubiquitous space heater, the passage of hours or days in small, cheap, unventilated offices that always remind me of unsavory roadside motel rooms.

I go back to Mitch's inquiry—"Tell me about you and Jim"—but I don't see what he's getting at so I do what I always do in moments of confusion—I start talking, hoping something meaningful will work its way out. "Well, he's tall and I really like that. I look down on most men." I could have said anything. He's a glazier. He rants about politics. He scours the Internet for information. He is Eli's best friend. He speaks in complex sentences even though he watches a lot of television and says "nothin'" and "ain't" and "fookin'" when he wants to come off plebeian. He's a man of enthusiastic appetites. Sex. A good martini. Brie. He's unapologetic. Honest to a fault. Loves the asinine movie *Spanglish*. But I say something obvious and surfacey: He's tall.

"I see. This is about a man and a woman."

I nearly choke on my coffee. Well, in fact, yes.

I stare at Mitch. This idea is new and explosively sexy. Out of nowhere I see my hormones, like some wide-necked fullback, barreling through the door, slamming me to the ground. I think of Jim, his body on top of mine, his big hands locked around my face, his fingers clutching at my hair, his mouth boring down on mine. I feel my pelvis tip reflexively. I am in big, big heat. I've never felt so exposed. God help me.

Yet. I can't help myself. I adore the idea that Mitch has posited, of Jim and me as simply man and woman. Jim and I are standing, now, facing each other. We are naked. A modern-day Tarzan and Jane, who, along with Ricky and Lucy, were couples models for me. Lucy talked back. Jane did not. Me Jane.

I'm so turned on, sitting there on Mitch's couch, that I start to spew a panicked sweat. An X-rated hot flash. I can't shut the flood of hormones down. The background fantasy is now impossible to turn off. Jim slides a pillow under my head. He's on his knees and he straddles me. He slowly places his penis into my mouth. He asks, "Is this Okay?" I am helplessly pinned but yes, oh, yes, this is fabulous.

I blame Mitch. All this talking has made me orally fixated.

Mitch chews away on those oily omega-3-infused bits of silvery fish, waiting for some kind of corroboration, I suppose. What shows on my face? Am I displaying looks of lust? I remember my mother yelling, "Wipe that look off your face." No poker face, mine.

Mitch is no idiot, either. He can read me. I want out of there. Need to get out. "You're right. Man and woman," I say, straining to climb out of that big low soft womb-couch. I clamber upright, rock a bit till I steady myself. I'm still feeling monosyllabic, primitive. "Got to go. Time to go."

Where is my exit vine? Why can't I fly the fuck out of here in one swift swing?

I get the hell out of Mitch's office and walk down Center Street to Main Street in downtown Gloucester. Instead of getting in my car and heading right to work, I decide to take ten minutes, stop for a fresh cup of coffee at the Lone Gull, do some deep breathing, and write down whatever I can retrieve from that nutty thirty-five-minute session. All I can come up with is "Man and woman." Just as well. My hands shake so hard I can barely write.

As I drive to work I think about one of the first things Jim says to me after we become lovers. "I've thought about this and I know what to do. I am going to be the man you deserve." He repeats this on occasion, I'm assuming, because he thinks I need to realize there are things I deserve. Mitch tells me, as well, that I deserve certain things in this life.

But what I always hear is something very different. What I hear Jim saying is: *I am going to be a man for you.* I think, to hell with what I deserve, which is probably eternity sizzling in hell. What I want is a lot of man.

"EVERYTHING IS FOREPLAY"

CHAPTER 6

Early Sunday morning I pull on lightweight running pants and a long-sleeved T-shirt and head for the Hudson River to run, more will than want. I've packed my running clothes, as I always do when I travel, and I push myself out of my comfort zone to find my way in the unknown.

That's always how it goes—tricks, mind games, and unabashed curiosity. Running in a new place fills in the details, gives me a deeper sense of it. It's also territorial, like a dog aiming its urine stream against a building or a man putting a diamond on a woman's finger. When I've run somewhere, like Queens, St. Louis, Houston, Marathon Key, or Ocean Beach in San Diego, it opens up to me. An elderly woman on her knees weeds a little patch of pansies. A mailman smiles as he slips letters into a slot on a red door. A man shoveling snow yells out to me, "Look up. There's a full moon."

Today's run is hard at first. I'm a little hungover and sore from all the sex, have subsisted on catnaps and cheese and crackers, feel totally hollowed out in the middle. The only thing going for me is that I'm getting used to this state of being.

Gradually I loosen up, stop thinking, and let my body take over. It's slow going but so what? I'm here. I'm doing it. At my age, with so many of my friends suffering knee and hip pain, I consider every run a gift.

I listen to the song list on my iPod—Hudson River Run—that I created an hour earlier to sync with my mood and my energy. It's all longing and it's all mournful—Meat Loaf, Iris Dement, Michael Jackson, Prince, Tim Buckley, Bruce Springsteen, Tom Rush, and a few rousing, long chants by Krishna Das. I sing along with Das's call and response and that's when I realize that nothing could be more perfect than this.

Wait. Never second-guess the limits of extremes. There's always more. In a moment of breathtaking profundity, I glance to my right and catch sight of the Statue of Liberty, a stalwart beacon, rooted in the river, lotuslike in its sturdy serenity. You need know nothing to comprehend her message: *Welcome. You have made it this far. What else can you do? Anything is possible.*

The very idea that we in the United States can think like this, can take on the idea of opportunity as our personal inspiration, is the point. I run in the direction of that beacon. I am doing this because I can.

The river's choppy and I'm hit by spray as the water slaps against the retaining wall. Doused, I am surprised to taste salt in the water and realize that I am not so much changed by this weekend as I am enlightened by it. A statue in a river clarifies things. A splash of water brings it home. No one can stop me but me. There are 360 degrees of access. For a woman of a certain age, as I am, who came up on the second wave of feminism, who protested boisterously, who had to fight for responsibility, power, and authority at work, who had to perform at double-time to merit promotion, and who had to raise her voice, to risk condemnation to be heard, this idea of opportunity towers above all else, like the Statue of Liberty, who faces down the Hudson's deep and relentless currents.

When I turn back, I see that I must buck a headwind. It's gusty but it's still warm. No hat. No gloves. It feels so free.

I get back to Jim's apartment and find that he has left the door open a crack for me. I step in, pull the door closed, and twist the dead-bolt till it snaps and locks. I feel safe and warm in the shaft of light beaming through his living room window.

He's in the kitchen, grinding coffee beans. I go over to him, stand beside him as he makes a pot of coffee and buttered toast for us. We're quiet as we watch coffee drip from the Melitta filter into the glass pot. There's the faintest tinkle as the tiny stream feeds the growing pool of coffee. I think of the trickle of water that flows from the southern end of Fourth Connecticut Lake—a tiny, remote swamp you can circum-ambulate in under an hour—in northern New Hampshire. This grassy pond feeds all the deep and grand Connecticut Lakes and the 407-mile-long Connecticut River. It's amazing what's possible from tiny but consistent effort.

Jim reaches down and lightly runs his palm along my butt. I sense that he is just feeling it, checking it out because it's there, and satisfied, goes back to the coffee making. This brief, silent gesture is, by far, the sexiest thing he has done to me yet. It is, remarkably, the most powerful memory of my weekend.

"I like it when the line on a woman's underwear shows," he tells me another time when we are, for some forgotten reason, discussing panty lines. I am struck by his remark. It is revealing of his sexuality that he has this refined body of preferences. I have no such cabinet of delights when it comes to men and I grow extremely curious. Let me in. Show me the depth and breadth of your sexual tastes. Tell me exactly why you like this. Is it the way the flesh bulges ever so slightly right below the panty line? Does it add something tactile to the woman, who, in the current style of fashion, wouldn't be caught dead with a visible panty line? Is the line a rigid, delicious counterpoint to the buoyancy of the mounded flesh? Does it call to mind the grip-ability? Is it, by definition, a line of demarcation that, by extension, contains the butt? Cups it as a hand might? Does it draw your eye and hand to it, suggest a layer of palpable dimension? Does the way the line impacts the flesh imply the nature of that butt—soft, hard, flat, round? Does it give you a sense that you could slide a finger under that elastic and go to the forbidden? I want to demand this information emphatically. Yet I squelch the urge to query. These sexual revelations, spoken as fact and without emotional overtones, are potent aphrodisiacs for me. He can mete them out, one at a time. I love discovery. I love where it takes me.

. . . .

It's two in the morning and everything is new. Not just this new day in mid-December but everything, from the way the glass of water on my nightstand tastes sweet and soft to the metallic clank of the street sounds—to the way my nipples tingle and tighten when Jim slides his hand onto my belly. I will him: Move your hand up. Don't tease me like this. But he draws his hand away, its imprint burning a hole in me.

My reticence is my bondage. I am powerless.

I catch myself sulking and edge over to him. He draws me in as we enter the last hours of our time together, our bodies locked, my thoughts wanting to turn melancholy. This sex fest is almost over. It's back to reality for me.

Jim's still and quiet. I try to be the same, out of respect for the behemoth, the bull that has ravaged me again and again. He's sixty-seven, he's amazing, and it's a workday. He keeps his exhaustion a secret.

This has been a wonderful weekend. I have no regrets about any of it. I'm capable of walking away with nothing more than a goodbye. I got everything I wanted and more than I expected. There are a lot of parts to my life in New England. I know this. It's a rich life that I've made for myself, a life I enjoy and that feeds me, despite the troubles with Eli and the nutty boss and the long hours and my own demons.

I would like it if Jim would say, "This was wonderful. I want to do it again." But he won't. I already understand that. He is enjoying this for its newness. He isn't even making up his mind about me. He's just here, now.

At fifty-eight and sixty-seven that's all you can ask.

Once a man dropped to his knees and begged me to withdraw my request that he move out of my apartment. He wrapped his arms around my legs, pulled me between his knees, and implored me to reconsider. I stepped out of the entanglement of limbs, like a sticky spider's web, and moved away to another state. This never impressed me as an act of love, but of desperation. A better kind of love is Jim reaching over, his fingers homing in to the place he seems to like best, exploring two small dips where my inner thighs meet my crotch. He tugs gently at my pubic hair. He does this another time, not quite so gently. His soft warm lips open into my ear. He hums his baritone sound directly into me as he slides his fingers into my vagina—call and response all over again.

His art is sex. He hums and I open my legs and let his fingers go deeper. It's like a lullaby. It's saying, Rae, it's okay. Let go now.

. . . .

I note every detail of this newness. I'm an artist sketching a scene I want to have for later. Later, in my fantasy life, in bed in Rockport, or driving to the mall or in a meeting with the director of new media, I will be able to create something sensual, multidimensional, something almost real, something akin to an emotional hologram.

Here, on the last day, is the sketch I make of us: We're in bed. I'm naked, stretched out on my right side, facing my new lover. He is naked, too, just like I wanted. How strange to get what I want. The getting hardly matters, though, because there's the reality of what just happened to consume the ensuing moments. Milestones are meaningless unless you are a historian, and I am not a historian. I am a woman in heat, plain and simple.

He has wrapped one long arm around my shoulders and wedged his left leg tight against my crotch, which feels scratchy and wet against his smooth taut Swedish skin. I've jammed my right hip hard into the back of his thigh and I've slung my left leg over his. A tension, something electric, holds us in this fully charged embrace. I am weightless, our position a levitation.

I view all this from outside myself. What I see first is a da Vinci, a detail of precision fit. Jim and Rae. It even sounds precision engineered. I feel, through some vein in his thigh, his heartbeat in my vagina. The steady *ba-dum, ba-dum, ba-dum,* like the slow, insistent vibrator that takes matters out of your own hands, that ramps up the urgency. My own motor, as Jim calls the tiny rhythmic pulses my pelvis makes, engages again.

I scan this bedroom scene, composed in tones of black. This is a Rembrandt, a study of shadow, of chiaroscuro, with a smudge of illumination on my naked butt as the sum of city light penetrates the linen curtains and finds, faintly defines, a crescent of flesh.

A truck brakes hard and squeals to a stop. A fire engine wails down 23rd Street. A couple of drunken males hoot. And then, nothing at all. This Chelsea apartment is one of a thousand similar apartments, Jim's with windows facing into a quiet, private courtyard.

I think about the story we heard that afternoon as we came back from a walk through the Village to buy Jim's favorite Costa Rican coffee beans. A man jumped out of his apartment window and died in the courtyard. This news strikes me as terribly sad and I am inclined to dwell there, in the sadness. Perhaps the natural antonymous response to sexual euphoria is melancholia.

What must it take, I wonder, to slide open the window, remove the screen, climb up to the ledge, compact your body, and somehow propel your concentrated, raw, fucked-up self out there into the emptiness. By choosing this method you give yourself time to reconsider and time for regrets. Jumpers are among the greatest of the self-loathers, have the hottest-burning hate.

I slide out of bed and peer down into the manicured courtyard, with its symmetrically situated benches and ornamental shrubs and small lights outlining the pathways. This garden was erected in defiance of the slop we humans spew.

The story gets worse. The concierge says the dead man was married to one of the psychiatrists practicing in the building. Jim and I look at each other when we get that news, then look away before we say or do something stupid. We agree, as we ride the elevator to the tenth floor, that the man must have hated his wife. It will ruin her business and disable her clients.

I pull my eyes away from the courtyard and raise them to the bank of windows in the London Terrace apartments on the other side. Bedrooms. Living rooms. Bathrooms. I see a naked woman wrap a scarf, sarong-style, around her waist, sit in a chair, and nurse her baby. Another man lies on his back in his bed and repeatedly kicks a sheet off his feet. He seems, from this distance, more infantile than the nursing baby. I, too, am in somebody's sights for I stand in front of the window naked, staring out, wrestling with the generalized anxiety that comes with this territory.

I come back to bed and Jim reaches out an arm and pulls me into him once again. Finally he puts his warm mouth to my breast. Did he, too, see the baby nursing across the way? Finally he suckles. He does this noisily, pulling at my nipple with his lips, rolling his tongue back and forth, drawing desire through me like sucking juice through a straw. Now he's slurping and sucking and moaning. Whatever gestures we make toward decorum, whatever precise garden paths with their boxy hedges defining the boundaries of our meanderings, all of it falls away instantly when we indulge our urge of the moment. And, of course, we will. Nothing, not tidy walkways, not double-glazed windows, not marriage, not the ornate wooden frames encompassing the anguished German poet's portrait, keeps us human beings in check.

I stick my finger in Jim's mouth, feel the hardness of my nipple alongside his tongue, love the effort and the expertise, fall back, and let him take anything he wants.

HOME

CHAPTER 7

I 'm trying without much success to come up with funny captions for the *New Yorker* cartoon at the back of the magazine, something I do almost every week. It used to be for my own amusement; now, I present them to Jim because I want him to laugh. Like many of the things he does, his laugh is all consuming, full-bodied, manly. And unrestrained. His face is never more alive and beautiful than when he laughs. His inner child shows himself—free, wicked, ready to test the limits—and I reach out and grab because getting the man-boy to climb all over me, to smear on the kiwi-scented oil, to lick it off like I'm his lollipop, that's when it gets really good.

Afterward, he turns his head toward me. "Rae."

"Jim." I'm incoherent, but I remember his name.

"Look at me."

I do that. I open my eyes and there he is, looking earnest and concerned.

"What?" I ask.

"There's a problem."

"Problem?" I instantly come to. This isn't normal. It isn't like us. We don't have problems. We have sex.

"About this stuff. The scented lotion. I don't like it. I can't taste you."

I look at him, more man than boy now. "Jim" is all I can get out.

"Yes?" he says, sliding back down between my legs.

I love this man.

. . . .

It occurs to me, as I indulge in this recollection, that I should be worried. I'm fifty-eight years old and I can't seem to get enough.

I go to back to the cartoon, a little dispirited. A man and a woman are in a kitchen with an outsize toaster. Texas toast comes to mind. Wordplay. For me the cartoon contest is like the Sunday *Times*' crossword puzzle, a socially sanctioned indulgence that doesn't make you gain weight or spend money or feel guilty. It's good brain calisthenics and I'm worried I need it.

I carry a cup of hot coffee and a favorite pen to my reading chair and take half an hour once or twice per cartoon. It's a bit like work at first, getting into that tiny freeze-frame of a world, inhabiting it like I'm the one about to snap off a wisecrack. Once I'm in there, the one-liners roll out. Out of twenty or thirty captions that come to mind, I preserve ten or fifteen.

I hand Jim the magazine and surreptitiously monitor his response as he reads each of the captions. He laughs. I want to know, "Which one is that?" Like sliding my finger alongside his tongue when it's preoccupied with my nipple, I investigate. "Show me."

Nothing strikes me as that funny right now. I'm distracted by this emerging idea that my insatiability is freakish. I believe my appetite for Jim is *unprecedented,* way outside the norm. It's chemistry on steroids.

No one I know speaks of having such experiences. This is especially worrisome to someone like me, whose peripheral vision corroborates that I'm in the normalcy spectrum. I spy no friend of a similar age who is fully engulfed, as I am, by a love affair or who boasts of a compelling sexual life. Even in books I don't often come across women in fever like this. Is Anna Karenina my only role model? Good god. How about Glenn Close—a case study in female attraction, Hollywood style? In that interpretation, the woman boils the family rabbit and opts for homicide instead of suicide by locomotive. Aye. Women who are hot for a man, red zone hot, are so obviously fucked.

What's normal for a woman like me? There's movie sex, where two handsome, sexy people, most likely intoxicated, wildly sling three-inch heels and Hermes ties as they clamber onto the kitchen table or at least use it as a stabilizing instrument in their frenzied copulating. There are the remarkably beautiful young women in the Victoria's Secret ads for whom a thong makes good aesthetic sense. Then there are the people beyond middle aged, like myself, more than half of whom regularly copulate, enjoy oral sex, and do so into their seventies. In secret. As universally joyous as the act of sex is, it's subjected to vicious ridicule if it's practiced by older people.

I recall hearing an author speak at an annual conference sponsored by the American Society of Journalists and Authors. She had published a book about sex for middle-aged people. She was a beautiful woman, a fitness instructor, who wanted to get middle-aged sex out of the closet, so to speak. The email she received after publishing was so upsetting that she said she had to stop reading it and pay someone else to monitor it for her. It was full of hateful invective and name-calling.

For those of us over fifty who don't have the time to scour the Internet to locate like kind or to seek out palatable porn, we're having sex in a vacuum. While a Viagra ad is at least an acknowledgment that we're still interested, it's about as erotic or evocative as having sex on a slab in a morgue. In their drive to hold us within the bounds of good taste, and to pacify an FDA that seems to believe old-people sex is a health hazard like coconut cream pie, the ads further provoke derision. Just check the Internet for Viagra spoof ads.

As a marketer, I know that my first order of business is to understand my client and my client's target market. Cialis ads talk to Baby Boomers, most likely those in the upper age range. We came up during the sexual revolution. We had sex in the mud at Woodstock in front of our friends. Now, according to the ads, we're consigned to our own individual clawfoot bathtubs, aimed off into the sunset, in the surf. Is the tide coming in or going out?

The bathtub feels cold to the eye. I object, feel physically repulsed. It's white and sterile. The two naked people are separated by two thick walls of porcelain. Bodily smells and fluids spiral down the drain. I guess the idea is that the tub is a good place to chill while the Cialis kicks in. And while that's happening, the sudsy water plumps the old, dry skin. In a spoof of this ad, the woman looks at the man and says, "Did you take it?" He says, "I can't remember."

Exactly.

My real concern isn't sexual dysfunction, it's dementia. My lust for Jim scares me. I'm in the age zone when anything can go wrong. I'm guessing Baby Boomers like myself—as a group, independent-minded, entitled, nonconforming—are not going to handle dementia well. The bright side for our caregivers, who will be desperate to shut us up, is our already-acquired comfort level with mind-altering drugs.

My zeal for Jim feels a little familiar to me, like that sort of irrepressible abandon that old people have when their boundaries begin to fail them—a gloating indulgence in excess. I think of those women who wear purple hats and red dresses and dine in museum restaurants. They order pastel-colored cocktails and share confections adorned with mounds of whipped cream that look like wedding dresses plopped on plates. It's scary. I think then of the ones who trouble me the most, those who talk loudly in theaters despite the social norms, despite the hisses to be quiet, and despite the on-screen admonitions to silence yourself and your phone. They never do. Am I one of them?

Aye, I mutter again. Aye. Aye. Aye. I don't mean to but I say this out loud: I'm never going to get enough.

Jim hears this and I'm horrified. He's moving from his desk to the couch, a copy of *Harper's* magazine in one hand, a mug of coffee in the other. It's hot in the Chelsea apartment, even in winter, and he's wearing shorts and a T-shirt. The window's wide open yet I see a delicious sheen on his arms, something I could stand up right now and lick. He's sweating. He barely misses a beat as he sits down and sips his coffee. He turns pages till he gets to the Harper's Index column and says, just loud enough for me to hear, "It's always here for you."

• • • • • • • • • • • •

After sex, Jim talks to me. His mouth is against my ear as I lie on my back. "This is my sandbox," he says, running his hand along my body. "All these parts to play with." He rests his hand on my hip bone. "I like this," he says. He touches his fingers to my pubic hair and runs them up along my inner thigh. "Look," he says, lifting his head to peer between my naked legs in the candlelight. "I love this bend." He traces the right angle my thigh makes with my pelvis. "I love the way it looks." He lays his palm on my concave belly, which is soft and empty and dips like a child's wading pool. "I like this very much."

I understand the nature of our love affair. It's not personal. Not yet and maybe not ever. Jim and I both know that all women can create titillating angles in repose. All bellies beat warm and soft after sex. All ears crave sweet nothings. What we have is sex to distraction. Sex that's transcendent. Sex as remove.

The good thing about this kind of sex is that it's empty. We don't have any of the sticky stuff that might glom things up, stuff like love, expectation, frustration.

Jim has other guarantees for me, as if "it" always being there for me wasn't enough. "I don't give up," he says.

I've noticed. He tests my outer limits. Is it one orgasm? Five? Ten?

I smile over at him as he debates where to place his hand next and I think, *This sandbox isn't saying.* Without pride, clothing, and the inclination to say no, a woman has very few secrets. Let my capacity for Eros be my secret, at least for now.

. . . .

I part Jim's company at 24th Street and 9th Avenue around 7:30 in the morning. He's going to his shop in DUMBO, Brooklyn, and I'm going to my office in Salem, Massachusetts. We kiss goodbye—a lackluster event. We're done with each other, at least for now. He turns south and I continue east. I note that once he turns away, he never looks back. I know right then that he never will.

I drag the banged-up little suitcase east on 24th one block to 8th, turn left on 8th, and walk north for ten minutes to 31st Street. I will always relish this walk, whether it's to Jim or away from him. It stretches me, shakes out the niggling worries, deepens my breath, and physically reorients me. It returns me to myself. Each time, I'm embarking on a journey. Each time it's away from one life and toward another. My friend Rod Philbrick's uncle, a spy, wrote a memoir titled "I Led Three Lives." Well, I'm gaining on him with two.

I'm not sure how the spy managed his transitions, kept it all straight, but I have this walk. It's here on 8th Avenue that I get my bearings.

Then I'm back in the lower levels of Penn Station. It feels as if I never left. The delis, the newsstands, the bakeries, and the coffee shops, they become the sentries that signal creature comforts and familiarity. They, too, help to make this radical shift, this turning of the channel, more doable.

I marvel at our ability to accept transitions, from naked embrace to the cold scrutiny of armed guards, from delicious abandon on hot, damp sheets to snow and ice and shoulders bunched like fists at the ears. Planes and trains show us our capacity for instantaneous adaptation. So do secret lovers. I walk into my house that evening, say hello to Eli and the cats, and ask, "What would you like for dinner?"

. . . .

I witness the way Jim turns back into his life and I don't, at first, recognize how easily my own life recaptures me. In mere minutes I'm fully engaged with the mail, the cat litter, the magazine deadlines, the six or seven performance evaluations I must write in the next week or so. And so much more.

I tell no one about my weekend. It's almost as if it never happened. I've unpacked and returned the suitcase, and now I watch as the little bruises on my arms, from where Jim restrained me with his teeth, fade into nothingness.

Jim and I, meanwhile, pick up where we left off with our telephone relationship. It's not long before I see that there are two Jims— the physical Jim and the phone Jim. We speak briefly while I'm out running, when I'm in the car, or for a minute now and then when I'm at work. This is different from the long weekend. This is two people getting to know each other, avoiding touchy subjects like want or the future, sharing each other's day, sounding off explosively about the war in Iraq, the shocking ineptitude of our president, the arrogance of the administration. Unrestrained rants about politics and the economy and the power structure belie a deeper rage but I am content to let that be. The politics, the greed, the wanton disregard for the welfare and future of the populace, the killing of innocent people in Iraq and Afghanistan incite bottomless rage all on their own.

. . . .

One morning, a week before Christmas and just a few days after my first weekend with Jim, I step out of the bathroom after my shower. I feel rushed, as I always do on mornings that I run, because I know I'm going to be late for work.

Eli comes to meet me as I gather up my briefcase, lunch, and purse. "Jim called," he says.

"He did?" I'm flabbergasted.

"Yes. He called on your cell phone and I answered it. He's coming for Christmas."

"He's what?" Flabbergasted, nothing. I'm horrified.

"We talked and when I saw that he didn't have plans, I invited him up here."

I begin to understand. Jim called me on my phone, Eli heard it and fished it out of my purse. Jim, caught by surprise, just went along with Eli and pretended he called us to talk about the holiday.

"He can't come," I say, the second time I've bullied Eli this week. "It's out of the question. We don't even celebrate the holiday anymore and we said this year it would be low key." That part is true. I plan to take the day before and after Christmas off to read, start fresh files for the new year, and relax.

Eli nods, as if he understands and agrees, which he couldn't possibly. Jim is a treasured friend and Eli would like nothing better than to sit around on Christmas Eve and drink Wild Turkey with him.

"Besides," I say, "Jim hates Christmas as much as you do."

Once I'm in the car driving to work, I start to calm down. I call Jim. "What the hell?" I ask.

He's pretty worried himself. "I fucked up," he says. "Eli answered your cell phone and it was after 9:00 AM. I thought you'd be at work by now."

"I'm never at work at 9:00. I work till 7:00 so I have no compunctions about getting in at 9:30."

"Well, I'm coming for Christmas."

"No you're not."

"I'm not?"

"I already told Eli it's out of the question."

We're both relieved. I still don't know if I'll ever see Jim again but seeing him against the backdrop of Eli and Christmas and all the pent-up want would be ruinous.

．．．．．．．．．．．．

Want is a sickness, an insane obsession that runs its course. A serious case of it can last more than a year and is linked to chemicals the body produces, as doctors who read brain scans can now attest. Once the rush of chemicals subsides, once the snow melts, you get to see what's really there. A rusted tricycle? A trellis with a couple of broken rungs? Maybe it's a pot of gold. . . .

Jim's a mystery despite what he says. "I'm transparent," he tells me. "You get exactly what you see." The reason I believe this is because I want to. There's no Rae watching out for Rae.

After insanity comes Phase II—preoccupation—when another set of chemicals kicks in. This batch produces warm, loving feelings. If not, then you can invoke that old standard—"There's no chemistry"—and move on.

It's early on and I see no end to the obsession.

One of the photographers I supervise is working in one of the large galleries. In the hours before the museum opens to the public, it's quiet and empty except for a few guards assigned to keep an eye on things. Dennis is shooting introductory panels to a major exhibition opening soon. It's very dark in this room and he's got a few soft lights rigged on stands and a scissor lift to elevate him for certain wider views of the show.

He paints with light, which means he's swinging a small, hand-held lamp in an arc across the face of a large wall to illuminate certain words with fleeting, thin light. Swish. Release the shutter. Swish. Release the shutter. It's a low-light exhibition, to protect the many works on view. Why wouldn't I be thinking of Jim's strong, sculpted profile in candlelight, the way his round, white butt looks utterly succulent as he pulls off his underwear, the way his penis, when he offers it to me, gets hard in my hand?

He tells me, "I love it when you hold my penis," and I marvel at how something so simple can be so erotic.

I watch the photographer a little while, transfixed by the sweep of light, by the sudden sense of the head of Jim's penis soft against my closed lips. I open up, little by little, surround the sweet smooth head with the pillowy, inner sides of my lips. I touch my tongue to that small slit from which ejaculate surges like lava, and I use my tongue to take measure of the buoyant shape as if I were running my hands along a marble sculpture.

God. I feel vertiginous, a bit sweaty, the swaying lights like one of the small boats out in the harbor rocking side to side one breezy evening, the tiny light at the top of the mast swinging to and fro, to and fro. It is so easy to slip from that tiny point of arcing light to slow, deliberate fucking, Jim on top of me, pushing, pulling, mere centimeters, just the head of his penis in and out, in and out.

. . . .

As Christmas approaches, lots of holiday treats are delivered to my office. Baskets of fruit, a coffeecake, cheeses, nuts, tins of cookies, a box of brownies, fudge, and other foods arrive from friends, staff, and vendors. Occasionally the deliveries spark festive little respites from work. We take a break, gather around the conference table where the bounty is displayed, and talk and nibble. When people we know walk by our office/gallery space, we invite them to share.

Both Eli and I have been subsisting on fruits, vegetables, and fish. But it's the holidays, so, on my last day of work before my short vacation, I take one brownie from the table as a surprise for Eli. It was made in Tennessee, sent to us by one of our graphic artists as a gift, and it has a name like Decadent or Killer. It feels heavy and dense and soft. It could weigh as much as half a pound. I almost don't take it, think about leaving it for the staff, but there are six of them and so I decide it's okay to bring one. Though Eli hasn't been eating sweets, he loves them.

It's the day before Christmas Eve and I get home from work early, around three or four. My short vacation has begun and I'm surprised at how happy I am. My daughter and her boyfriend are coming for Christmas dinner, Eli and I both have good books to read, and I'm working on a writing project that I like. Jim and I speak frequently and we laugh a lot. It's all good.

Eli, I see, has begun the holiday feed right on schedule. He's cracking open and eating pistachio nuts by the handful. A gift from a neighbor, he tells me. I hand him the brownie and he opens it and starts to wolf it down. Take it easy, I warn, these are your first treats in weeks.

He says the brownie is delicious and offers me nuts and bites of brownie, which I decide against.

I sit down for a couple of minutes to make a shopping list and then tell Eli I'm going to Trader Joe's, a half-hour drive from Rockport. He says he has a stomachache. "You're not used to eating such rich food," I say and bring him a small glass of seltzer water.

Eli's nowhere to be found when I get back two hours later and I feel an eerie quiet all around me. There's an emptiness that doesn't feel right. Other than the absence of Eli and an ominous sixth sense that I'm not yet trusting, nothing else suggests that I should worry. So I put away the groceries, change into jeans and a sweater, and sit down to read. Reading doesn't hold my attention so I push the book and newspapers aside. My thoughts bounce erratically.

After an hour or so I finally admit it: Something's wrong. Eli's car is parked behind the house and it's nine at night and nothing like this has ever happened before. He doesn't just disappear for hours.

I call Jim and tell him I think Eli must have gone to the hospital because of his stomachache but I'm not sure because there's no sign of trouble and, besides, who calls an ambulance for a stomachache? And why hasn't a neighbor stopped by to tell me since everyone will have noticed an ambulance's flashing lights and Eli writhing and moaning on a stretcher? And why, if it's too late to stop by, hasn't someone called at least and why isn't there a note? Everything's just as I left it except for the missing Eli. I tell Jim I'm going to call the hospital ER to see if he's there.

A nurse tells me Eli's in a lot of pain, has been medicated, and seems to have some sort of intestinal blockage. This news is further assurance, in my own thinking, that it's the brownie.

I'm surprised to hear they're waiting for an ambulance to transport him again, this time to a larger hospital in nearby Beverly. They'll move him between midnight and 1 AM.

I call Jim back and tell him what's happening. I'm concerned but not panicked. I'm sure it's the brownie and make a joke out of it. That heavy stuff is a mass, a humongous clump of fat. I can almost visualize how it's being squeezed from his esophagus through his stomach and into his upper intestinal tract, excruciatingly slowly, like a half-gallon can of Crisco lodging itself in some narrow bend. It needs time to work its way through his system. My guess is that he panicked and called an ambulance because he tends to get extremely painful indigestion. Everything about this fits and there's a certain logic that assures me of a quick resolution. What I don't take into consideration is the holidays, how all the doctors are away till after the New Year, and how hospitals, deaf to my input, often take medications and treatments to the extreme, making things worse—especially for those who suffer from mental illness and rely on drugs that interact with narcotic painkillers.

My voice is shaky, I'm tired, and I'm going to have to drive to the hospital to deliver a list of Eli's many medications. They should have this information in their computer because this isn't his first visit to ER and this hospital. Going over Eli's meds with a nurse will take time and patience. Eli uses several medications to help manage his bipolar disease and to help him breathe because he has COPD, which includes emphysema and asthma. There are other disorders and other meds, too.

What's important to me is that Eli adhere to his regime. If he misses any of his doses, his behavior worsens. Or, if they give him the narcotic painkillers that interact with the lithium, he quickly cycles between the extremes of severe depression, rage, and mania. My biggest job when I get to the hospital will be to stop them from giving him drugs that will induce a bout of depression.

It won't be easy. Past experience has shown me they want only to silence him. An entry like "excitable" on his chart spells serious trouble for Eli. They dope him till he drools. And when they send him home, the drug interactions then become my problem. Just three years before, I moved into a nearby inn for three months after the hospitalist prescribed high doses of Percocet for severe pain due to herniated discs. This cost me $4,000 for housing and expenses, and it cost Eli $14,000 in credit card debt because, while manic, he charged everything from an ergonomic office chair he never used to a CD changer he never unwrapped to a rotting antique beaded African belt.

The hospitalist, the doctor assigned to treat Eli when he was hospitalized for his herniated discs, didn't consult with me and it's unclear whether he spoke with his primary care physician or his specialists, such as the psychiatrist and Eli's pulmonary doctor. This usually spells disaster for the mentally ill, who spend years of trial and error working out a drug regime with their psychiatrist.

Eli was, in fact, readmitted to the same hospital the day after his release from this episode. This second admission was for severe asthma and bronchitis, which he'd developed in the hospital and which, despite the nonstop coughing that provoked vomiting and cries of alarm from his roommates, they refused to treat with anything but Robitussin. Following that were three months of rages, the $14,000 spending spree, and one attempt at suicide. He stopped the Percocet on his own and his depression and rages disappeared.

I tell Jim: Poor Eli. He must be scared. He hates hospitals. If he didn't take the time to leave a note it must, in fact, be pretty bad. The only part that doesn't fit is this transfer, in the early morning hours of Christmas Eve, to a bigger hospital fifteen miles to the south of us.

It's so unusual to be home alone at this hour of the night, I say. If Eli weren't in trouble, I'd actually savor this.

Jim suggests we have a glass of wine together before I leave. What a good idea. I pour some red wine, sit down, and put my feet up. We talk and laugh and sip wine for a few minutes. It almost feels like we're together again. When I hang up I'm feeling relaxed and ready to head to the hospital.

. . . .

It's 11:30 when I park my car and approach the emergency room by way of the ambulance pavilion. A sign says that this is the only way in after 10 PM. Standing beside an ambulance and staring quietly into the darkness is a firefighter I know from Gloucester. I don't ask but assume he's just brought someone to the hospital. He's so absorbed, so still that I assume the person he recently touched and treated and tried to help has died. What must that be like? I note that he's not in uniform and that he's in no hurry to get back to the station.

I pause to speak with him. I appreciate this opportunity to talk, to discharge some of the anxious energy that's built up during my fifteen-minute ride through the dark wintry streets of Cape Ann. So we chat. I relax, muster courage, and will an infusion of energy to face whatever's next.

The earlier optimism drains off the minute I step inside the emergency room. Oh, no. Nurses and doctors stare at charts and computer monitors, noncommunicative inside a central glass administrative area. They're all too busy to look up when I approach. Eventually I say hello and wait to be acknowledged. I'm finally told where I can find Eli and that it's okay to go see him.

. . . .

I hardly recognize Eli. He's naked under a sheet. He seems bony. He's wet with sweat, his face is an alarming shade of gray, and he's moaning. A tube runs from what must be his penis, under the sheet, to a plastic bag pinned to the underside of the gurney. Jesus. What is this?

"Eli?"

He opens his eyes and looks in my direction. I see that he's already hopelessly drugged.

"It's bad." That's all he says.

"IT'S GOING TO BE A LONG HAUL"

CHAPTER 8

A nurse tells us the ambulance is on its way. She says that Eli has a large blockage in his lower intestine, based on the x-rays, and that they need to halt any further ingestion of food and fluids until it clears up on its own or until further tests reveal the nature of the trouble. They're talking about operating, she says, but a surgeon will call.

"Wouldn't he have had some warning signs before this?" I ask. "He's been fine. It's just that he ate this enormous brownie on top of a whole lot of pistachios." Eyes roll at this simplistic cause-and-effect explanation, so I shut up and wait with Eli for the ambulance to take him to Beverly. Maybe digestive juices, like the other juices that facilitate our bodily functions, deplete as we age. Eli is sixty, after all, perhaps too old for the enthusiastic consumption of holiday treats.

I gather up Eli's clothes and his messenger bag and drive home. I leave my car parked on the street for the rest of the night, which is against the law in Rockport in winter. I hardly care. It's after 2 AM and I'm in shock. I collapse onto the couch fully clothed and wait for a phone call.

●●●●●●●●●●●●

His condition is worsening, I tell Jim after spending most of the following day with Eli. I'm hesitant to get into too much detail. This is my problem, not Jim's. I'm concerned that Eli's ordeal and, more to the point, my worry and stress and preoccupation with this perplexing drama are going to derail the love affair. When Jim said "Everything's foreplay," he wasn't referring to catheters. Suddenly my life is equal parts want and worry.

Eli is barely coherent. He can't even have water or his medications. Unbelievably, I'm told there's no IV form of lithium. I spend an hour or two online looking to see if any of Eli's medications can be administered intravenously. The answer is no and someone at the nurse's station tells me earlier in the day that they sometimes use a strong antipsychotic in these instances. Lithium doesn't so much treat the symptoms as it prevents them from occurring in the first place, whereas this medication seems more like a chemically induced straitjacket—immobilizing the patient. At least that's what it seems to be doing to Eli.

It seems preposterous that a medication like lithium, so commonly used, can only be taken orally. So for the first time in three decades, Eli is off all his meds—cold turkey. This can't be good. And there's no one with any expertise to consult. It's Christmas Eve. I leave messages with all of Eli's doctors and ask them to call me back. No one does; not now, not ever.

It's a confluence of bad things, I tell Jim. Like a perfect storm of maladies.

. . . .

On Christmas Day my daughter and her boyfriend come to dinner as planned. I make coq au vin and serve it with mashed potatoes. It's comfort food. We eat quickly, without appetite, and then drive south to the hospital. Inconsolably thirsty, Eli begs us for water. He tells my daughter: "They say I can have soup now. So it stands to reason that I can have water, too. Please bring me some." I see that he's still getting fluids and nutrients intravenously.

My daughter brings him water, as requested. His hands shake as he holds the thin, pointy paper cup she gets from a dispenser over the sink. He takes a few desperate gulps and holds out the cup for a refill. It's then that I realize he's lied to her. I grab the cup and toss it in the garbage. He falls back on his pillow, spent from the effort.

. . . .

Eli's much worse on Christmas Day. He's more disoriented, more feverish, more of a zombie. The nurse at the desk tells me he still can't have anything to eat or drink. "But it's been three days," I say. "He'll be fine for at least a week," she replies.

"A week? But he's thirsty."

"They always are."

Jesus, I think, *healthcare* is a misnomer. There's no "care" in healthcare.

"How will he be fine?" I ask. "He isn't taking his meds."

I see, hovered over some paperwork, the same hospitalist who treated Eli the last time. This doctor, the liberal dispenser of Percocet, is responsible for months of hardship and eventually, for Eli's decision to declare bankruptcy. Yet I must not alienate him because, once again, he's in charge of my significant other. And, since Eli and I aren't married, the privacy issues often prevent me from getting information on Eli despite the healthcare proxies and other signed documents I have.

"Doctor, what can you tell me about Eli? What's wrong with him?" I have to call out because he's sitting in a far corner of the administrative area that's encircled by glass. He calls back that he'll meet me in Eli's room in five minutes.

My daughter, her boyfriend, and I stand around Eli's bed and make small talk among ourselves. At one point we pull out gifts we've brought Eli. We open them for him. One is a wind-up toy, which we all play with for a while. Eli's touched by these little gifts and he seems appreciative of the attention.

Time passes and the doctor doesn't arrive. Only the most severe cases are hospitalized right now, so we assume he's dealing with an emergency. Eli slips in and out. We try not to engage him. He's not really present, but we can get his attention when we need to. It's best to let him hover in this uncomprehending zone, a place where there's not as much suffering.

When the doctor finally arrives, he tells us a surgeon is going to meet with us.

"When?" I ask.

"In a day or two."

"What?" I'm not getting it. "We want to know what's wrong with Eli now."

It's late afternoon on Christmas Day. This floor of the hospital is so empty it echoes. I continue, "Eli had been doing just fine. What's going on?"

The doctor again says the surgeon wants to talk to us.

"But you must know what's wrong. How can you treat him if you don't know what's wrong with him?"

He gives up the resistance and says, "He's got an extensive mass that's spread throughout his digestive tract."

A spreading mass? For some absurd reason, I think of the great molasses flood in Boston's North End in 1919. Focus, I tell myself. Pay attention. I kick at a curl of red ribbon on the floor and it catches on the toe of my boot. The doctor's implying a malignancy. I lean against Eli's bed and attempt to catch my breath and curb the dizziness. I feel stupid, unable to process the information. I can feel my eyes blinking like hazard lights.

From his bed Eli moans, "Shit. I'm going to die." He's heard everything.

I hold Eli's hand and say, "This can't be true." The doctor walks out when we all start to cry.

The next morning I bring a friend with me who wants to say hello to Eli and we see immediately that he's in terrible trouble. His fever is so high that the cold compresses we put on his forehead instantly dry up. I run to the nurses' station and tell them I think Eli has a severe bladder infection because there's blood all over the sheet where the catheter is and there's blood in the urine pouch. A nurse says it will take three days for a culture and I say, "Bullshit. All you have to do is look. His urine is red. And Eli says he's been complaining all night to the nurses about how much it hurts."

The nurse shrugs and walks away. This is simply unbelievable. I head to the nurses' station and find the hospitalist. "Come right now," I say. "You've got an emergency."

He sees the trouble and within a minute or two, a team arrives wheeling a large mobile unit of some kind. They check Eli's vital signs. They take a lot of blood and they take some of the urine and spin the dark, rusty-colored fluid right there. They even do an EKG. I'm so jaded at this point that I suspect they're doing all this for show, like guerrilla theater. But then the doctor looks up from the readouts and says, "Get him to ICU."

. . . .

A couple of days into Eli's ordeal in ICU Jim asks if I'd like him to drive up so we can spend the weekend together.

"How about some R&R?" he asks.

This is like being asked if I want a hot fudge sundae.

"Of course!" I say. "Hurry."

We laugh and with that laugh, I feel lighter and happier and hornier than I've felt in weeks. What a wonderful man Jim is turning out to be.

After all that fantasizing building up to all that sex—it's as if part of me froze. I don't yet realize it, but this hot and cold is more than just the stress of Eli's acute illness. It's the pattern that long-distance lovers fall into to protect themselves. Cool at departure. Deep freeze during the intervening weeks. Warm as the rendezvous nears. Hot the day before. Unendurable the day of. Jim calls it "countdown."

The idea of Jim driving to me is a turn-on all by itself. But it's also a tremendous relief. It's been a hard, exhausting time. And although I nightly regale Jim with dramatic stories from the hospital bedside, I keep it as upbeat and positive as I am able. I want the love affair separate, protected, only for special occasions—like an Easter frock. More to the point: I want the love affair and I want it intact. I uphold my vow to do nothing consciously to imperil it.

Yet, it's been so lonely. While it's easy to respond to upbeat Jim in kind, I spend hours of each day locked inside an intensive care unit. You have to be buzzed in and you have to be buzzed out. And there's the big extended family I've come to think of as The Grievers. They've fully inhabited the Family Room. Stuffed animals, a cooler full of soft drinks, stinky running clothes, blankets, and pillows are strewn all over the floor and chairs. Priests occasionally stop by to sit with The Grievers. I arrive each morning for coffee and permission to enter the inner sanctum of suffering, death, and, sometimes, healing, and I'm surrounded by this enormous family. I watch as, one by one, members are called to the bedside of the failing matriarch. One by one, they get buzzed in. One by one they say goodbye. One by one they come back to the Family Room to wait, in tears. At least they have each other, I think morosely.

Eli's family is, of course, nowhere to be found. The easy answer is that they have problems of their own. I've been understanding of this since I met Eli. I share none of the dramas with them and expect nothing of them. But their absence, and their resentment of the demands he's made on them over the years, is harsh. I care for Eli by myself. He's my responsibility. If I don't honor my love and caring for him, if I don't share this problem with him, I'm sure he would become homeless and perish. I will do anything to prevent that from happening to him.

I wish so much for some Grievers of my own. If Eli's family were there with me, if there were an extended family in my life like The Grievers, my role in his life would be very different. I'd be a loyal friend. I'd be there for him. But at the end of the day I'd go home alone to my own bed and my own life, trusting the others to pitch in and help the man survive and make a decent life for himself.

. . . .

His days in ICU seem to drag on. I sit with the physical body of Eli, but not the Eli I knew, in the mornings before work and in the evenings after work. While with him, I work on my laptop, make work-related phone calls from the Family Room, try to reach his doctors, chase down nurses, work to befriend everybody who has anything to do with him, and keep up some kind of connection with Eli. So, with Jim's offer, a huge weight lifts. This feels a little like sharing. I thank him and look forward to Friday, when he'll arrive.

It occurs to me that Jim's offer is, in fact, much more than a proposed rendezvous between two lovers. It's a statement of his own about responsibility. He's a responsible man who sees someone he likes in trouble. He is compassionate. He wants to help me and he offers just what I need—distraction and the release that comes with laughter and wonderful sex. I am so grateful I send a prayer of thanks in his name out into the universe.

That night I have my dinner, as I often do, in the hospital cafeteria. They serve salmon and baked potatoes. It tastes really really good and costs $5. I chew on lettuce and think more about Jim. He's coming in just a couple of days. Our first weekend together, so full of sex and wine and sleeplessness, has the recall of a dream—foggy, far away, shifting, hard to pin down. Not so strange, really, to get nervous and excited and scared all over again.

• • • • • • • • • • • •

A doctor, a friend of Eli's, visits him in ICU. I know her, as well, having had dinner with her and her husband a couple of times. She comes into Eli's glassed-in ICU room, with its own x-ray equipment and sink and operating room setup and sees me bending over, speaking to Eli.

"Rae?" she asks.

I say hello and we hug. "You look so beautiful," she says.

This seems so inappropriate in so many ways but I remember saying something just like this at the funeral of my friend's mother. "What's different about you?" the doctor asks.

I shrug, embarrassed. My friend, Eve, is in the room. She drove two hours from New Hampshire to be here. She said the same thing when we met downstairs in the lobby. And the day before, while picking up a book at the bookstore, the manager caught sight of me and said, "You look luminous." I haven't slept, have hardly eaten, and worry all the time. I work ten-hour days, spend mornings and nights in ICU, leave messages for doctors, and watch the comings and goings of The Grievers. How can I be luminous?

I ask the doctor if she's seen the CT scans and x-rays. Yes, she says and begins drawing on a scrap of paper. She sketches an esophagus, a stomach, and a bit of the upper intestinal tract. A couple of times she erases and redraws parts of it. She then uses the side of the pencil to lay down a thick black area, like an oil slick, that extends throughout all three. This laying down of the black mass takes a long time and as she works on her sketch, my legs begin to shake.

"This is what it looks like," she says.

I am flabbergasted.

"Is he going to die of this?" It looks to me like the entire bottom of the esophagus and much of the stomach wall are host to the black mass.

She only says, "It's going to be a long haul."

I know right then that I cannot go the distance on this. A tooth-ache sends Eli over the edge. I once broke into tears in his dentist's office after spending a night with Eli in tooth pain. He's horrendous. Unbearable. Abusive. A dental assistant in the office took me aside and told me her husband was bipolar. When they're in pain, everything goes haywire, she said. You'd better hope he never gets back pain. Of course Eli did get back pain and I lived at a B&B for three months.

So what am I to do with a man who has no stomach and a possible colostomy bag—which happens to be among the things Eli has always feared—and who is undergoing chemotherapy while off lithium? This is a toothache times a trillion. I take the paper scrap and head home. Everything has changed, as I knew it someday would. And now, there's Jim, who has begun to say: Take care of yourself. Choose you. If it comes down to it, you need to choose yourself.

The shape of the new year, all twelve months stretched before me, is already beginning to make itself known. The year appears like a landscape that I'm beginning to discern, as if through a lifting fog. I see life and death issues. A man in serious peril. A lover too good to turn away from. A woman on the downside of middle age facing painful, life-altering decisions. Roads not taken now to be reconsidered. Change.

. . . .

Things clear up a bit as I drive. I have been asking Eli to move out almost every day. This will force the issue, since I no longer have cash reserves to support months in a nearby B&B. And for the past year, we've had several meetings with doctors, including a nephrologist, about the lithium toxicity that is now having a deleterious effect on Eli's kidneys. They are showing the first signs of failure. It won't be long before we'll have to find alternative treatments again. We've tried before with disastrous results.

I must somehow try to save Eli and save myself. The difference now is these are mutually exclusive efforts.

. . . .

Jim parks his car in the town parking lot instead of in front of the house. The neighbors see everything and he agrees that we should be careful. This is still Eli's home. I respect Eli but that only goes so far right now. I need Jim to be here even if it's just for sex. What else can I ask of a man I hardly know, even if he's an old friend of Eli's? And we decide on the phone in advance that he shouldn't go see Eli because it would only frighten him. A spontaneous visit from Jim is as rare as Last Rites.

You can't miss Jim as he walks up the street. He's taller than almost every other man in Rockport and there's a visible strength that comes from his broad, sturdy physique. Not to mention, he wears a brightly colored micro-fleece cap that complements his frequent smile and looks a little like an abstract painting made while smoking pot. My friend Keith sees him and says, "Jeez, he looks like a movie star."

I meet Jim at the bottom of the stairs and walk him up. It's very awkward at first, almost as if I must get to know him all over again. I don't realize it now, but in fact every rendezvous will be just like this one. I hug him, kiss him, tell him I'm so glad to see him. Privately I look him over and think: He's a complete stranger. Did I actually sleep with this man?

The phone rings just as Jim takes off his coat. It's my sister from Los Angeles. I tell her Eli's very sick, which she knows, and that he's in intensive care and has some kind of spreading growth. She knows this, too, probably from speaking with my father. She asks who's been around to help and I name a few people, including the Christmas visit with my daughter. She starts to list for me the ways I've spoiled my daughter, possibly with the goal of showing me why I won't be able to count on my daughter for anything. Suddenly I'm very tired and don't know how I will live through another word of this. "I don't want to have this discussion," I tell her and hang up abruptly. I look over my shoulder to see Jim standing right behind me and I wonder what he makes of me at this moment. He doesn't say a word.

. . . .

I stuff my cell phone into my pants pocket. I'd like to turn it off now that Jim's here but I must not. What if the hospital were to call? What if Eli dies? Since my love affair with Jim began, my phone has been my constant companion. It's smooth and small and warms up in the palm of my hand when I take a run with it or when I hold it while waiting for a scheduled phone date with Jim. I sometimes think of the pit of an avocado when I've got it with me, its organic shape fitting so naturally into the cup of my hand. Usually when I drive, I drop it between my legs. When Jim calls, as he usually does when I'm heading to work, the little thing vibrates and buzzes. It's Jim, I think, and reach down for it. The phone has become a bit of a comfort to me.

"Would you like a martini?" Jim asks as I turn back to him after the phone call. I tell him yes. While he begins to pull together everything needed for martinis, I root around in my refrigerator for hummus, grapes, olives, feta, nuts, and some of the crackers and paté we ignored on Christmas Day. There are also a few thin, spicy cookies that a Swedish friend made and left on my door stoop on Christmas Eve that I haven't even opened. As I unwrap them I think—if only Eli had eaten these instead. I spread everything on the table like a picnic, our first of many in Rockport.

Jim pulls two chilled martini glasses from the freezer and into them he pours the iced, shaken gin to which he's added just a touch of dry vermouth. These are exquisite drinks, all crystalline and arctic cold. On the surface floats the thinnest skin of ice.

"To you," says Jim, as he carefully passes me the martini and we gently clink the rims and toast. We dip our heads and sip. Just delicious, I tell him.

I let the gin bring me to a new focus, something other than poor Eli, for the first time in over a week. It's so easy now to turn to Jim and his radiant smile and his animated talk of the drive up and how fucking cold it is in my house and how the best martinis have this fabulous ephemeral touch, a frozen sheen adrift on the glinting expanse of gin, and how, with everything going on with Eli, he is very glad he could make it up. We laugh and talk and taste all the foods and sip the martinis till the glasses are empty and our bodies turn liquidy and loose. Then we head up to bed and make love.

. . . .

We fall asleep for an hour or two. When I awaken I'm still afloat, riding the high of that elegant martini. Outside my tiny bedroom window a nor'easter has taken hold. I can feel the ocean waves crash—boom, boom, boom—one right after another. The beach is getting a savage pummeling. It's windy and wintry now. The whole room sways and I fight that sense of vertigo that happens when you're three stories up and at the mercy of a fierce winter storm. Alongside me in the crawl space that runs the length of the attic, I hear a deep, low moan as if the air is being sucked through a tube. Though this small attic room is unheated, our naked bodies have warmed the air. We are safe here in this tight cube of a space while sand and salt and snow and shingles fly like confetti.

I notice that Jim's voice has joined this stormy chorus, though he's speaking in harmonics again—something parallel, something that sets a slight buzz running through me, something persuasive and hypnotic laid on top of the stormy night. His voice is low and deliberate. He's telling me to do something. I don't really discern the content at first but hear the urging, the prodding, the gentle instructive nature of the message. I do as I'm told. I move slightly and he pulls the pillows out of the way. He's saying something about rolling over on my stomach, moving up to my knees, asking me if this is okay, telling me to lean forward a bit, spread my legs, a little more, wrap my fingers around the thick tubing that forms the outer edges of the headboard. His hands reach around and grab onto my hip bones. I arch instinctively. I let him in. I follow his whispered directions, arching again, this time against his pelvis. His lips are soft and wet on my neck. For a second I feel safe, lulled by the quiet insistent tone and the warm touch of his tongue in my ear. His teeth clamp into my shoulder. He bites down. My hands sweat and I work to hang on to the pretty filigreed ironwork. My eyes open and I see that I am looking into great tumult. Huge waves now slam into the street below. They soar over the retaining walls and they smash into the cliffs that run up the coastline. All the boundaries are broken now. Jim's in the bed I've shared with Eli for eighteen years.

It's like we've never fucked before. Jim's low growl builds to a roar as the house and the man and the whole world shudder and shake and let go. When he screams the only ones to hear are me and the wind, a wild wind that has already grabbed this and taken it away.

I lie quiet, afterward, wondering how it is that I can find a part of myself that's still so unburdened, so open to laughing and playing and endless sex. I've always been good at compartmentalizing, even in extreme cases. But this is different because Eli's situation is dire and demanding and it has drained me. Or so I thought.

I look over at Jim. He's quietly sleeping, his mouth closed, his breathing slow and steady, his beautiful face relaxed. He's on my side of the bed and I'm on Eli's so even this long-cherished comfort zone is askew. As I drift off I think about what will happen next. Jim will go back to Manhattan on Sunday and I will go back to the hospital and carry on with the wait. Still no word from the phantom surgeon. Still no calls from the psychiatrist. No one from the hospital consults with me. Eli is too out of it to talk to the medical staff when they do show up. I tell the few people I see at work between Christmas and New Year's—when all is eerily becalmed: Never get seriously ill during the holidays.

So they keep Eli in a semicoma, almost like a hibernation, where he functions at low ebb till things at the hospital return to normal after January 1.

. . . .

Jim's visit is so short. But two things happen this weekend that mean a lot to a woman who wants more of the love affair. One, Jim drives all the way up to New England in the dead of winter and sits in a hospital hallway while I visit Eli. This is great. It's sex with benefits. Two, he says he'd like to come back in a few weeks. Since we have no idea what to expect at that time, we decide we'll stay in a hotel in Salem, where I work, and take a holiday.

When it's time to say goodbye, I walk Jim outside to his big, banged-up Suburban he uses in the city to haul equipment and crew. He's pulled the truck up to the house so he won't have to carry his suitcase across town to the public parking lot. As always, I worry about my neighbors though I tell my downstairs tenant, a friend, in advance about Jim's visit.

"I have a lover," I tell her straight out. "He's coming for the weekend."

"Really?" she says. "How nice." I know she means it.

. . . .

Jim tosses his suitcase into the back seat and I stand next to him in the street as he prepares to get into the driver's seat and leave. He turns, embraces me, kisses me, and continues to hold on. "There," he whispers into my ear. "It's done. They know I'm here now. That I'm your man."

. . . .

After New Year's Day, I find that Eli has been moved to a private room on the oncology floor. There is always an aide sitting at the end of his bed. It's always a woman. She always watches his every move. Better her than me because now he's gone all the time, hallucinating and enraged. I assume it's because of the withdrawal of all his medications combined with the lack of food and water. There's nothing left of him that I recognize, not even the physical Eli. He's lost twenty pounds, his skin is covered in purple, bloody blotches, and his legs are swollen to three times their size. Since the infection and his stint in ICU, he's been unable to urinate and must always wear the catheter. Another awful thing is his stench. It's the worst kind of barrier. Who would want to visit him now? Or help care for him? It's as if he's rotting.

I walk in one night after work and find him half sitting up, listing to one side, mouth hanging open. He can't focus. He doesn't know me. He's drugged. He sways to and fro trying to get a fix on the new object of movement—me—as I approach. I see that spittle drips off his chin and when I do catch sight of his eyes, I see that one eye crosses and the iris looks black instead of brown. I guess his eye looks like it is a different color because it's fully dilated. I'm sure he's had a stroke, but at this point, fuck it, I just drop my briefcase and let myself slump into the chair at his bedside. I, too, have finally given up. I feel like they have won.

. . . .

One day the doctors send Eli downstairs for a series of intestinal x-rays. This involves injections of dye into his bloodstream and timed x-rays as the dye works its way through his system. He yells and fights the people in radiology. This ordeal goes spectacularly badly. They have to keep injecting him with Valium to knock him out enough to get an x-ray taken, then wait while dye works its way farther along. While waiting, he's restrained and allowed to writhe and holler. When it's time for the next x-ray they sedate him again.

The technician is a stout, muscled man who says, "No worries. I can handle this," and I wonder, where do these angels come from? I'm relieved. Normally I would be expected to handle Eli. Instead of managing Eli, I spend my time talking with him, trying to connect him to his surroundings and to what is going on here, but he's utterly gone. I hold his hand and talk, on and on, hoping the sound of my voice penetrates his fear and anxiety and disorientation. His yelling and shouting continue till it's over and he's back on the stronger meds.

We're not told the results of these tests but I receive a call a day or two later from a social worker who's talking about moving Eli out of the regional hospital, either home or to another facility. I track down Eli's most sympathetic nurse and the hospitalist and tell them I can't have Eli come home in this condition. He has to be eating. He has to be back on his medications. He has to be able to pee and I have to feel safe with him. For some reason they heed my concerns and transfer Eli to the locked psych ward at the Addison Gilbert Hospital in Gloucester. Now he's in a new environment, surrounded by a couple of dozen elderly men and women suffering from dementia. They are sweet souls but Eli can't see this. It's incarceration and he's deeply offended. His fever immediately shoots up again but this time, they say, it's the flu.

This is the second of nine hospitalizations for Eli. The year 2007 will be, without question, one of the worst years in his life. No one should have to suffer this much, especially considering the suffering of his childhood and the loneliness and alienation that followed. His suffering has bound me to Eli more permanently than any wedding ring ever could.

After three weeks at Addison Gilbert, during which time he is allowed to begin eating again, they prepare to discharge him. I tell them, once again, I cannot have him home with me. He is not on lithium, he is unstable, he's still very ill, and I cannot be responsible any longer. Jim and my therapist both reinforce one key point, which they repeat again and again, as if I cannot hear or cannot remember: If there's a choice, choose you.

I stand in Eli's hospital room, before a social worker, a couple of nurses, a doctor, and Eli, who's woozy from another in a series of high fevers, and tell them he can't come home. They make me say this to Eli, as well. And I do. I say, "Eli, you cannot come home." He says, "I can't believe you're throwing me out of my own house."

There's nothing left to say. I leave and go back to work.

. . . .

The social worker consults with Eli's doctor friend and together they find him an adult foster care home to move into. I make the trip with Eli and the doctor to his new home, a residence in Lynn.

He's released to the care of a woman. Though she's young and has lost custody of her children, she's trained for this work. The kids live next door with their dad, her ex-husband, who occasionally spends the night. Another man lives in the house. He's morbidly obese and immobile. He's also part of the adult foster care program. He has diabetes, is unable to keep himself clean and it shows, eats all the time, and never turns off the television, even in the middle of the night. He also keeps the volume turned all the way up because he has lost his hearing and refuses to wear his hearing aids. I suspect Eli will grow to hate it almost immediately because it's been years since he's even watched television. But he warms right up to the woman, who's petite and cute and lively. She jokes with Eli as scores of papers are passed back and forth, signed, and turned over to the doctor. I help count out Eli's pills. Then we go into his new bedroom and unpack.

The arrangement is short-lived. According to Eli, the woman feeds him a can of Campbell's tomato soup a day in return for a daily food allowance that would buy a garage full of Campbell's. She calls the doctor and says Eli is hostile. Eli, in turn, says he's hungry.

When the crisis hits, I am in Houston visiting my father, who is seriously ill himself.

My cell phone rings while I'm standing in line waiting to pay for a pair of blue jeans at Dillard's, a belated Christmas gift from my father and stepmother.

It's the adult foster care program administrator, the doctor who helped us through this crisis and who is a friend. She tells me that Eli's caretaker isn't comfortable with him, that she's afraid he might become violent, and that he's already had some episodes.

I'm not surprised, of course, but I can't say this. "What happened?"

She tells me they had a fight. Something about matches and lighting the gas burner on the stove.

"Was Eli trying to cook?"

"Maybe."

"She isn't feeding him. Has he told you this?"

"He's complained about it, yes."

"I'm not clear on why I'm getting this phone call."

"We have to move Eli out of there and I can't find anywhere else for him to go. Frankly, he's not a good candidate for this program so he's terminated. As of today I've terminated him."

I'm in such a panic I can barely keep my voice down. "But what makes you think I can handle this?" I whisper. "He's not back on lithium and his psychiatrist in the hospital has refused to talk with me. If there's a plan, nobody's informed me. I can't do this. I won't do this." I realize where I am. I look around. The polite Southern women in line with me drop their eyes to the floor.

"So what exactly are you telling me?"

She says that the doctor won't put Eli back on lithium because of the kidney problems. The medications are indeed an issue. It's going to take a couple of years to get his new meds adjusted. It's going to take some time.

"What?" I'm absolutely incredulous. Two years of rage and chaos?

"We're here," she says. "We're at the house."

I repeat what I'm hearing. "You're at the house."

She confirms this.

"At my house?"

"Yes."

"Why are you dumping him like this, before he's well? And without my permission? Who's going to take care of him? He has no money. There's no food. And he has that catheter. If you can't handle this, if that supposedly trained woman can't do this, how can I?"

She can't be held responsible for Eli. Friendship only goes so far. Eventually she has no choice but to hang up.

I imagine what it must be like there in Rockport in January, what the neighbors must be seeing right this minute. The doctor pulls up in her car, gets out but leaves the engine running, opens the trunk, pulls out Eli's stuff, and sets it on the granite stoop. It's snowing. It's twenty-five degrees. Eli slowly, painfully unfolds out of the car. He cannot yet urinate, he has a satchel containing over a dozen bottles of pills, each with specific and confusing time and dosage instructions, and he's confused by the moves and the malignant-mass death sentence that's still hanging over his head. All the pills in the world that aren't going to work like the lithium worked. Weak and sore and tired and abandoned, he tries to work the key into the lock.

I approach the register at Dillard's with my skinny jeans and a handful of cash and all I can see is Eli, arms full, trying to make his way into the house. Will he even be able to climb the steep stairs? He's been summarily dumped.

A few days later, while waiting for my plane to depart Houston Hobby Airport, I call Eli's doctor friend. "What was wrong with Eli?" I ask. "Remember that drawing you gave me? That spreading mass? What about all that cancer?"

"Right," she says. "I honestly don't know. I'll call you back."

She checks his medical records and phones me a few minutes later. "There's no cancer. There's nothing there."

As shocking as her statement is, I realize I'd never fully stopped believing it was the holiday brownie. I don't ask how the surgeon and other doctors who read his MRIs were so misled. I simply hang up, relieved that my suspicions are fact and that Eli isn't riddled with cancer.

INCIDENTAL WOMAN

CHAPTER 9

My way of compartmentalizing helps right now. At work I find I can zip from task to task like my brain's on roller skates. I experience a certain mental dexterity and an emotional detachment that I don't have the right to expect, given all that's happening. There's also a calm and an ease to this approach that keeps me level. I zoom out—take in the big picture when I organize; zoom in—drill down to handle specific tasks while the others quietly wait their turn.

I learned this behavior young and very well. It let me move away from disturbing events and on to other things like homework or riding my bike or getting back to sleep. It feels like switching channels on a television and I get through the year because of it.

At work, I snap off Eli's telephone rants about Campbell's tomato soup and loud television and whatever else and turn to examine the slanted, frilly typeface an earnest young intern chooses for a poster he's designing. I make some notes about readability and send it back for him to redo. I reread, from a second design proof of *Connections* magazine, an article about an installation of tiffins, or Indian lunchboxes, and stumble a bit over the article's opening sentence. I ask the editor to break up the sentence to make the story easier to get into. Later in the morning I walk outside with a staff member whose personal calls made in our open office space are starting to annoy people. All I need to say is, "Please make those calls outside on your cell phone on your lunch hour." She gets the message.

Jim is the one channel I cannot change.

All I can do is try to turn down the volume of Jim as I move through these demanding days. I wash my hands in the ladies room and feel his teeth biting into my trapezius muscle like a tomcat mounting a female. In the mirror I catch my shoulder lift, as if in response. I bend to lace up my running shoes on a snowy morning and he's back there, angling his pelvis against my butt. I want to arch my back, feel the heat of that perfect fit. Even in sleep I'm encircled. I make an effort to turn over in my bed only to find I'm somehow pinned. It's Jim. He grips my hair so hard I can't move, can't twist my head, can't push back though I need to because it hurts and I want loose. He pretends to play nice for a tenth of a second but suddenly shoves huge fingers into my vagina and I shout "No!" but my nipples harden and his mouth zeroes in and the only "No" after that is the one before "Don't stop." This isn't a dream. It isn't my body tangled up in the sheets. It isn't imagination and it's not recall. It's the miasma of Jim, lingering long after Jim has gone. It's a heavy-lidded, breath-choked, musk-scented, sweat-soaked, all-encompassing echo-world. I navigate the echo-world as I wrestle myriad matters in the here and now.

• • • • • • • • • • • •

At first, my trip to see my ailing father in Houston feels like a turning point. Flying west at the tail end of calamity is not quite the geographical fix I'd opt for if there were choices available, like Tahiti, but it's still radical—a stark leaving behind of almost everything except Jim. We speak once in the morning, briefly, and again for a long conversation before bed. I do not tell my father or stepmother about him, so they must wonder about all the laughing in my bedroom late at night. Eli, after all, is still ill and newly relocated to the adult foster care home in Lynn.

But I am very ready, however foolishly, to believe Eli is no longer just my responsibility. In celebration, I arrange my itinerary so that I will fly from Houston to JFK for a long weekend with Jim—our third, before heading north again to New England. The excitement of the pending rendezvous stokes the energy of each conversation I have with Jim. He sounds as happy as I feel.

One evening I describe in dramatic detail the exasperating loop we get stuck in while driving around Houston's beltway. We circle the city three or four maddening times. It was utterly miserable, I say, because my father refused to let me consult a map. His preposterous face-saving remark: "Those things are never right." The telling is hilarious release. I feel as if I'm in recovery. And why not? Eli is safely housed with a trained adult foster caretaker.

This, I tell myself, is the new normal. Eli is in good hands, better hands than mine, in fact, because I must impose such rigid controls—controls Eli despises—to meet my needs for peace and civility and appearances. I am, after all, my father's daughter.

The joyous thought repeats—I'm finally by myself.

Now there are no excuses. I must read more. Start reviewing books again. Never miss a day of writing. Run every other day regardless of the weather. Eat well. Live a writer's life. Be a good mom by being less of a mom, as grown daughters everywhere understand. Renew my neglected friendships. Publish often. Make money. Smile regardless. Get fitter. These are my promises to myself, now that I am free.

It never occurs to me to include my love affair with Jim on my to-do list of vows. He comes naturally. He feels easy. He is like dessert except without the calories.

I stay at my father's house a week and live every second embracing the Southern lifestyle. Freshly brewed iced tea with lemon and sweetener. Mmmm. I love it and drink glass after glass. Grapefruit and avocadoes are my staples. My Cajun stepmother's scrumptious cooking includes a killer gumbo. This is sensual overload, but I have already proved that I can handle it.

And the Tex-Mex food. It's better than no Mexican food at all so I lobby for it as often as feels polite. Behind all of this is something deeply embedded, something utterly primal and key to the sanctity of my life: Delicious food at a friendly table—it's a functional, satisfying stand-in for the nuclear family and nurturing and, perhaps, even Mother.

When very young, I trailed, transfixed, behind Enrequita, my smiling Mexican grandmother, as she worked long hours in her kitchen. She showed me every step of her food preparations while I tagged along. She used her hands to explain because she didn't speak English. Except for her daily predawn trip to Mass at Our Lady of Sorrows, where my grandfather earned the living as head gardener, she seemed housebound.

My father's mother ground her own spices with a mortar and pestle, made a legendary turkey mole that took hours of exquisite tending, and whipped up spicy shrimp pastes she spread on toasted corn tortillas as snacks for my father and his brothers when they watched football games on television. Former track stars and football players themselves, they never tired of sports.

Enrequita showed me the way to shape and cook directly on the gas flame those tender, warm, and soft flour tortillas she supplied at breakfast, lunch, and dinner for twelve sons and daughters and their hungry young families. The line for Sunday dinner at the small house on Anapamu Street in my hometown of Santa Barbara would sometimes spill out of the house and run along the walk. Homemade blood-and-milk sausages sizzled on the grill and at least once in my recollection, a pig was slaughtered, quietly and probably not entirely legally, in the back yard (How else to feed those tall, lanky football players on a gardener's wages?)—just blocks from I. Magnin and the swank El Paseo restaurant.

My father eats with the same gusto he always had. He, like many of his siblings, developed adult-onset diabetes. Many of those once-virile, once-indestructible athletes are now dead or disabled. So, except for Jim, I enjoy what I relish and what comforts, such as Tex-Mex, in strict moderation.

Every morning I go out for an early morning run before it's too hot and muggy. The goal is to twice circle the Bear Creek two-mile track. Then I like to cross the narrow road and hang out at the little zoo, where I cool down and renew the acquaintance of the goofy-looking emu, bison (a sign reads: STAND BACK. BISON CHARGE FENCE), red-tailed hawk, great gray owl, pot-bellied pig, and other animals that have ended up here. Many are old friends and I look forward to these visits.

What a transition this is. It feels like I'm floating, aloft in a temperate updraft between my real life and this, here in Houston, where I drift wherever I'm pointed. "Let's run out to the drugstore to get your dad's prescriptions." "How about watching *Lawrence of Arabia?*" "Would you like to help me whip up some of my delicious homemade pralines?"

"Sure." "Why not?" "No problem."

I write and read. I sit by my father as he watches television. I drive with my dad and my stepmother out to the country—dusty, flat expanses dotted with scrub brush, live oaks, and the occasional herd of Texas longhorn cattle. On a back road across from a swamp in the middle of nowhere we come to a rundown place encircled by pickup trucks. Here the staff works up a sweat cooking and serving monumental piles of deep-fried catfish, hush puppies and french fries, and a hamburger that's possibly as tall as a toddler. There's a perpetual burger-eating contest in progress and the restaurant walls are covered with snapshots of people in various stages of burger consumption.

One day, my stepmother and I leave my dad behind and drive to NASA in Galveston to see what now looks like something from the dinosaur age—the command post for the first lunar landing. The NASA trip further restores some continuity to my scattered life. I remember this place. I saw it on television. Watched intently. Dug out my Polaroid and took pictures of the command center and the moonwalk while it was broadcast on the television.

The West is home. The farther west I travel, the closer to Santa Barbara, the more of myself I rediscover. I wonder, as we drive back from Galveston, whether Jim feels this way when he flies west to visit his ninety-seven-year-old father in Arizona.

In the evenings, things slowly wind down. We gather at the kitchen table for as long as my father can endure the back pain. We talk, have wine, and snack on appetizers while my stepmother chatters happily from her workstation nearby.

My father is eighty-one and still every bit the Mexican alpha male he was in his younger years. Though women still turn to admire him in the airport and restaurants, he suffers from several debilitating physical problems, including a recurrence of prostate cancer, severe back problems, and the ongoing challenges of congestive heart failure. He's still a tall man, he has thick, beautiful white hair that always catches me by surprise and no wrinkles at all, and he retains a trace of the old virility he put into good practice during his football-player years.

And though my father's a recovering alcoholic with a horrific past that included violence and abusive behavior, blackouts, and arrests, he's now a mellow man who savors his nightly glass of merlot. I never expected to enjoy my father's company, much less enjoy drinking with him, but that's what we do every evening before turning to the ubiquitous television. It's sweet and relaxing. One evening while we are having our glass of wine together, I nearly knock my laptop computer onto the floor when I make a quick turn. My father, Angelo, says, "You'd better watch that drinking, Rae." If only someone sane from my family were here to witness the absurdity of this moment, I think. But there's no one else who would know just how ridiculous it is—other than Eli.

And though I miss Eli, often deeply, it's not Eli I call when I want to relate this funny, ironic story. It's Jim.

One rainy morning I decide to accompany my father to his gym, which he visits three times a week. He needs a cane, at the very least, but more realistically, a walker or even a wheelchair. His pride intervenes, however, and so we enter his gym very slowly with neither cane nor walker. Some people greet him heartily but others succumb to an open-mouthed double take as he unsteadily mounts the recumbent bike. I step up to the treadmill directly behind him. Together we get our cardio workouts over with.

My last night in Houston and a fierce lightning storm is this very minute detonating right outside these windows. In the living room, I hear Carolyn draw the drapes across the patio windows. She and my father try to shut out the blinding strobes and thunderous din, as if to neutralize at least one of the paroxysms bearing down.

The tension's been building. This morning I ran early, in advance of the worst of the heat and humidity. My playlist for my Bear Creek Park run, across the highway from my father's house, is called Houston Slog. It's been so hot and steamy that I've resorted to inspirational music, like the Krishna Das chants, to keep me going, however listless the effort is. Dread thick as the stultifying humidity hangs over everything. Lightning provides temporary release.

I'm glad to have had this time with my father but I'm always on red alert because he and Eli are very sick and in danger. It's hard to relax. In the Buddhist tradition of daily reckoning, you envision a moment when the people you love leave you. On the surface this seems like the perfect exercise for me since I've got one channel just for disaster awareness and you might say that's my default station.

Your loved ones move on, get sick, die. You die. No. I mean that I die. I'm supposed to practice knowing that I die. I'm supposed to envision my death—the ultimate loss. So far, I've never given up anything I wanted for any reason.

*My Buddhist teacher tells me the practice brings us to readiness.
Practice now. Prepare yourselves. He beseeches us to practice so we don't
have to suffer quite so much. What matters most are our relationships, says
the Lama, who asks us what good an iPod does on a deathbed. He also
says: Nothing stays the same. Everyone goes away.*

*Connectivity is the thing that sustains me above all else. How do you
train for the fact and the metaphysics of free fall?*

All the important people in my life are still alive.

Thus I have the most to lose.

*Tomorrow I leave for New York. I love my phone conversations with
Jim right now because they're so much fun, and fun is the polar opposite
of what happens when I contemplate me in my pine wood coffin sliding
into a 1,800 degree Fahrenheit furnace. Jim, a big presence with a bigger
energy, doesn't leave openings where the dread can wriggle in. On top of all
that, he's responsible. He calls, follows through, keeps promises, arrives on
time, dresses up and looks nice for me, washes the dishes, makes the coffee,
delivers the ecstasy with a smile that says, "More?"*

"Okay."

*That's my little voice, invoked to conceal the gluttony that drives my
obsession with Jim.*

I like new. I enjoy not knowing and not fretting. I love the mysteries.

*Does Jim like leather? (Don't know) Butts? (Most probably) Lima
beans? (Yes, with butter and pepper, just the way I like them) Sexual
enhancements? (Not yet) Me? (So far)*

*Interactions unfold in unexpected ways. Words are spoken in patterns
never before heard. His repertoire of kisses is not yet fully delivered. His
testicles, large and heavy—a surprising and luscious handful—straddle my
anus, rise and fall to create a debilitating ecstasy, while he rides the missionary*

position to fruition. Here, in the realm of new, expectations and anticipation cloud the joy of what is. You must abolish all to fully partake of new.

Yet my discipline needs work. I slide into my signature bad habit. I assume the worst, especially now. Anticipation, in its negative state, is a clever predator with, I believe, a special fondness for new. Mitch asks me if I use this tendency as a talisman to protect myself from the very thing I dread. That is, a made-up version of something awful is certainly better than a real something awful. It won't work, he says. Bad things will happen, says the Lama.

I use these journal entries as my daily practice. Here is where I count my blessings, as instructed, and here's where I imagine the details of my dénouement.

Meanwhile there is life to be lived.

When I was eleven, while baby-sitting a neighbor's toddler night after night, I fell under the spell of a poetry anthology I found on a bookshelf. I read many of the poems so often they became committed to memory. There, in that restless young divorcée's spare apartment, late in the long evenings when she was who knows where, I came across the idea of joy. Sara Teasdale presented it as if it were novel and counterculture and impossibly rare. It was.

In my household, joy was an obscenity. Displaying it incited my mother's ridicule, and worse. So I coveted the hope and promise Sara Teasdale revealed to me in "Barter." Right then, I determined, joy and peace and beauty were mine to take, if ever I were to find them.

> *Life has loveliness to sell,*
> *All beautiful and splendid things . . .*
> *Give all you have for loveliness;*

Buy it, and never count the cost!
For one white, singing hour of peace
Count many a year of strife well lost;
And for a breath of ecstasy,
Give all you have been, or could be.

No problem! Not only would I barter for loveliness, I would sell my soul for it!

Did this message burrow itself into my subconscious? Am I that impressionable that it serves as my operating manual forty-seven years later?

"Are you excited?" Jim asks while on the phone. "Yes," I laugh, thankful for the way I can compartmentalize. Pine box. Me in it. Click. Jim dripping warm oils between my legs. Aye. Click. Eli subsisting for a week on canned tomato soup. Click. Jim, fresh out of the shower, his silver-white curls setting off the broad plains of his face. Turning me inside out like a fucking schoolgirl. Click.

"How about you?" I remember to ask. "Are you excited?"

"You better believe I'm excited. I can't wait." I love his uncensored enthusiasm.

From rendezvous to rendezvous, I don't really believe I'm ever going to see him again. Now, though, with just hours between us, it seems as if it's actually going to happen. I'm almost there and what we do, at this fabulous and long-awaited point in the cycle, is to joke and laugh.

Before we hang up, I mention that by now, Eli is asleep in our bed, back home, just where he wants to be. He's tenacious and he needs me.

"He's in your bed?" Jim asks. His voice has dropped to a register I've not heard. It's menacing and dark and hard.

"Yes," I say. I'm starting to see the problem here.

"That's my place now."

I'm quiet. All the laughing has suddenly stopped and I'm listening to silence.

Jim has one last thing to say. "This could be a deal breaker."

. . . .

By the time I leave Houston for New York I know Eli is back home. But there are layers of denial. One, I'm far away and Rockport doesn't quite seem real any more than snow does in this eighty-two-degrees-and-humid climate. Two, I'm not going to Eli. I'm going to Jim. He draws me like a supercharged magneto hauling a freight train off its tracks. So, after receiving the shocking news of Eli's return home while at the Dillard's sportswear counter, I turn the channel back to the life I'm living at the moment.

Before Jim's arrival at JFK, I rescue my suitcase from the carousel and spend ten or fifteen minutes engaged in a series of communications with an oddly dapper homeless man whose mismatched vest, slacks, and jacket are nonetheless fetching. There's a certain look he's going for—engaged, tidy, purposeful. He's in possession of a small, worn suitcase that sags in on itself, appears empty, and is 90 percent unzipped.

I'm not paying attention when I plop down beside him. I realize he's a vagrant only when he politely asks for both money and food. His diction, like his ensemble, is awkwardly formal and just a tad off.

I like this man and, without hesitation, give him what cash I have left over from my trip and the stash of food I hoarded while aboard the plane. To end the string of thank-yous, I walk the length of baggage claim a couple of times. No problem. I need to move after the long flight and I need to prevent the formation of blood clots. But the man approaches me again, his suitcase still back by the chairs. What do I have left to give? I caution him, "Be sure not to leave your stuff unattended. Security is very strict these days."

"Security?" At that, he heads right back to where we'd been sitting. It's then that I see, just beyond the bank of three seats, a huge stack of belongings. He'd carefully wedged everything behind a large display of rack cards and a stairwell. He was set for the night until I invaded his space.

Then it hits me. If it weren't for me, this could be Eli right now.

· · · · · · · · · · · · ·

Jim meets me at JFK. I'm in baggage claim, as planned, when I catch sight of him striding along the walkway on the other side of the plate glass window. I wave and smile.

Finally.

I watch him until he disappears into the doorway, headed my way. Several thoughts collide: He's such a welcome sight. It's been a long time. The rendezvous requires intricate planning and sizable expense. Vexing eventualities routinely intrude, conspiring to upset the plan. And yet, here we are.

When Jim and I find each other we have one small, disappointing, meaningless kiss. Is this because he shuns public displays of affection? Well, he's back to being practically a stranger, in any case. Once again, I know the phone Jim better than the real Jim.

He takes hold of my suitcase—that part I like—and we head out to the street. Geno, one of his subcontractors, does the driving because Jim's car is in the shop. I am so ready for Jim but find, to my consternation, that Jim is all business. Am I invisible? In no sexual scenario—no matter how kinky and no matter how you spin it—in no way whatsoever do I find this the preferred behavior for one's lover at the outset of a torrid affair. But Jim has channels, too, and right now it's switched on getting the hell out of JFK.

After a hasty follow-up hug he takes a seat up front with Geno while I squeeze in back alongside toolboxes and ragged-looking window frames no doubt rife with slivers and other paraphernalia belonging to a man who restores stained-glass windows.

It's ten degrees and breathing feels like I'm sucking straight pins into my lungs. Back to shallow breaths and Clinique moisturizer. Whatever benefits my skin soaked up from the Southern humidity are immediately wiped dry by this winter wind. At first the disorientation of lifting off in hot Houston and touching down in frigid New York City keeps me too off-kilter to take any of this very seriously.

Jim, I note from behind, is wearing the colorful ski cap his daughter wishes he would lose though I find it's starting to grow on me. Or perhaps it's the emerging contrarian in me. I'd like to tug it off and touch his hair. More than that, I'd like to reach around and run my palm along his thigh. I know just how it will feel and I could do that from where I'm seated but, of course, I do nothing but fantasize.

For the first time, I notice that Jim's wearing one of those rugged Carhartt jackets and blue jeans. The guys must have just left work because there's sawdust in the creases of their clothing and they smell like sweat and turpentine.

I'm frankly annoyed. Is this a proper welcome? Now I'm finding it a bit of an effort to shrug off whatever expectations might have accrued, expectations like a warm welcome or sexy hello kiss. Yes, I'm happy to be here, within inches of Jim and en route to West 24th Street where we'll finally have a proper hello. But. . . .

Jeez. I'm cramped and crabby. I'm smashed in the back seat of a stinky truck with construction workers wearing clothing that looks and feels like coarse sandpaper. There's barely an acknowledgment that I'm back here. I reach out to tap Jim on the shoulder, to say, "Hey, what about me?" but harness that impulse immediately because the idea of touching coarse sandpaper is the polar opposite of what I thought I'd be touching at this moment. Why couldn't he have gotten his Suburban fixed sooner?

I'm freezing and hungry and my long limbs are very tired of being twisted into knots. I just got off a plane, after all. Nothing good is happening back here. I hope Jim understands the risks of rendering me invisible.

We're quickly bound up in lanes of idling traffic. I'm a knot within a knot but psychologically I'm erupting. No compartmentalizing clicking into place now, that's for sure.

I hear Jim telling Geno which way to go and how, precisely, to do it. A boss or a control freak, I wonder? I caution myself to pay attention. I don't like control freaks. But something in me gets very interested. His voice has a touch of that deep roughness I love. It's partly from fatigue and partly because he exercises those lower registers when he wants to establish control.

It's starting to feel like the foreplay here is wordplay. Jim directs every turn Geno makes. Jim tells him when to switch lanes, when to speed up, where to turn. Geno's from Russia, but he's a U.S. citizen and has lived in the city for decades. He follows Jim's directions and I sit in the back seat, like a well-trained schoolgirl, with my hands folded neatly in my lap, waiting for my turn.

. . . .

It's hot—sauna hot—in Jim's apartment and I notice that he's closed the bedroom windows and the bedroom door. God. I'm going to suffocate. Things feel claustrophobic and complicated, like maybe I'm still disgruntled even though I'm here with the man I adore and want so much that my vagina contracts when he finally beams his brilliant smile my way.

Jesus. Jim grins and I melt. It's as if I'm living in one of those goofy songs I grew up listening to in the '50s and '60s, songs I'm sure brainwashed me. Feminism was the course correction required after lyrics like "To know know know him is to love love love him and I do, yes I do, yes I do" or "I've hungered for your touch a long, lonely time . . . I need your love. God speed your love to me." We were a society of girls rendered submissive by songs.

With Jim, it's pure chemistry. Submission isn't quite right. I practice submission by intent, wildly insistent submission. I aggressively submit.

It's not about domination. It's about standing face-to-face with him. The natural order now achieved. It's that simple. That important. My body opens up, turns soft and wet, welcomes him, wants him in. My nipples take shape, protrude, reach for him, like tendrils looking for their place to anchor, to latch on to. Thus commence my acts of shameless and furious want, want that propels me 2,000 miles to him

at 500 miles an hour so he can put one finger in one place inside of me
that shuts me up and drops me to my knees.

. . . .

He smiles. I smile back. Who can resist? Next thing I know, my underwear are wet. In that embarrassing, out-of-control moment I flash
on another time, thirty-five years earlier, when my body responded
viscerally. Every time my newborn daughter cried and every time I'd
stop in awe as her toothless smile widened and rendered me helpless,
my breast milk surged and dripped. They sell pads for leaky breasts but
what is there for a woman whose vagina is clinching and spewing and
communicating an impatience verging on dysfunctional?

My body has a mind of its own. Right now it's very hot for Jim. It's
almost as if I'm a spectator. This is out of my hands. This is the ultimate
horniness. Yes. I'll have your babies. Yes, I'll do whatever you ask. Yes,
I'll pull off these wet underwear and expose all the parts of this fifty-
eight-year-old body that behaves like a lovesick schoolgirl but looks
like that of a well-used, postmenopausal woman.

Ahhhh. No worries about babies, at least.

Things start rough, somehow. He's kissing me before my clothes
are off. Kissing and undressing. Kissing and getting onto the bed. Kissing and breathing. All of it is desperate. I needn't have worried about
all the wetness. We're both immediately sweaty and wet, the way he
likes it, the way he planned it.

I want on top. I like it on top and have never been on top with Jim
and it's starting to feel like I never get my say in sex. My determination
fixates on one thing: straddling Jim.

When I try to climb onto Jim, which isn't easy because he's twice my size, he pushes back. He's got my wrists in his hands and I can't get an advantage. I don't understand. I try several times and each time I make some progress, he slides me off, which is easy because we're both so slippery. We're kissing and his tongue is buried in my mouth and I love this so much, this sucking need that just comes over me. I pull him in and hold him close like I'm absorbing him. But this isn't a cooperative effort. His tongue turns to muscle and I feel skewered. I suck harder, fight back, climb up, and slide off, again and again. My brains—all those little vesicles stuffed with niggling items like *proof ECHO booklet, start up the mail delivery, buy a thank-you card*—are all fog. I'm bewildered, as if I'm drinking shots of tequila in a packed steamy bar and the crush of all of humanity squeezes me like a juice orange till I'm empty.

It feels like mud wrestling but it isn't. It's sex and it's the heat of sex. We're kissing and I'm crazed. He's got my arms in his hands now, and I'm not sure why, but he's fighting me on this. I use my legs, slide one over, and wedge it deep between his. Then the other. I'm on top. He's laughing. He let me get here.

This is utterly delicious. He's rubbing my nipples with his palms. God. I fought and won. Do this all night. Please don't stop.

I inhabit this zone well. This mindlessness, the fog, the rapture suits me. This is where I let go. The one place.

I do let go. Fluids pour out of me. There's so much of it. He's soaking wet. He must realize I've done this but he's right with me in this moment and he's on to the next thing, moving, taking hold of my hips because I've become so still and quiet and deep in the zone where my brain is one massive sensor hooked into the places he touches and the places I touch. There's nothing else. I'm all body.

I ride this out as long as I can stand it, until all I can do is fall forward onto him and let the orgasm squeeze deeper. I hang on to Jim. Ride it out. I am sure this is all unconsciousness. What I experience next is a new sense of myself. I am a piece of writing paper, something that will flutter, eventually, to the ground, something that settles without sound, that's free of gravity, free and empty. A fluttering and lifeless thing. Coming to rest.

He throws me off him. I land hard on my back and he crouches there, animal, between my legs. He pulls my legs up over his shoulders and slides his penis into my vagina. It all seems to happen in one movement. I'm pinned again. His arms immobilize mine. His eyes are training at that cosmic place he likes so much, couched in pubic hair, where the penis slides into the vagina. Living porn. He's transfixed. In and out. In and out. He's relentless. A voyeur. I'm incidental. The orgasm explodes. He screams.

TO LOVE HIM WELL, LET HIM GO

CHAPTER 10

While I'm still at my father's in Texas, Jim invites me to a party in SoHo. "Would you like to meet some of my old friends from the Gurdjieff Work?" he asks. I don't hesitate for an instant. "I'd love to." The party is scheduled for the Saturday night I'm to be in Chelsea.

Though I know that Jim is easygoing, generous, and inclusive, I'm touched by the sweetness of his offer. Then it occurs to me: We're going to have to do something besides sex, something that involves speaking and other people. Does he realize this? We'll have to behave as a couple, talk as a couple, relate to curious people our shared anecdotes—such as?

Of course, it's all foreplay, just as Jim says. In the abstract, going to a party where I'll see Jim interact with his old friends and possibly old lovers—surprisingly intriguing—strikes me as more delicious foreplay, just different.

In the early stages of a love affair just about everything is different and new. Once, when I talk to Jim about the long, swinging cycles of separation and reunion, of hot and cold, of detachment and interest, he says, "I don't experience that. I'm enjoying the newness."

Ah, yes. An honest reading. I listen to what Jim is saying. I try not to flinch. I make a concerted effort not to hold on when the instinct is to latch on and grip hard those things I value tremendously. A ballet teacher, a Lamaze coach, a tennis coach, a ta'i chi instructor have all said something similar: *Loosen up. Relax those hands.* A Buddhist lama, working earnestly to help his followers, cautions us: *If you want to keep something, give it away.*

. . . .

Jim is telling me to scoot down in the bed. He's already taken my clothes off. He's already kissed me, sucked my nipples, slowly pulled my bent knees apart, touched me, rubbed me, set me on fire, and I hear him, a distant voice, low and soft, through some deepening fog. "Scoot down," he whispers. I don't know what that means because now my world is reoriented. There is only him licking me and there is me wholly revised: a slow growing flame where once a child emerged, where once a final menses flowed, where now my total consciousness resides, where my entire being has come to coalesce expectantly. He seems to know I'm given over. He understands I don't know what he means so he takes my hips in his hands and slides me down, helps me move. "That's right. Just a little more. Good. Good."

I'm pleasing him. Doing what he says. Obedient little girl and naked woman and compliant devotee and craving cunt. He made this happen.

Here is an obedience so mindless it's dangerous. This must be how it is when you are hypnotized. I hear his voice, a rumble in my vagina, and I say, "Okay."

He's on his knees. Somehow his penis is already inside me and how I know this is the way its muscle flexes and releases, flexes and releases. This man is close to orgasm. This is going to be fast and furious. This is exciting, like nothing else I can imagine or have ever imagined. Suddenly he grabs my legs and pulls them up, slides them on either side of his head, rests my ankles on his shoulders. I am bent in two. His enormous torso bends toward me. I don't break. He goes for my breasts with his mouth. He kisses my mouth. I still don't break. This is rough and harsh and, yet, he's right here, his mouth on mine, his eyes wide, looking at me, seeing me.

. . . .

Yes, I know. I need to stay open, to always be in touch with the good part. And keep it right there. Keep it at that. I clench my vagina. Dig my fingers into his butt. I bite into his bicep. I get it out of my system. When it's over, I smile and open my palm. He strokes it with his fingertips and we are done.

. . . .

"What kind of party?" I ask Jim when he mentions the gathering.

"It's a catered dinner, a birthday party, at their loft. You'll like it. David's a photographer. The other David is an editor and he has a new business doing something like what you do. You'll have plenty to talk about with them and the others." He tells me they've known each other through the Gurdjieff Work for as long as three decades, working together, studying, listening to lectures, having discussions, meditating, and sometimes living together on retreats. They'd gather several nights of the workweek and most weekends. Eli was also once a member. Jim belonged for twenty-five years but quit at least a decade ago.

"Why did you leave?" I ask.

"I was still yelling at my kids," he says.

I know, from hearing Eli talk about it, that it was more than a program of spiritual and intellectual enlightenment. In close proximity for long periods of time and work, people hooked up sexually. Sometimes they married. I am not the first woman that both Eli and Jim have gone to bed with. It happened while they were in the Gurdjieff Work, too.

The very idea of going to this party with Jim is a turn-on. Walking down the street with Jim is a turn-on. A love affair is self-indulgent. And this love affair with Jim is like no other I've had. The attraction has never been so primal, so elemental, so utterly without extraneous distractions. Just a man and a woman.

I have never really had a love affair. Not like this. This is European. It comes with twisted sheets and drunken siestas and salty olives we slide into our mouths and suck. It comes with preoccupation and sly glances and perfect balance. I'm centered. I belong here. This is luscious and prolonged and hot. It intrudes. It bleeds through all the channels I've been so good at separating—work and running and Eli and daughter and friends and writing—and it's corrupted all the parts. I have lunch and settle for a peach to keep me thin. I buy emery boards and decide on nail polish, too. I need a running bra but I'm touching something silky and black and eyeing the $65 price tag. I read the same sentence ten times and still don't know what it says because he's right here, right now, shoving his wet finger into my mouth.

Yet I continue to present as the picture of decorum. I see pictures of myself Jim takes with his digital camera and I appear prim, a bit severe and bookish, especially when wearing glasses. I object to this look. The severity suggests an uncompromising woman, someone like my mother. I see the way the lips are set and the gaze simmers with focus and intensity. I see my mother in her lab coat biting back a nasty slight or releasing it with a hit of venom as she slides a hypodermic needle into a half-collapsed vein, despising that aged ailing person she, like all of us, will become. This is who I see looking back at me. A bloodsucker. "Take it down," I say to Jim after I study the picture.

"I like it," he says. He gets his way and I see the good side. It doesn't give me away to the children or others who come into his cluttered apartment. I look, in fact, like a tightly clenched fist. He, on the other hand, sees the conquest, the woman he gets down to who has cast off the dark lenses and white blouse and pursed lips and the extravagant bra. He knows about that soft underbelly, beating like a heart.

There are other pictures. These I do not see and do not know the disposition of. They are taken right after sex when Jim is still naked and radiating a male musk I want desperately to roll in. Once again I'm denied. He finds his camera and circles the bed, photographing. I twist my head in his direction, smile if I can, eyelids weighted with sex. He wants documentation of what he calls *fuck-addled*. I pull a corner of sheet toward me to hide some of my nakedness. I smile fuzzily. I don't care. I'm at my most adoring. I'm tenderized, a product of his prowess. He wants a record of this more than he wants fifteen views of my drowsy image. He keeps circling. I try to come to but it's impossible. Sex is so much the drug.

This is okay, I think. I'm allowed one last fling. We're making it a good one.

Jim contemplates similar thoughts. One day, out of the blue, he turns to me and says, "It's occurred to me that you are probably the last girl-friend I'll ever have." Who, at our age, wouldn't think that? A protracted fit of heedless abandon—so adolescent and still familiar—ensues.

It feels gluttonous. My Catholic school training—leave at least one bite on your plate—is in the distant past. The deeper I get into this, the deeper I'm willing to go. I know this is just another love affair in a world of love affairs but to me it's more. There's a connection between what goes on in bed and what goes on in my head.

This is an adventure, like John Muir exploring the High Sierras. I know about that, how you get to the top of one crest and the next one, hugely curious and all-enticing, attracts you despite your apprehensions and trail fatigue. In this love affair, I'm Rae, getting older, curious, poking about in the unexplored regions of my female psyche. What's in here? Am I changing the way Suzanne Braun Levine says we change when we enter our "fertile void" or am I just becoming more of me? What's this party really about for me? What if . . . ? How . . . ? I push back at these questions and try to relax. I'm learning something. The more I loosen my grip, the more interesting everything looks.

Jim repeats, this time as if his work is all done and mine has just started: "Why not just enjoy the free fall?"

. . . .

Before the trip to Houston, before the party, I visit my hairdresser for my monthly cut and color, as it's called. It's in this small studio in North Beverly, where my hairdresser and salon owner Jeffrie hovers and attends to my hair needs, that I am subjected to my most sobering reality checks. Gray roots, tired eyes, a softening of all the severe features looks blankly back from the full-length mirror, asking bluntly, "Who the hell are you?"

Epiphanies happen while under the hair dryer, waiting for the mix of copper, brown, and red dyes to set. I consume, while undergoing the camouflage treatment, *Cosmopolitan, People, Us, Vogue*. I am told that a little more than half the people between sixty-five and seventy-four have sexual intercourse, masturbate, and have oral sex. Oh boy. Years more of this! Between fifty-seven and sixty-four, that percentage is 73. This news is downright shocking. I thought old people didn't care about sex. I'm not even thinking about myself because I'm not old. Back in Jeffrie's chair, however, after the dyes have taken hold, I see the lie I tell myself. I'm old. Dyes perpetuate the lie, but only a little.

• • • • • • • • • • • •

It's still very cold on Saturday night when Jim and I set off to SoHo for the birthday party. God, I think, where am I? This place is a far cry from old-timey Rockport, with its fishing shacks and seagull paintings and clam chowder. I'm not a shopper but SoHo is different. I want to go in each shop. I want what they have.

Each storefront has its own allure, like a fantasy world. Competing for attention, their window displays are works of art unto themselves. On this black winter night each window glows like hot coals in a campfire, which I find incredibly appealing. There are stores with nothing but sneakers. I don't care about this. There are jeans, jewelry, purses. I like purses, but these are big and bright and have lots of flashy hardware.

I love the lampshade store. Big round parchment lampshades— orange and purple and pink and yellow—hover like balloons caught and momentarily stilled. I think a globe of colored light like this would be wonderful in my office in Rockport. Here I am, seduced. Here I am, wanting to possess again.

It's cold and we keep moving. Wait. Chocolate! I poke my head into an expensive, oddly sterile chocolate store where I spot a chocolate bar containing bacon smoked over apple wood. Other chocolates are seasoned with exotic ingredients such as French sea salt or Aztec chipotle, cardamom, and sweet Indian curry and coconut. Don't mask the flavor of $12-a-pound coffee with hazelnuts and vanilla. Don't infuse my chocolate with green tea. Don't make love to me with the TV on. Focus and purity. All the key pleasures in the unadulterated form, please. I am not so inured that I must experiment with rapture.

We move on. Some streets are cobblestone and sidewalks are cracked in places and uneven. We watch our step and take care where there is ice. This is a bit like New England.

Oh.

I'd almost forgotten myself. I'm far from Eli and all that he and I have to face. Yet, by this time tomorrow, I'll be home and Eli will be there, too, for the first time in two months. I'll think of nothing else for a time, except, of course, Jim and whatever it is we do tonight in bed and whatever it is I want him to do that he does not. There is always that, the dark and scary realm of unspoken need that neither dares yet approach. And just like that, thoughts of Eli slip away.

To get into the couple's loft, Jim presses a button at the street level and someone buzzes us in. The door lock snaps opens and we enter a small vestibule. There, we call for the elevator, which takes us directly to David and Carol's living space. Perhaps I tense up because I feel Jim's large hand slide up the nape of my neck, underneath my hair, and this makes me feel small and vulnerable. I absolutely love it and forget about being scared.

Twenty or thirty friends have already gathered. We are among the last to arrive. Most people already carry drinks and appetizers served by a catering staff dressed in black. The setting is splendid: crystal, silver, candlelight, flowers, and all those slim black figures proffering intensely flavored, highly colorful diminutive works of gastronomic genius.

I see a balcony overlooking the street and it's there I meet the David who's an editor. The balcony seems to be part of the fire escape system, but there are a few chairs and a table that claim this section of platform and turn it into something sweet and charming. It's far too cold to sit, but David takes the time to smoke a cigarette and I briefly inquire about his work. I also explore the large, digital photography studio located at the opposite end of the loft.

Jim and I slowly and systematically make our way to each of the many small groups of people talking and laughing. As the noise level increases, the circles tighten in. Yet Jim insinuates himself with ease. He introduces me to every person at the party, adding context to each introduction. I find this group of people warm and welcoming, and I am further touched by Jim's consideration. The introductions are so friendly that I am able to move about on my own, picking up threads of the earlier conversations.

Eventually Jim takes a seat in a rectangular arrangement of couches and I see that he is among the senior members of this group. He enjoys a whiskey, chats, and laughs wholeheartedly with the men and women he joined.

We give David a book of Robert Polidori's contemporary digital photography of Havana. As David turns the outsize pages, I am struck by similarities between the powerful aesthetics of Havana and this group of Baby Boomers, of which I am one. A fading elegance is everywhere about me. The gorgeous architecture of a tropical Havana, like good bones, supports a life lived zealously. Yet nothing stays the same. Havana has been muted by weather and neglect and wear and tear. Her grand structures—mansions, hotels, and ballrooms— are reconfigured, partitioned and reinhabited to accommodate what is. Polidori's portraits of a dulled and peeling city describe in minute detail the unapologetic ways we adapt for survival. These are mesmerizing, high-resolution portraits and they beg extended examination. I've heard that Polidori has backed off the color enhancements. It can look garish and unnatural on something crumbling at the edges, as I would look wearing red lipstick.

I look at the eyes around me, fixed on these pages as they take in layers of relevant messages. These are eyes that bespeak a similar mellowing. These are people tempered by time and attuned to subtle variations of tone. We have evolved from the wholesale embrace of the spectacular to the appreciation of subtler beauties. I've replaced my own saturated vibrancy—thick black hair—with Jeffrie's quieter tones of copper and auburn and brown. Other women go a different way.

They choose to send a jarring message announcing their indefatigability. They wear purple dresses and red hats and walk, en masse, into an art museum or a restaurant.

After we eat, David calls us all into his studio. Two by two, he photographs the couples. Sometimes a couple is joined by a third person. These are old friends and longtime couples, except, of course, for Jim and me. And I am one in a long line of women Jim has brought to such events.

Couples play with each other. Some grab props like stools and wide-brimmed hats and glasses of wine. Almost all ham it up. This makes me nervous. When it's finally Jim's and my turn, he slides his arm around me and I grin at David though I don't feel it. It's perfunctory and I know what this means. Lately, unless I feel the smile, it doesn't show up in the photograph. This moment is forced and there's nothing I can do about it but be a good sport. David takes the picture, studies it awhile, and says, "One more."

Something's missing. We're not a couple. We're lovers who barely know each other by the light of day. Our conversations during the party begin with "I" rather than "we" and very few people inquire about me, as if already anticipating my disappearance.

A week later, the photos show up in my email inbox and I delete them without ever looking.

. . . .

Sunday morning I tell Jim I don't want to go home. This remark is unnecessary, alarming, and selfish since there's absolutely nothing he can do about it. It's made worse by the fact that I have a choice in the matter and I go ahead with it. "I don't want to go to Rockport. I can't believe this is happening. I can't believe they brought him back and just left him there."

I'm filled with dread. My worry is that, because Eli is unstable and I have no idea what his medicines are anymore, I once again have no control over my life. His mood is my reality. His rage is my nightmare. Because his hospital psychiatrist has refused to speak with me since Eli was admitted, I have no idea about the current status of his treatment and state of mind. What will I be walking into?

Jim says the only thing he can say. "Stay here till you decide what to do." I say no, walk out the door, pull my suitcase up 24th Street and north along 8th Avenue till I get to Penn Station. There's nothing cathartic about this walk of doom.

It's when I'm on the train, moving away from Manhattan, the Empire State Building shrinking into the background, that the gravity of the situation really hits me. We've gone through two months of hell and Eli is far from well. He still wears the catheter because he can't urinate and, since his discharge, he doesn't even have a psychiatrist. There isn't even someone to call when Eli gets in trouble, which he will.

. . . .

On the train ride home I stare out the window, my back to the person in the seat beside me, and let myself cry. I miss Jim. I resent what I face. I'm angry with myself because I have no action plan. I'm angry with Eli for acting out. And I'm very tired because all I did all weekend was fuck when I should have been defining and solving this problem. So, on the train back to Boston I cry. I sleep. I pass over the Connecticut

River and wish I could take her north, to her source, a place I climb to every summer on the Canadian border to listen to quiet, to breathe in cool, pine-scented air, to witness, again, to be reminded, again, of how something so magnificent can start with something as minuscule as a trickle from a pond, and to marvel at all there is for us to behold if we just hold still and see. I try to hold that thought as I move up the Eastern Seaboard, along the shore, through the old cities of red brick and lofty spires and decaying mills, to the quiet village of Rockport, where Eli awaits, wondering what's next.

"I WANT YOU NAKED"

CHAPTER 11

Eli is reading when I get home after the long train ride from New York City. "How's Angelo?" he asks, assuming I just got in from Houston. I'm ready for this. On my walk from the Rockport train platform to my house—fifteen minutes if I take my time—I reorient myself. I breathe in the healing salt air and send up thanks for these delicious, deep, cleansing breaths. I open my eyes to the world around me and look outside of myself. It's mid-January and many of the beautiful Christmas lights are still up in the yards and windows and along Rockport's Main Street. I take long, strong strides and let my body stretch, flex, and relax. I feel all the sore parts—nipples, vagina, biceps—acutely. I slam that door tight. I won't dare call to say goodnight to Jim. I can't imagine hearing the sound of his voice right now. My throat constricts as if I'm about to cry again.

Stop it.

I step into the restroom at Dunkin Donuts and wash my face. I don't look like I've cried for three hours but I look very tired.

When I get upstairs and see Eli, I simply say hello and everything snaps right back to normal.

"My father's good," I tell him when he asks. "And we had a pleasant visit." I look around. Boo, our black cat, sits beside Eli on the couch and Lila sleeps at his feet. Nothing seems to have changed.

Strike that. Eli is skin and bones. His left eye still doesn't focus correctly. There's a bulge on his inner right thigh where he's attached the urine bag. His skin is mottled with bruising. His hair is long and straggly. But he's still the Eli I love and the Eli I once chose to live with.

"What happened at the foster care house?" I ask.

"She threw me out. I complained because all she fed me was canned tomato soup. I tried to cook a sausage and she went ballistic. I was starving."

"Did you raise your voice?"

"Of course not."

I believe Eli and I don't. He's often loud but he doesn't hear that in himself. It doesn't always mean he's crazy or out of control. "You seemed to like her," I say.

"She wanted nothing to do with me."

The story of Eli's life.

The incident is classic Eli. He's a challenge that some people accept in order to have access to the rest of the package. I wonder, are the new meds actually working? He seems so centered and sage. When I ask about them, Eli explains that he's on a low dose of lithium but they're backing him off and replacing lithium with newer antipsychotic meds. In a few weeks' time we'll know more because he'll have been entirely weaned.

What a bad joke this is. We've been here before but Eli claims no memory of previous attempts to wean off lithium. He's desperate to rid himself of drugs altogether and will do anything to orchestrate that. Even going off one of the many meds he takes or taking a lesser dose feels to him like release from prison, a common metaphor that, by extension, casts family members who warily monitor daily med rituals in the reviled role of jailer. I don't say any of this out loud because I don't want to upset Eli. In theory, I agree. Eli needs to be off lithium, not just because it's causing kidney failure, but because he says that it dulls him and interferes with his ability to write poetry. This is a common complaint. I don't doubt it but I resist. I believe it's more important to live a good life than a long one but who am I to say? It's not me who's confronted with such hostile choices. Without lithium, Eli's quality of life will radically plummet. Don't go there, I warn myself. When did empathy ever serve the jailer?

It's at this precise point in the conversation that I must be hyper-vigilant. Eli is extremely impatient when I ask questions, especially questions about medication. He wants me out of that loop. He doesn't want me in his business or controlling his life. So I need to think carefully and ask one or two questions, at most, with days between these difficult *grillings*.

Eli's impatience has taught me patience.

I always knew the day would come when patience gave way to fear. We now have no doctors or social service agencies to help us through this scary transition. We are on our own. By myself, I won't be able to force Eli to get a doctor or call a hospital for help. All we do have are a handful of prescriptions and no advice about what to watch for or what to do when there's trouble. Without lithium we look forward to cycles of rage and depression. There will be no room left for Eli. He didn't ask for this. It's not his fault. Which makes my solution just that much more heartbreaking.

I want out. Somebody wins and somebody loses. Jim and Mitch are background voices. "It's you or him. Choose you." It's not fair but I have long known a world where fairness has no role. The sick irony is that I must perpetuate this ugliness. The message behind all my panic is very clear: Get out or die. I must be safe. And, for the first time, I know how good safe feels.

Yes. Eli must be out of the apartment before the lithium has left his bloodstream.

I tell him he's got to look for another apartment. I'll pay, I tell him, though I have no idea how I can afford a mortgage payment and rent. He says he'll start looking.

Each evening, when I get home from work the answer is the same: No, there are no apartments. No, I didn't find anything today. No, I didn't look. Why should I?

In late January we have a bitter cold snap. Temperatures dip to the single digits. When it gets this cold a sense of impending crisis pervades every movement—conscious or mechanical. Nothing's immune. It's a dangerous time.

Things slow way down. Things go quiet. In effect, everything outside the perimeter of the heating elements freezes rock hard. Birdbaths. Dirt. Tree limbs. Fingertips. Pipes. Cars. Even the saltwater harbor with its relentless tidal shifts freezes. An ominous sea fog hovers, almost inert, atop the open ocean. Heating oil runs out. Space heaters produce carbon monoxide and people suffocate in their sleep. A claustrophobic homeless man refuses a ride to a shelter and turns to a solid on a Boston sidewalk. I take a run and my hands ache halfway through my route. I veer off, away from the ocean and the brutal windchill but I have no choice but to keep going. I rip off my gloves and suck my thumbs, which absolutely throb.

· · · · · · · · · · · · ·

One night during the cold spell I have several after-hours meetings. Everything's complicated by a fever, chills, and a brain-numbing head cold. It's 11 PM and all I think about on my drive home is how wonderful it's going to feel to slide into bed and bury myself under the heavy down comforter. I put my car in the off-street parking lot down the street and face down a brusque wind as I trudge up the hill to my house. In the dead of winter like this, everything I do is twice as hard.

I find Eli in the bathroom with the door ajar.

"Are you okay?" I ask from the other side of the door.

"No," he says. "My urine bag is broken and the replacement bag doesn't work." He pushes open the door and there he is, naked, standing in a pool of urine, the catheter hanging from his penis and feeding urine straight onto the floor.

"What?" At first I can't take this in. It's too ludicrous to be believed.

"I've been waiting hours for you to get home. You've got to find a pharmacy that's open all night and get me a new bag."

"You don't have another bag?"

"It doesn't work."

"Where am I going to find an all-night pharmacy?"

"How should I know? Boston, I guess."

I nearly fall to the floor with despair. "Boston?"

"I don't know. You'll have to call and find out."

He hasn't done anything but stand there leaking urine.

I slam out of the house. I've never felt so angry and I've never been so loud. I slam every door I can find. Bathroom. Downstairs. Screen. Car. Amazingly, nothing breaks.

In the car, I scream. I scare myself. I've never behaved like this. Never tasted what's buried. Unbelievably, the car barely starts even though it was running a scant fifteen minutes earlier. I want to call Jim. I'm utterly enraged. Of course I stop myself because I'm hysterical and if I scare myself, what would this sound like to him?

I drive through Rockport, speed limit twenty mph, at seventy. It takes every bit of control I have to slow it down to forty because part of me wants to drive into a wall. Once on the highway, I take it back up to seventy, eighty, eighty-five. My little Grand Vitara can't do much more than that, even with its six cylinders. Going fast isn't a choice I make. It's me, shot into outer space.

Where am I going? I don't even know.

I race on.

Eventually I realize I need help.

. . . .

I regret making the call immediately, as I knew I would. I can't even tell Jim what's wrong, exactly, other than the fact that Eli is back in the house standing naked in a pool of pee, that I am on a drive at midnight, zero degrees Fahrenheit, to find a urine bag and I don't even know where to go or what to ask for since the standard bag, according to Eli, does not attach to his catheter whereas the standard one used earlier did attach. What I say finally to Jim is *sorry sorry sorry*. I should handle this on my own. I shouldn't let you see this about me.

He yells into the phone, "Shut up."

I'm stunned. I want to hate him, along with everything else.

He's yelling still. "Do you think this bothers me? Do you think I want you hidden?"

I'm flying through space. I don't care what he wants. I need oxygen. I need something elemental, like air.

"What do you think this is all about between us?"

How should I know? Stop it. I will him to stop the yelling. I will this to be over.

"You've got it all wrong," he shouts. I don't like the way he sounds shouting. So shrill. So hysterical.

"I shouldn't have called," I cry. "I just can't take this anymore."

"Don't you get it?" He's still yelling.

"No."

"I want you naked."

Naked: Nothing left to hide. Revealed. Exposed.

Then what?

. . . .

Three nights later, a Friday, I get home from work, still very sick, and Eli is there, defeated. I don't even bother to remove my coat. I walk straight to my computer, search for Craigslist, examine the listings for roommates, and call everyone who needs a roommate in the Boston area. I like the Buddhist in Medford. I practically implore him to let us come by right that minute. He says he'll think about it. Minutes later he calls back and says yes. I throw on my coat and I take Eli by the hand. Come on, I say. This man called Tenzin is a Buddhist. Eli's a Buddhist. He's Tibetan, last from Dharamsala. Eli's Zen, last from the Bronx. Maybe this will work. Three weeks later Eli, silently crying, prepares for his move to Tenzin's apartment. "This is the end of Eli and Rae," he says, rising one last time from the couch to finally go. I watch him cry all afternoon. I say nothing. It is a torture I deserve.

....

Jim flies to Arizona for his annual visit with his father, who's now ninety-seven. His brother lives in the area, as well, so he stays with Dave, sleeping on the couch and fending off Dave's fat, beloved, slobbering pit bull. Together they make the trip to their father's assisted-living apartment where all three play pool, share meals, and drink beer. Jim calls one night and says, "He's going to make it to one hundred."

Dave lives in a mobile home in a bowl-like expanse of loose and rocky dust in a place called Golden Valley. Chicken-wire fences, cactus, and makeshift sheds help break up the huge flat terrain into parcels that men and women have purchased and made their own.

Perhaps the "golden" comes from the fact that this no-man's-land sits on a gigantic aquifer that developers are readying to tap into. At the moment, however, Golden Valley doesn't seem like much of a community. It's just scrub brush, a smattering of double-wide trailers, rusty trucks tucked under tin-topped carports, and packs of guard dogs that bark at coyotes, buzzards, humans nuts enough to trespass.

Golden Valley bears vestiges of the Wild West mentality. Neighbors shoot rifles at each other with occasional admonishments by the sheriff. Snakes wind through the loose dirt, headed for shade. Air cooling units called swamp coolers pump away in the tiny abodes, making them marginally habitable in 110 degree heat but, nonetheless, habitable.

I notice, with alarm, that Jim seems to get more distant with each phone call. And even the phone calls decrease in frequency. What's this about? I don't understand that he's sleeping on a short, uncomfortable couch with a dog that won't leave him alone and that his younger brother, so happy to see him, talks nonstop. Whatever the problems, Jim is receding into the sunset like the Lone Ranger. I stop myself from questioning this and just engage in conversation when the opportunity arises.

When Jim gets back, he tells me he'd been on the phone with his ex-girlfriend and Dave called out, "Hi, Rae." This was hurtful to the woman, who knows me, but not about the affair. So right then she guessed. She asked for Jim to come by her Manhattan condo two days later, on a Saturday, to talk about this.

I listen to this story carefully, say little in response, and keep my voice steady when I say goodnight. It's hard because the adrenaline shoots through me like a fireworks finale on the Fourth of July. Something about Jim going to her place to talk this through feels wrong to me. I get off the phone as quickly as I can.

I loathe this because it's way more than I want to handle right now. What the hell was I thinking, getting into a relationship when I have so much already on my plate? Another emotional upheaval would do me in.

I feel kinship with that thunderstorm in Houston—dangerously explosive—though when I call Jim back I work to hold myself in check. No, I tell him, I don't like saying this but, no, it is not a good idea to go to your ex-girlfriend's apartment right now, under these circumstances. I don't like it. What's the point, exactly? You know where this has the potential to lead. Only go if you are okay with that as an eventuality. I'm not okay with it.

I see that I must battle for my man. With Jim so detached these days and a former lover of many years in tears, asking him to come to her, things are precarious. I surprise myself with this phone call. Yes. I have to fight for my man. I don't know how but I know for sure that I'd better. More so, I'm claiming him as my man and I expect him to tell his ex that new boundaries have been imposed.

On the other hand, I can't know what Jim intends nor can I know the power of her pull. I don't say the words, but *deal breaker* hangs like a rabid bat. Please, don't go there, I whisper after hanging up. Don't go to that fatal place.

He calls back a few minutes later and says, "You're right. I'm not going."

"GOOD GIRL"

CHAPTER 12

Jim takes me to the Peninsula Hotel at 5th Avenue and 55th Street. It's a five-star hotel but we're not here for the $1,500-a-night feather bed, the copper-plated footbath with lotus blossoms floating on the water, the spa's jade hot-stone massage, or the delicious rich-people watching. We're interlopers in heat ready for the next thing.

I'm dressed New England casual—black jeans and a boxy hip-length black leather jacket like Boston tough guys in Southie or the North End wear. I pull this on every winter and think Sopranos or Whitey Bulger or *Mystic River*. I like my jacket. It keeps me warm and the sturdy leather would render me relatively unscathed should I, for some reason, skid along the pavement. Disaster scenarios are my mental Muzak. As usual, I wear my insulated Merrells. Jim is similarly clad in jeans, a black lined windbreaker, and his ubiquitous abstract-art ski cap. But he is so striking, to my thinking, that he could stride right into Windsor Castle, demand an audience with the queen, and get it.

We've just left MoMA and tea with a museum colleague of mine. We had a lovely time with my friend and the Eames chairs but Jim thinks we're ready for something a bit meatier, more of a wallop to the flesh and the crotch. He doesn't put it that crudely but we're both thinking: change of pace.

We climb the red-carpeted stairs of the Peninsula, nod thanks to the doorman, who, to his credit, looks through us and not at us, and step into the plush chambers of excess, tastefully restrained at the entry level and carefully attended by an alert staff.

I note each detail. It's not every day that I have a martini with a lover and learn the bill is over $60.

Jim and I are interlopers here. We're invading the sanctified premises of the perfectly poised. Chin up, I say.

We take upholstered seats at a table and Jim orders two Tanqueray gin martinis, very cold, olives on the side. The Gotham Lounge is nicely sequestered on the mezzanine, a flight of stairs up from the lobby. From my seat at the balcony table I can see the comings and goings at the bank of elevators. It's a bit like a warehouse loading dock, with all the package-laden people heading up to deposit their purchases.

A waiter in a tux arrives, formal but friendly, to proffer a silver tray arrayed with diminutive bowls. One holds olives—black, green, oily, salty, garlicky, spicy. Jim immediately samples them, apropos of his enthusiasm for all things sensual. Also positioned on the tray I note a small bowl filled with bits of salty, crumbly sharp cheese. Jim plucks a nugget, pops it into his mouth, and licks his fingers. I'm embarrassed, not by his manners, but by the memory of the way he licks his fingers after they have been inside of me. Here in the Peninsula, amid all this pomp and posing, Jim places the tip of his index finger into his mouth, sucks rather noisily for a few long seconds, slowly slides it out. Aye. He catches me watching, smiles, and brings a bit of cheese to my mouth. The tips of his wet fingers push against my lips as I let him feed me.

I see now where we are going, having been delivered this tasty prologue, and I am gone, transported to a scene on Jim's bed, on top of Jim's sheets—Jim, talking to me, kissing me, whispering *Sweet Rae, good girl, sweet thing,* as if he knows what's coming, cooing *Sweet Rae, move over here,* as if he knows what I'll consent to—anything—*like this,* as if he understands how much more I risk to be open than any of the others, uttering *Sweet Rae* as if he feels sympathy for me, poor me—*Sweet Rae*—and he settles there, where he lives, between my legs, slides his fingers fast and deep before I am quite ready for this, deeper than I could have imagined possible, he invades my core, he holds still then, claiming and inhabiting my core, which isn't enough for him so he spreads his massive fingers slowly, deliberately, and makes a pressure so powerful my head pounds and the slow reckoning takes shape—abduction or, no, sublime surrender—and all the parts of me ring with the urgent warning that I will soon be ripped in two, but he persists, maintains the unrelenting pressure this side of unendurable, while the core of Sweet Rae is raped and plundered. At the moment when I arrive at the brink of my primal scream, after which I will cease to exist, he touches his tongue to my clitoris and I writhe desperately, moan for god, for Jim, fight Jim, try to push him away, but he is a rock implanted in my core and I fall back, possibly dead.

I say this to him, again and again: You own me now. You did this to me and you own me now.

What I don't say but what I really mean is this: *Please. Be careful with me.*

I think of little Lila, my female cat, who rolls onto her back when I walk into the room, who squeaks and calls and makes herself cute so I will come to her. While on her back, her head tracks my every move. This is utterly adorable. I go to her. She squeaks. I run my hand along the precious expanse of her soft belly. She squirms and purrs. I'm the only one. My pleasure is sublime.

It is while I'm with this thought, it is while I once again start to sense the precariousness of my own proffered-soft-belly situation, that the waiter arrives and presents us with two icy, elegant martinis, crystal clear, quaking with possibilities, a perfect skin of ice as ephemeral as October snowflakes, for our lips to touch and melt. Thank you, I say, and move my eyes to Jim. We toast. To you, he says. Thank you, I say, again, and we take our first sip together. Delicious.

Transformative. That's the word. I feel different now, like a man must feel. I've taken my orgasm, come out of it, perked up, liquored up, turned a page. Next pleasure, please.

I momentarily pull out of my heat-induced fixation on Jim to note my splendid environs. A few sips of this mega-martini and I'm afloat. The feeling's mellow, narcotic. It radically narrows the field of vision but heightens the focus. This blissful intoxication suits lovers. *I see only you, in keen relief.* This is heavy duty, but the firm, accommodating upholstery seems to have my physical self well under control. I'm safely ensconced. I relax into my altered state, rotate my head, train my tunnel vision on the next thing and the next.

I think I'm seeing billionaires directly across the room. They perch erectly, for the most part, on couches or in chairs like mine.

At the polished bar a few solo women talk and laugh with each other and the bartender. I get the impression they are here to take a break in their busy day, have a drink, move on. I catch Jim eyeing the women, something I know he does but I never want to see. And I never, in my wild Latina heart schooled by the jealous antics of my father and the youthful Padilla brothers, want another woman to see Jim looking when he's with me. What do these women think when my man gives them that look? What does this inferred breach of loyalty say about me? About my man and me?

I pop an olive in my mouth to staunch the seething gut.

There's a story my siblings told, closer to lore than fact, perhaps, but I liked it and believed it. Shortly after my parents' divorce was final, my father tossed one of my mother's suitors through our kitchen window. The unfortunate bush pilot from Alaska got the message: Hands off. She's mine and no silly piece of paper comes between her and me.

Of course. Now I understand.

In those old and storied Wild West days, channels switched madly from lust to possession to machismo to rage. Maybe Jim should know this about the ways of my kin. I've seen bloodied noses, guns, kitchen forks, and butcher knives repurposed as weapons, a phone book torn slowly in two merely to demonstrate murderous might.

Come to think of it, I, too, could flex my machisma.

I turn my intoxicated gaze to the prettiest of the women at the bar. Her neat, round butt, contained nicely in a pencil skirt, touches upon her barstool, weightless, like a butterfly lighting on the stamen of a tiger lily. Impossible, but it happens.

In this Peninsula lounge, a dignified mix of men and women engage in amiable chitchat. The women seated with men are younger.

The men wear suits, presumably because it's Midtown, 6 PM. They are either leaving work or stepping out, between appointments, for a tête-à-tête. Women wear skirts, dresses, heels sculpted into works of art. Must these paeans to rich feet touch pavement? Must they encounter even a hint of dog piss? I slide my own boxy feet under my chair.

What a sight. Small rectangular shopping bags embossed with logos like Gucci, Armani, Coach, their thin, twinelike handles erect, are arranged in artful repose at their feet, like pets. The look is de rigueur, as if the shallow bags were designed for placement beside pointy Jimmy Choo patent leather leopard-spotted pumps. It's a look that connects with me somehow. Squared, sharply creased shopping bags, low to the ground, sometimes a pouf of tissue lufting gently, the pointy patent leather toe, the plush carpet. It works. I note a bit of action as a long silky leg swings across a knee and a satin-tipped toe kicks the air seductively for a number of beats.

Jim has two martinis and I handle just the one. We rise unsteadily, wait for the ground to level out, take a test step or two, then slowly move across the carpet, down the stairs, out the door, down the second flight of stairs and out onto Fifth Avenue into the enveloping pandemonium.

. . . .

We wait on a corner for a bus that takes forever to arrive. It has started raining so a number of people, Jim and I included, cram ourselves under a glass-covered bus stop. Jim moves his body tight against mine, his pelvis pushed into my left buttock, and he locks it down. Snap. We are a single unit now. Good god. Yet who cares? It's cold and wet. Each person here grapples with his or her own discomfort.

If there's any thrumping, any small gyration from either one of us, it would be imperceptible. And I do. I push back against his pelvis. I let my butt work itself into his slightly parted crotch and I maintain the pressure, push back a little, sense the shape and position of his penis there behind the zipper. This is the level of closeness I need at any given second of my life.

His entire body is engaged, flexed, meeting mine. This is my favorite thing, the whole fabulous length of him pushed against my upright body, me straightening, pulling up, stretching each vertebra to get the most length, the most expanse of body against body. All this while afloat, baffled even, the consequences of a bowl of gin and vermouth and a splash of hormones making themselves known second by second. Everything new. Take a breath. Another surprise.

The bus pulls up around 6:30. It's jammed with a rush-hour crowd. Jim and I disengage our bodies from each other, carefully climb stairs that have magically descended to curb level, and make our way to the middle part of the bus. This is a double bus of sorts, with two compartments for riders joined at a flexible, accordionlike midsection. In this center, which twists and bends, Jim takes a seat. To get my bearings I remain standing. Immediately people take seats on either side of him and before I know it, the empty seats have disappeared. The jerky motions make me feel like I'm on an amusement park ride, like a teacup that spins and jerks one way and then the other. I'm drunk and now I'm disoriented. I remain where I am, grasping a pole.

It's hot. I'm sweating and lurching and pretending I'm not. Jim is seated, watching me, grinning. We take a corner the way a cabdriver would, recklessly and fast. I nearly topple but regain some balance. He's still watching. Still grinning. I'm still drunk when he pats his knee, as if to say come here Sweet Rae, settle here on my lap, no need to fall, come here, and I almost succumb, almost sit on his lap, when one of those transporting moments overtakes me and I see myself on his lap, bent forward, his hard penis ramming my crotch, me too drunk to protest, loving it mostly, and I move toward Jim to actually sit on his lap. A split second before I squat, I notice something. All the people are looking at me, looking at Jim, his hand patting his thigh, his grin, and they are watching this, waiting, wondering if I'll do it, sit there on his lap, engage in that obscene drunken dance. I shout "No!" I jump away. I refresh. Clear out the fantasy. Marvel at what almost happened. The people around me see that I have come to my senses. They lose interest and go back to their paperbacks, Chinese newspapers, and cell phone games.

Jim, ever delighted, shrugs his shoulders as if to say, "Worth a try," and I marvel, once again, at the trust I have in him.

. . . .

Early one February morning Tenzin, Eli's roommate, calls. It's 1:20 AM. I have trouble understanding what he's saying, in part because Tenzin is Tibetan and he's lived, until recently, in Dharamsala, but mostly because the call wakes me out of a sound sleep.

"Tenzin?" I recognize his voice right away just as I know from the first ring that Eli is in trouble. "Can you say again what's wrong?"

"Eli," he says. "Roommate. He's a little sick?"

"He is," I say.

Tenzin is silent for a while. I wait. I'd like to help him out but I'm scared of what's coming next.

"He is not here," Tenzin says.

I'm sure Tenzin is no alarmist, so I ask him if he thinks something's wrong.

"Perhaps. He's a little more sick. He broke things in his room."

"God," I say. I want to apologize but something stops me. Instead, I thank him for calling.

"Alright." Before I can say or ask anything else, he's gone.

I try Eli's phone but my call goes right to voice mail. I leave a panicked message. "Call me, please."

I pray: Please let Eli be alright. But this prayer, however earnest, has nowhere to go. I don't have a god.

I do have the free market economy. I've turned Eli over to a stranger in exchange for money. This could only happen here, in the United States, where there's no extended family, no viable social network for the mentally ill, and no easily accessible, affordable medical system in place to help people with these complicated, off-putting, and life-threatening problems. Sure, there are hospital psych wards for temporary confinement and day programs here and there. But there's no systematic, continuing care. It's the Dark Ages for Eli.

Eli, now beyond lithium, is in his own free fall, though this is free fall in hurricane-force winds because he's jerked around from scared to angry to despondent to okay to immobile to hyper hour to hour. He calls me several times a day, sometimes terrified, sometimes to say, "I think it's going to be okay." When he doesn't call, I know he's suffering the most. How can he possibly survive this exhausting chemically induced ride?

Since the hospital discharged him without a psychiatrist but with a long list of medications to take, he's on his own. If he gets crazy again, he has been told to go to the nearest hospital. There he'll be assigned a new hospitalist and a new drug regime. So far, there's no continuity in care.

Psychiatrists are, in many cases, hamstrung. Those who've treated Eli have been detached and abrupt, in part due to his combativeness. In their defense, they understand the limits of their usefulness. They work to maintain their clients through trial-and-error treatments but there are periodic breakdowns—indicators that the regime isn't working, combined with the poverty many that are mentally ill experience, which further limits treatment options. It's all the same dysfunctional system, whether you're the patient or the physician. Why don't psychiatrists organize, speak out, demand change? There is nothing so resistant as the status quo. All I know to do is try to keep Eli alive and off the streets.

. . . .

In a commerce-based culture like this one, I consult Craigslist and find an impoverished immigrant fifty miles away who moves people's households for a living. He rents U-Hauls, hires day laborers, and shares the weight of each family's stuff with his helpers. He's forty-five years old and works seven days a week or as many days as he can find the work. He has no car of his own and often works through the night to transport the family's belongings, unload, and return. To help make ends meet, he accepts a fragile, acutely ill man into his home.

This is the best our country can do.

Tenzin has a young son who lives with him at least half the week. Because this man is kind, or because he's a Buddhist, he phones me when he should be resting his body and recharging himself for the next hard day. He learns quickly to distance himself, however, from this problem. This will be the only phone call Tenzin ever makes to me.

I'm sorry that Tenzin has to endure this degradation to his lifestyle but I realize, of course, that Eli's unraveling has begun, just as I expected. These medicines are not going to hold him. And there's no one to call and nothing I can think of to do.

And yet I'm relieved. This meltdown could be happening right here. How much more yelling and worry would my downstairs tenant put up with? And how would I handle all this again—the rage aimed at me, the destruction of objects in our home? I imagine this time I'd act decisively. I'd explode in my own fit of rage or I'd collapse in paralytic despair. Possible scenarios: My heart would stammer and stop. I would throw myself in front of the Rockport train. I'd hurl myself off the A. Piatt Andrew Bridge. Whatever form it takes, it's a full-body primal scream and it's already halfway up my throat.

. . . .

Behind the office furniture and rugs and cameras and apartments available on Craigslist are stories of breakups and transition and loss and, entwined with any change, new beginnings.

I recall the night I used Craigslist to find Eli his apartment and his roommate Tenzin. After we viewed the apartment, Tenzin walked us to the door and told us he'd call us back the next morning. I drove Eli to a pharmacy parking lot a mile away and stopped the car. "Do you like the place?" I asked him. "Is it important to you that he's a Buddhist, like you?" Eli answered yes to both questions. "Then I'm going to call him now and lobby a little." Eli took the phone. He told Tenzin that he liked the apartment very much and wanted to be his roommate. His voice shook as he spoke. All this was happening so fast for him. I could see that he was trying to do the right thing for me as much as anything. Tenzin told Eli he'd call back in a few minutes.

Others had already made offers to Tenzin. He'd told us this right away. As I sat in the parking lot that evening, I imagined Tenzin thinking about what this old man, as he sometimes calls Eli, would mean to his life. I believe he had some idea because Eli is different. I believe that Tenzin took the time to think this through. He couldn't know exactly what he was getting into but he probably thought it was the lesser of the evils—the worst being a bunch of college students, like he had before, who drank too much and who made his and his son's life miserable. I also believe Tenzin has less fear and more seren-ity and greater physical strength. He is better equipped than I. And he needs the money.

. . . .

It's 2 AM. I'm worried about Eli. It's an impossible situation because Eli doesn't want to be found. What do I do? Why won't he answer his cell phone? Should I call the police?

My phone rings again. It's Eli's Buddhist teacher, Stephen. Even though Eli has studied and meditated with him for the last five years, we've never met or spoken. Now, at this improbable time of the night, he's calling me. Does he know something? What's wrong?

"Have you heard from Eli?" I blurt. I don't even know if I started with hello.

Stephen tells me Eli has been in touch by phone and he's in trouble.

"Where is he?"

"In his car."

Oh no.

"He sounds scared. He's been drinking."

"He doesn't drink," I say.

Stephen's quiet.

"God." I don't know what else to say.

"I told him to come here as soon as he feels it's safe to drive."

"Thank you so much."

"He's having trouble getting back on his feet after the hospitalization, isn't he?"

"It's complicated," I say.

Stephen waits for me to say more.

"I don't know what he's told you about his condition."

"I can see he's struggling," says Stephen.

I decide to tell Stephen that Eli's bipolar and that he's having problems with his new medications. I don't know that Eli wants his Buddhist group to know.

"There are people in the group who are mental healthcare professionals," Stephen says. "Maybe they can help."

This last thing stops me cold. Help? Help with Eli? I hadn't even wished for it, hadn't even resented the lack of it, hadn't even contemplated the concept of help.

I can find no words . . . so I mutter a quiet "thank you so much."

The only sounds are Stephen's quiet breath and me crying.

"What do you need right now?"

I say the first thing I think of. "Housing. Eli needs his own apartment."

"No. What do *you* need right now? What can we do for you?"

"And he needs a psychiatrist."

"And you?"

"What do you mean?"

"How long have you been with Eli now? Is it eighteen years?"

"Yes."

"Eighteen years."

"Yes." I can't seem to stop crying.

"A long time."

What's wrong with me? Why can't I think of anything to say? Why can't I stop crying? Why do I feel so utterly lost and beholden to this stranger's good will?

"Are you okay?"

This call is supposed to be about Eli, about Eli being suicidal, about Eli driving into a tree.

Stephen continues. "You've been good to Eli. You have been compassionate. There are other ways to be compassionate."

Freedom. I'm being rescued. Freed. Unbound.

Saved. I am getting saved. *There are other ways*. Four words can save a life. A wise man knows this and places a phone call at 2 AM.

· · · · · · · · · · · ·

It's hard to set a guilty person free. I'm worried that this phone call is going to hurt Eli. Stephen is Eli's resource, not mine. Stephen is practically all Eli has. I can't figure into this. I have to repair any damages.

"I don't know how much Eli confides in you," I tell Stephen, "but I wouldn't want to do or say anything to interfere with his relationship to you and Buddhism and the group. I value the relationship between you and want that to go on. It helps Eli. He's changed since knowing you and since he started going to sangha," I say. "You've probably noticed. It's a remarkable thing and I've always wanted to go to a meeting with him to meet you and tell you how much I've appreciated it.

"One time," I continue, "Eli came home from a meeting and said that Buddhism didn't matter, that meditation isn't of value if the study and the work should hurt or deprive the home and the family. He took these lessons to heart. He told me this came from you."

I want to keep going because it's a relief to express the gratitude I'd held in for so long. "Until December when he got sick, he was more serene and centered. He was a devout student and he respected you and wanted to learn and be a good student. He told me this is what he's always wanted. Once, after driving home from *sesshin,* he walked into the house, sat down, and said that he had never been so happy. He worked hard and was proud of himself."

I hope I don't sound disingenuous. Am I groveling? Can he hear that I am sincere? Will his Buddhist friends even want to deal with Eli after this? Is his behavior too threatening? So many worries. . . .

"Thank you," says Stephen. He's crying, perhaps out of relief or maybe it's exhaustion. It's beyond late. Almost 3 AM. Here darkness and emptiness intersect. We're most vulnerable now.

Especially Eli. While I'm linked to another life, Eli's all alone, like the dying are alone. Vulnerability like this is a force, a siren that calls your name and you cry *okay yes okay help me*. You finally stop fighting and do what she says and what she says is *Let it all go*.

Don't do that, Eli. Don't let go.

Poor Eli. I see him face-to-face with this nightmare that wakefulness and whiskey won't dissolve, holed up in his battered old car in an empty parking lot somewhere in Boston, off kilter from all the chemicals he applies to the problem, waiting for the moment, an opening, into which he can inject a single hopeful action—turn a car key—to attempt an escape, even for a few hours, to the arms of compassion. Long strong arms, holding all of us.

. . . .

It starts to occur to me. Eli has called for help and help is there. I can relax a little bit. I can slide down into my bed, onto my pillow, under my comforter. This phone call is not the summons I expected. I don't have to get up, dress, drive to Boston, gather up Eli, take him to ER.

There is a voice coming out of the darkness, tearful, disembodied, insistent. "You don't have to do this anymore. You have acted with compassion."

I think of Jim. I can't yet bring Jim into this; I can't reveal the ways Jim and I are not compassionate.

. . . .

Stephen is there, still, letting me feel his presence. When I try to say thank you he thanks me instead. He tells me he hasn't cried like this in a while. He says he's been moved by our talk. He's a minister, as well, who presides over all of the milestones, from births to weddings to deaths. He's seen much. This call, which started out about despair, ends with ways to encourage a life. Perhaps it's nothing at all but an idea, a twist to what already is. But hope resides in the thought and not the fact.

We've said everything each of us wanted to say. Eventually I press *End* and the call is over.

. . . .

The next morning my incoming email folder is filled with messages from sangha members who ask about Eli, who tell me they've set up a phone tree, who remind me to call anytime I need help. They are going to make him food and keep in touch by telephone, too. And they'll visit him. He's with them now. Stephen sends an email, as well, thanking me again for the conversation and telling me I can call him anytime. He gives me phone numbers and wishes me well.

. . . .

One Saturday early last summer I stopped by a crafts fair in Rockport. I was poking through the bracelets and earrings and mugs and plaques when I saw a small pile of pamphlets on one of the tables. It announced a new, local chapter of a nationwide grassroots support group for people and families coping with mental illness. I filed the pamphlet, knowing someday I would call these people and ask for help.

In January I call and leave a message. The woman who calls back tells me the monthly meeting is scheduled for the following Wednesday in Gloucester at the AIDS resource center. "You should stop by," she says.

This is easy. I drive straight from work to Gloucester. A friend of mine is director of the AIDS health center, so I know where the building is and where to find the meeting. I head for the large dining room, which serves well as a place to meet and talk.

There are snacks, including homemade cupcakes and potato chips. I pile some chips on a napkin and pour a cup of coffee. Everything is free and almost everyone smiles and says hello. A friendly woman, one of the leaders, approaches and introduces herself. Welcome to NAMI, she says. Have one of my daughter's famous cupcakes and make yourself at home.

NAMI—the National Alliance on Mental Illness—is a support network for the mentally ill, their friends, and family members. In Massachusetts this grassroots organization is visible, politically active, and knowledgeable. These passionate people have worked years to accrue powerful tools: information and knowhow. They are tied into the state's mental health networks and they lobby their government representatives by phone, email, and in person. They march. They speak out at the statehouse. They rally around legislation and organize email and letter-writing campaigns. They tell you which psychiatrists are good and which ones to avoid. They say things like: *It doesn't always matter what the diagnosis is. It's all the same medication.* They do things like give you their phone numbers and email addresses and say: *Call me anytime.* I do that, countless times over the next several months. And they call back. I learn how to work the system. They give me names and phone numbers and together, Eli and I get him signed up for state support programs and a mental health caseworker. I even bring Eli to a NAMI meeting. He listens, takes part, and says to me after, "I like those people. They are good people."

At my first meeting, Eli is still residing at what some refer to as the Gloucester hospital locked ward, before his move to the foster care home. I join the group gathered around the table. All of us here have friends or family who are mentally ill. In an adjacent room, some of these loved ones hold their own meeting.

We read the rules out loud to each other and introduce ourselves, telling why we're at the meeting. A married couple and another woman from Rockport lead the meeting. I must be careful how I tell this part of the story as we all pledge to protect our anonymity. I do so by changing the names.

NAMI is impressive, nationally and locally. It seems there's nothing about the mental health system and no one in the system these three regional leaders don't know. System, however, is a misnomer, for there is nothing systematic about mental healthcare. It is all about crisis intervention. And NAMI trains us to be tough advocates able to stand up to police, hospital administrators, even our elected officials to help those in trouble.

One couple appears to be in their seventies. They still care for an adult child who has been hospitalized, they tell the group, more than twenty times. The husband and wife are deeply concerned about what will happen to their child after they die. The father has just survived a serious medical emergency, intensifying the urgency. He's back, fighting for housing, insurance coverage, occupational therapy, work-training programs—everything necessary to provide the mentally ill with tools so they can live decent, independent lives.

The woman seated next to me has said nothing, has not looked up, has not, in fact, moved. Her head droops forward and there's a heaviness coming from her that worries me. After I tell everyone why I've come, I tell her, "It's your turn." She remains silent. The group leader steps in. "Why are you here tonight?"

The woman to her left nudges her and says, "Helen, they can help."

We wait to see if Helen will rouse herself.

"My name is Helen," she begins. She tells us she's here tonight because she needs help. She cannot persuade her adult son to leave the house. She tells us the situation has become unbearable. "If he doesn't go now, I'm going to die. I cannot take it a minute longer. I know I'm going to die. Please help me."

Oh do I hear you, Helen. Oh how well I know.

Poor Helen. When is the last time she looked in a mirror? Took the time to comb her hair? Had a hot meal? Most disturbing, though, is the evidence of her plight. She has placed her right hand on the table in front of her. It is wrapped in gauze and languishes there, disowned.

The group leader, Michelle, gets to the point. "What happened to your right hand, Helen?"

She says her son broke her thumb. He didn't mean to. He just wants her not to talk so much, to be quiet. She's been trying to get him to move out but he just sprawls on the couch, day after day, watching TV. To make ends meet, she works two jobs and comes home, between jobs, to check on her son, cook, and go out again. He's supposed to go to college but he doesn't go. The tuition's paid and he's enrolled but nobody makes him attend classes. He doesn't do anything. He lies there and doesn't do anything.

"I can't go back there. I can't take it anymore. Please tell me what to do. Please. I know that if I have to go back there I am going to die."

There isn't a person in this room who doesn't have firsthand knowledge of this kind of exhaustion and desperation. There isn't a soul here who hasn't spoken some version of what Helen says now.

Michelle doesn't miss a beat here. "Let's see what we can do, then."

When Helen leaves, she's armed with phone numbers, names of people to call, and a list of housing possibilities. And she has Michelle and this group, people who've come close to giving up themselves and who get their strength by seeing to it that others don't have to suffer quite as much as they have.

"PRETTY GOOD, EVEN FOR ME"

CHAPTER 13

I don't want to say no to Jim. Not ever. I wake up early, wanting Jim, running my hand lightly over my breast, my rib cage, my belly, thinking of him doing this, wondering why his hand feels so different on me than my hand, when I begin to understand how important his touch has become. It's Friday morning, late in February, nine hours before the start of my fourth weekend with Jim. I'm not sure, at first, what this idea of not saying no is all about but it feels important. First thoughts spring unencumbered to a fresh light. I take them seriously.

Perhaps I sense something about Jim; perhaps *no* is a turn-off. Perhaps I sense what's coming . . . sex in broad daylight, sex in front of a video camera, sex on the deck of my house, sex in positions that don't flatter an aging body no matter how many days a week I run or how few calories I ingest. I could so easily cop out. But what a mistake to set up a dynamic where *no* is always a possibility. I sense, as well, the disappointment and the ennui that come with limits.

This is an erotic resolution with a mission. I want an erotic life that builds instead of peters out. Why can't we dispense with the ravages of familiarity by using our brains? Isn't sex better if we're open and experimental?

Part of the challenge I sense here is the oh-too-true awareness that time is running out. I have absolutely nothing to lose. Why can't I be on a mission to prove that an erotic life does not have to stagnate, barring unforeseen health issues. What happens if I never turn away from Jim? What happens if sex is our number-one priority? Is this a novel idea? For me, it is. And though this vow hinges on deference, my objectives are quite obviously selfish.

I want Jim's full range of motion. I want everything during those few moments or scant hours when it's just him and me, alone, stripped of clothes and pretense and plans, wondering, open. This is scary naked. This is when the only conscious thought forming is *What?* What is next? The answer to that is *Anything.* Anything is next. No wonder this is the moment when life forms. It is the purest, most inventive time.

So give me that.

At fifty-eight I can finally appreciate it. Pull it off, perhaps. For all the years leading up to this, there has been so much in the way: fertility, social mores, children in the next room, a promising future, and all the *shoulds* and deferments that go along with it, so much fear and so much caution, ignorance of what's possible and confusion about what matters.

I want the best of Jim, all that his sixty-seven years of experience with sex and women and fantasy and longing have brought to him. God this is sexy. I wish for him to be unencumbered. I wish for him to perform as a high-functioning artist does, freely and absent any dis-abling self-conscious concerns. I desire spontaneous and creative flow. I will not shy away from him. I will not say no.

This morning I awake with an intense erotic curiosity—a woman's hard-on—and I vow, for once, to give a man license to be all that he can be. I want to know what Jim can do with this. I want to know where Jim will take us. Why not?

I am not absent in this equation. No worries here. Is facilitator a passive state? Is enabler an abdication? Is responder unworthy? Or is all this merely to justify my role as blissful recipient of the remarkable prowess Jim lavishes on me?

No wonder I say thank you, over and over, ad nauseam. How dare he question my gratitude? He likes me this way. Spent and stymied and monosyllabic. Jim. Jim. Jim. It's my choice.

Not saying *no* is not the same as saying *yes*. Saying *yes* means you still think you have some control. Not saying *no* is about relinquishing control and turning to nothingness. It takes courage. It's how I start my free fall.

You must simply *be*. Hardly simple at all, if not impossible. On every level, you must be. To be is to fully engage with all of your senses as you stretch to correspond with the world around you. This is an expansive role. To be is your most powerful state. Call it wordless rhapsody. Call it neural harmonics.

It's possible to make a vow to honor Jim's wishes because I've found that I can trust him. He's a gentleman in the old-fashioned sense. He opens doors and insists that I go first. He asks me if what he's doing is okay. He calls me three times a day. He brings me cinnamon toast when I'm too hungry to think straight. He stands beside me when I

throw up and says, "Poor baby." Oh how my appreciation of this loving man makes me want to bury myself in him. Once after exhaustive
fucking he says, "Have I killed you yet?" "Not yet," I tell him, knowing
that some sort of annihilation of my sentient self, is, coincidentally, my
desire as well.

So, with regard to fucking, sucking, licking, biting, hair pulling,
gripping and grabbing, and whatever else is done, Jim decides when,
where, what.

* * * * * * * * * * * * *

I recall a moment of tremendous euphoria I experience during a visit
with Jim in Manhattan. I'm in Chelsea, running south along the Hudson River Parkway. A man pushing his daughter in a stroller catches
my attention and points to the river. I glance right, over my shoulder,
and see four large U.S. military ships cruising north, led by a single
black helicopter with its nose dipped, it seems, in reverence. Sailors in
their dress whites stand erect along the perimeters of the ships' decks.
They are at ease, their feet rooted hip-width and their hands clasped
behind their backs. One ship after another passes us. God. This takes
my breath away. It's early Sunday morning, already one of the quietest
times in Manhattan, and silence falls as everyone stops to behold this.
The sailors remain at rest, the ships underfoot pressing on, quickly,
carving white frothy Vs as they buck the Hudson. Glorious pageantry
set against a shining blue sky and a diamond river. Runners, skaters,
cyclists stop to watch. Then the four ships, festooned in colorful pen-
nants, cruise away, beyond the scope of our vision, disappearing behind one of the piers.

I click on my iPod again and resume running. My playlist, Sunday Morning, is full of wildly impassioned love songs that recall for me the previous night with Jim. There are worse things to be than lovesick, I think as I pull this playlist together before rushing out of the apartment. In my world, in this moment, everything is foreplay. It's sensitized, rich, poignant . . . and worth remembering.

Though life is rife with coincidence, I am stunned when I hear Marty Balin exult, "You ripple like a river when I touch you, when I pluck your body like a string." His voice is as close to sex as music gets. And Gracie Slick, his partner in this eight-minute rhapsodic entanglement, responds as if plucked and stroked and stoned on endorphins. "Baby. Baby. Baby." Dirty talk. Call and response.

I swear, she is swooning.

Balin wrote this song in an enchanted state, marveling at the way it can work sometimes—a man brings a woman to the edge, where she is fraught but willing, open but scared, on fire, as alive as she'll ever be. There is only her brilliant lover in her sights. This is the purest form of responsiveness. She is the vibration. Touch her and see what happens.

My late-in-life love affair is special. I am the beneficiary of all the lessons learned from all our mistakes, our broken hearts, our successes . . . and our fabulously turned-on music.

The River Hudson. She ripples as I run.

Miracles here in the open, waiting to be found.

* * * * * * * * * * * *

Friday. Two PM. Everyone here in the creative services department pushing against deadlines. Friday afternoons are crazed, with lots of last-minute signage and flier requests to fulfill for the museum's weekend events. Since most staff are off preparing for the weekend or traveling, we are left alone and we get a lot accomplished.

I am the exception here. I'm fighting the pull of the weekend. It takes real effort to focus on the stack of papers in front of me as I await word from Jim. He'll arrive in the next hour or so on a commuter train from Boston, the last leg of his train travels north from Penn Station.

I haven't seen Jim in a few weeks. A lot's happened, especially with regard to Eli, and I feel different, now. My winning trick of persisting in the face of adversity can't work because I'm learning some things can't be solved or fixed. I'm so wary. I anticipate the next bad thing. How will Eli ever make it through all this?

Then, there are the complications with Jim. Our mutual deal-breaker threats regarding boundaries for our exes buzz in the background like excitable wasps. The last few weeks have tested my confidence. I want assurance that everything is okay. Asking for reassurance, as women know, is deadly. I must wait it out. I'll know the minute Jim steps off the train whether things are okay.

We planned this rendezvous a while ago, before Eli's move to the apartment with Tenzin in Medford. Perfect timing, it turns out. I reserved a room at the Hawthorne Inn, the beautiful, historic brick hotel just down the block and across the street from my office. Before the hotel and the martinis and the sex, though, he's coming to my office to meet my staff, visit the museum, and look around. Despite all the worries about Eli, I don't really expect trouble with Jim. I expect fun.

But there's still so much work to be done. I spend, minimally, ten hours a day in this place though my labors don't begin here. I'm home at my desk writing by 5:30 AM. I run at 7:30. I get to work by 9 or 9:30

and I stay till 7, when the guards lock up. Some nights we are allowed to stay later. My work is the better part of my world even though I know I will leave no lasting legacy here and I know that my boss will be quick to undo anything with my stamp on it as soon as I go. I have found no way to mollify his dislike of me, a dislike he spreads to his male counterparts in the other corner offices.

Bringing Jim here is risky. Linking him to this place adds to the degree to which he permeates my life, and it makes purging him that much harder—should he need purging. Wherever a parting lover leaves a memory, he leaves another piece of himself to grieve.

· · · · · · · · · · · ·

Question from Jim: What's off limits?

Answer: (1) Torture. (2) Anything less than full-tilt adoration of my daughter. (3) Large objects taking up space in anal cavities. (4) Graphic pictures of my vagina. (5) And, my journals. You must never touch my journals, I tell him, using eye contact like a drill bit. I bore down till he's afraid to blink. I harden my voice. I insist. Never go near them. Never read them. Never allow yourself to be tempted. And never let this prohibition pique your curiosity. Think of it, instead, as something blessedly irrefutable, like the Ten Commandments. When I die, my instructions are to burn all the short stories in the filing cabinets and the unpublished novels and the book-length ode to puberty in free verse and all the journals. I've got shelves of them. There's also a box of them in the basement, no doubt fuzzy with mold. They go back to my childhood. Don't open them. Don't read them. Don't. If you read even a single word, I will find a way to give you an ugly death.

. . . .

I was always a writer. I wrote my first song at the age of five. I wrote an embarrassment of poetry throughout elementary school. At twelve I wrote a science fiction novel. At fifteen I wrote a book-length poem, an homage to my libido, disguised as extended metaphor. After college I was a reporter and eventually an editor. I write to be read, except for those journals, begun in prepubescence as conversations with some anonymous other I never took the time to conceptualize. Now I use my journals as a way to think systematically about a problem or issue. The implicit goal is to construct an approach that feels true and right. Problems and issues aren't rocks; they're people doing something I don't like. Sometimes the problem is Jim.

I've suffered the life-altering consequences of reading a loved one's journal. When I was ten, I read the journal my mother kept when she first met and fell in love with my father. She was nineteen and he was a few years older. They were both attending the University of California at Santa Barbara, though they met at a church picnic. My father recently said of my mother, "The minute I saw her I knew I should run the other way. But she had all that red hair."

My mother's journal was a record of her infatuation with my father. The journal was a vessel into which she poured her emotional response to their brief, passionate love affair. I know, from having gone to City Hall to examine my parents' wedding license, that they were married three months before I was born. The fun ended there, as did the journal.

The journal could be construed as proof that she loved at least the idea of me because she had written my name—Rae Arlene Padilla—all over the inside covers. Perhaps it was her way of getting used to the idea of me, a surprise, something she later forswore with a zeal and frequency akin to daily prayer. *I wish you were never born.*

I discovered her journal, by accident, at the top of a full garbage can one Saturday afternoon when I was taking out the trash. I pulled off the lid and there it was, a book, cover jet black, just waiting for me. The coincidence of my being the one to find this amazing thing defies mathematical probability. There were eight trash bins and six apartments using them and twenty-four hours in a day. There I stood, trash can lid in hand, looking down on half-full bags of potato chips and soda bottles and newspapers. And the book. I picked it up and only by paging through was I able to deduce what I had. By then it was too late. I'd seen the words Muriel Jean Kronberg and *love* and *kissing* and *handsome* and *party* and *forever.* There was no mention of the pregnancy. Just variations on my name. This was not the Muriel I knew, but a smitten, uncomplicated, passionate teenager who couldn't begin to imagine the depths to which hatred would burrow in and build. I was better off without knowledge of her vulnerability and her capacity for joy. Now there is just that much more to lament.

· · · · · · · · · · · · ·

I've decided that when I introduce Jim to my staff, it will be as a friend of the family from New York City. We all bring friends through the place. The museum is a destination, as is Salem, with all things witchcraft to entice those with lurid curiosities. No one here will think to ask, "Family friend? What family? You have family?"

Jim doesn't have to be told what he must do: Smile. Show polite interest mixed with a hint of reserve. Most important, he must cinch those hot vibes with a tight yank on the belt. Say little and see much.

I'm doing this why? I push myself to venture outside of my comfort zone, take risks, stay open. So far I have no regrets. Risk, after all, is the precursor to gain. In this case, I want Jim to have a mental picture of where I work and I want him to see a little of what I do. I saw his shop in DUMBO, met his subcontractors, visited his job sites. I've carved something out, as well. I like creative services. I like my staff. I like the work. I like our "palatial digs," as the director of security once called our workspace.

The last thing I have to do before my weekend can start is get through twenty or so design projects in various stages of the production process. I look at color proofs of brochures, posters, banners, booklets, ads, etc. I note my comments on the proofs, review our clients' notes and feedback, decide which of the new designs is ready to present to my boss, which work I want to send back to the designers for tweaks, and which I think is ready to send to the clients. It's not unusual to run a project through six, seven, eight, or more rounds of revisions. One of my jobs is to work with everyone involved to try to keep these rounds of revisions to a minimum. When a mercurial or arbitrary personality is the client, the protracted revisions don't always make sense. Then I intervene, work with the client to determine what's really the problem, try to get closer to completion. It doesn't usually work, so my job shifts to empathetic motivator. I help the designers work through the numerous revisions without feeling too demoralized. I pass on any insights I have gleaned from talking with the client. I consult with my boss to see what he recommends. And sometimes, when the designer's frustrations peak, all I can do is say: If you want to feel creative, go home and write a book. This is work. This explains that paycheck you get.

The boss would argue that if they were good creatives, they would have gotten it right the first time. I get in trouble when I remind a boss, as I often have, that *right* is relative; tastes vary. More often than not artists create successful projects in spite of a boss's conservative or outdated aesthetics. That ability to produce handsome work that does the trick amid opposing and contentious direction is, in fact, where the true talent is expressed. Blame mounts all around. Designers, once heralded as brilliant, lose their luster over time. Sanguine members of the creative staff note the signals. The wise ones nod knowingly and move on to the next employer to begin the cycle anew. Adoration. Love. Acceptance. Generalized dissatisfaction. Blame. Disdain. Separation. That's the way it goes in the creative profession. You give your all and get out before you're fired.

I am in the *adoration* phase of a comparable cycle with Jim, I think, as I ponder the occasionally rude comments people scribble on the proofs. It's as if they don't realize a human is going to read this stuff. When I came to PEM, I pulled off heroic production feats amid endless infighting among newly hired deputy directors jockeying for power. Over time and with the help of my boss, I built a large and productive department. Now, though, I catch glimmers of my own obsolescence in these comments on proofs and from my boss. Those who are infatuated are more respectful. I see my future in the words: *Can't you find any other pictures of kids playing?*

With Jim, I'd better savor the moment because nothing this good can possibly last.

Never saying *no* is a nod to a future that's mere construct. But not saying *no* has advantages in the moment, also. So I decide, definitely, I will do this.

When Jim does finally call, I'm almost ready for the weekend to begin.

"We'll be pulling into Salem in about five minutes." He's very jolly. "Okay?"

"Of course, okay," I say. "I've been waiting for hours!"

He laughs.

"Don't go anywhere," I say. "I'll be right there."

Don't go anywhere. I'll be right there. Mantras sung by long-distance lovers.

. . . .

I have an eight-by-ten photograph of Jim taken in the middle of a street in Manhattan a few years earlier. He's wearing his Carhartt jacket and his crew stands with him. It's a group-and-grin shot but it's unusual. There's movement and intent and direction caught here. The men smile at the photographer, perhaps a member of the crew. They look genuinely amused, engaged, paused momentarily, perhaps to enjoy what might be the punch line of some hilarious off-color joke. Jim towers over all of them. He's clearly the boss, not just because he's taller and in the center, but because of the way he meets the camera, head on, full of life. I can almost sense his next move, he is so flush with energy and forward momentum. I imagine that as the shutter snaps, he's pausing, smiling, but more in motion than at rest, moving to the scaffolding, some wisecrack flung with a twist of the head, an arm flexing as the film advances automatically, a finger rising, aiming toward something outside the viewing field.

I keep this photograph in a folder on top of my desk at home. Sometimes, late at night, I go to my office, pull out the photograph, and pore over the details. I think: He looks so familiar. And then I see why. This is the man I've been waiting for all my life.

All those dinners together for all those years, had I looked, I would have noticed. The inverse is just as true. I didn't look because I knew.

. . . .

I take Jim right to the museum. As usual, the first hour together is awkward. It's as if I barely know him.

The cafeteria, in the large public atrium, is a nice place to sit, relax, and reconnect. He orders a cup of clam chowder, a staple everywhere in New England on Fridays and every day in every seaside town. In Manhattan, he orders Moonstruck's chowder every Friday. It tastes more like cream of celery soup than clam chowder, but it's near at hand and one of his favorite simple pleasures. "Guess what I'm doing right now," he'll ask me over the phone at 4 PM on Fridays in Chelsea. "You've parked your car and you're ordering chowder." This signals the close of another busy workweek and these phone calls to me are celebratory. A simple pleasure is truly complete when it's shared.

From the museum we walk to the hotel, where Jim quickly showers and changes into a clean dress shirt and jacket. "I want to make a good impression," he says. While I assume no one will think twice about his quick visit to the department, he's convinced everyone will notice. Though we've spent a lot of time conversing on the telephone, the time spent together in person amounts to less than five or six days. My lover, the man I proudly present to all these people I've hired and respect, feels very much like a stranger to me as I walk him around and listen as he engages each person in short conversations. People are very polite and, as we move on, each one turns back to his or her work, their faces and their body language remarkably inscrutable. Jim takes a seat at the conference table, just outside my office, while I finish my work. It's around 4:30 or so when I head over to the museum office complex with all the jobs and distribute them. On Monday morning, our clients will find new and revised work for their review.

"Let's go," I say to Jim on my return. We stroll next door, to a Hungarian deli, and purchase pieces of sausage, cheese, crackers, and chocolate for a picnic in our room. Across the brick walkway, we buy a couple of bottles of wine and a corkscrew. I'm anxious to get to the room. I've got my briefcase, my purse, and my overnight bag with me. Jim's carrying food, wine, and a long baguette. For anyone who cares to notice, there is no denying what this is all about.

Sure enough, I pass coworkers heading into the hotel tavern for drinks. "What are you doing here?" one woman, a friend and coworker, asks pointedly. She looks at us both with a smile. "My friend is staying here," I say. "Well, you two have a great time!" She laughs and walks toward the tavern while we walk to the elevator. So much for secrets.

In truth, I'd already decided Jim need not be so much of a secret now that Eli has moved out. I don't want Eli to know, yet, because I want him to have his own place and be settled a bit. My daughter, whose opinion I trust, said, upon hearing about Jim, "This is going to kill Eli." Perhaps. Or perhaps my daughter is tired of my sexual antics.

Eli, nonetheless, deserves stability and security and a medication regime that works. It's impossible to know how long that will take and whether Jim will even be in my life at that time. Until then, I keep secrets from Eli. Regardless of his needs, my decision to bring Jim to Salem and into my offices signals a reduction of secrecy in my world.

Eli's hub is now fifty miles southwest of here. My friend's recognition of what's happening is a relief—one less stressor.

. . . .

If there is one perfect weekend that serves as the standard for a love affair, against which all else is measured, then the Hawthorne is it. We have the perfect waiter. Perfect martinis. Perfect room. Perfect sex. Perfect food. Perfect. Perfect. Perfect.

Why does it start with a martini? Because I am fifty-eight and Jim is sixty-seven. Because gin disables all those inhibitions that come with age and that the mirror so rudely reinforces. Because every time we see each other again, it's like starting over. Because we are latent sots, inclined toward certain altered states. Because, if perfect states are to be found at all, a martini shines a light.

Why is this night, above all others, perfect? I say it's perfect because we connect. Brains. Psyches. Crotches. Preferences. Tonight I take my place beside Jim. I claim proximity, woman to man. May it always be this simple.

We sit back, relax in upholstered faux French provincial chairs, side by side, our backs to the wall. Though we hardly notice, we face clusters of low tables and chairs and couches and people engaged with each other. To our left is a large rectangular bar that seats eight or nine people who drink, converse, and eat the hot appetizers served free of charge in the early evening. The bartender is bounded on all sides by the bar. He has a large space in which to mix drinks and a wide wall of liquor behind him. He mixes delicious cocktails of generous proportions. We have one martini each and split a second, which goes unfinished.

Our waiter establishes right off that he is in service of our needs. "I will be your waiter tonight. Anything you want. . . . " Want. Oh, yes. He gets it.

Scott knows we are in heat. He's an empath, as they say in *Star Trek*, with manners. And though it's a bit uncomfortable to be so thoroughly known by a stranger, I stop resisting right away. He is the perfect servant of sex—handsome, alert, orbiting attentively at the periphery of our consciousness, competent, knowing. He sniffs out our outlandish pheromone fog because empaths are more animal than human despite appearances. If he were a masseuse, his fingertips would fall immediately upon those knots in our flesh where life's difficulties have lodged. We are in good hands.

Jim and I talk and talk and talk. We revisit our shared past in light of our new intimacy. *Did you expect anything like this? When were you first attracted to me? What did you think when I never answered your first email? When you said . . . , then I. . . .* The emerging details are as salacious as the half-tucked white blouse, his big hand spanning the small of my back as we take our seats, the show of soft breast lifted to him by a lacy black bra, the skirt hiked high up the hips from so much squirming, his musk mixed with juniper and Chanel No. 5 and the smoky wood fire popping in the hearth. We feast on ourselves in the retelling of the love affair to date. I am vaguely aware of the self-indulgence, the drunkenness, the scene we two must be making but it's a passing thought and there are other thoughts so much more interesting.

We go on with this inquiry and I admit to him, somewhat shyly, that I have always experienced him as a beautiful man. I tell him this story:

One night, years ago, I sat between you and Eli in your Suburban as you drove us back to Queens after dinner. Somehow Giuliani came up—this was post 9/11—and you railed. Forget cleaner streets, you said. Forget a taming of the criminal element. Giuliani, to save himself and some inept police officers after a shooting gone bad, had illegally released a young black man's juvenile record to the media. He did it to cast aspersions, to imply that this young, innocent man was to blame for being shot and killed. You were furious.

I clearly remember the ride, I tell Jim. *This* was it, the seed planted. All that was needed after that was a spark of actionable interest—like the night we ate pho soup together in Chinatown . . . so many years later.

. . . .

The part I keep to myself:

I study Jim's profile that evening in the Suburban. He's bluish in the dark, drained of all color, visually indistinct. Yet the big noisy truck barely contains him even as the night light paints him neutral. He is like the bass, turned way up, blaring out the windows as he races through the empty streets in some industrial section of Queens. He rants over the bang and rattle of the truck filled with tools and garbage and window frames. He scares me a little.

I take a careful appraisal as he uses both hands to steer over the cobblestones, around the corners, out of the emptiness, back and forth across lanes and in and out between cars. Holy shit. He's a cowboy.

He laughs and he rants. Jim really interests me. I love his explosive passion. I'm familiar with this, harbor something similar myself, but have found it a detriment. The difference is he lets his passion out. He has no shame about expressing himself, whereas I have devoted time, money to therapists, and hard work to wrestle this thing down. So who or what am I attracted to here? Jim? An alternate version of myself? The vicarious experience of passionate expression?

. . . .

I tell him that I was keenly aware of his physicality that night. That I took liberties from where I sat in the dark. That I caught a sense of my fascination and it unnerved me.

He listens to what I'm saying and I am surprised to see a few tears. What do they mean? My first thought: He appreciates being of interest. He is touched that someone notices. He's a big man who must hide parts of himself from others.

. . . .

Once, early on, we walk north along 8th Avenue from the Village. It's a zoo in this part of Chelsea—gay bars that open onto the sidewalk, crowds of partiers with drinks in their hands, outrageous behavior, and blatant flirting with Jim. I am with someone that 90 percent of the people on the sidewalk, male and female, look at twice.

It's through this chaos we navigate, on our way back to 24th Street, when we pass a small, empty burger joint with one homeless man sitting in the window. He has no food. I note this out of the corner of my eye but it's a fleeting thing and I am on to the next impression and the next. In New York City, every blink of the eye brings something new to see.

Yet in the split second that I see the man and forget about him, Jim not only sees him, he comprehends the situation, digs into his pocket for money, stops, turns back, enters the restaurant, and lays a wad of cash in front of him. When I notice that Jim is no longer at my side, I turn around to see him exiting the restaurant, I see the cash, I see the man reaching out, I see him pull a takeout menu from the shelf beside him.

Why did Jim do this? I believe it's because he cares that there are people who suffer.

It takes me to another time and place and another act of kindness. A man walks up to my mother. She and I are standing, of all places, on Rodeo Drive in Beverly Hills. She's just had her hair done and her BMW detailed. We're heading, now, for Bergdorf Goodman, where she will spend some money.

The man, who is in his forties and wears a suit, says, "I've left my wallet at home and have no money to get to work." She opens her purse, fishes around, pulls out a wad of bills, and hands him all the cash she has—around $60. She says to me, "I know that what he said makes no sense. I know that he probably lied to me. But why would he ask if he didn't need it?"

Show me your compassion and I am yours for life.

. . . .

It's as if we're in a movie. Perhaps we're enacting my fantasy here at the Hawthorne. Or is this a dream? I don't know anymore. Martinis. Lust. Jim. I lose track.

. . . .

The night at the Hawthorne begins to take shape weeks earlier, when I make the reservation for our room. What happens in the hours and days between that telephone call and the night in the tavern—as desire for Jim begins again to insinuate itself into all my waking thoughts—is neither contrivance nor fantasy. I anticipate the evening and imagine, precisely, the luscious warp and weft of details till I have something close to probable.

I fully expect that we'll be seated according to my wishes, against the wall and alongside the bank of windows—our own semiprivate little nook. A waiter, a lesser facsimile of Scott, stops by to take our order. Everything good? Sure, says Jim. We accept our drinks—Bombay Sapphire martinis. Jim sips and smiles. Martinis always deliver, he says. Based on experience, I foresee that we are offered chicken wings, when, in fact, it's quesadillas we actually nibble with our drinks.

Jim gets feisty in my virtual scenario. He's lively and irreverent—a bit of a handful. I don't resist when he slides his long left arm around my waist and slips his hand under my already untucked blouse, along my back, under my bra. I fully expect that he will touch the flesh of my breast, feel my heart beating at twice its normal resting rate, slide his fingers around my nipple. Who's to know? He will do this, compromise me in public just as he compromises me in private. I see how he is already. I understand what turns him on.

He doesn't care about my nipple. My breast isn't the thing. It's true what John Updike wrote: Women must think sex is all about them. But I know better when it comes to Jim. My breast, the erection of my nipple, the way he squeezes and releases, squeezes and releases, is the way he has of separating the woman from her propriety. I will not say no. But I will do anything, anything at all besides that.

. . . .

I do not anticipate what really happens—that we never touch once we are seated. We sit, laugh, and talk, dip into the martinis and olives, and never let a hand drift across a forearm or a finger touch a shoulder or a palm. Touching, in fact, is verboten. I dare not rest my arm so that it touches his. He never kisses me, of course. His hand never slips to my knee.

. . . .

After an hour and a half of verbal foreplay, we push up from our tavern chairs, thank Scott and leave him a sizable tip, walk to the elevator, ride up to the sixth floor, find our way to the door of our corner room, unlock it with the key card, and stumble in, kissing and groping.

By now I'm at the edge of desperation. Jim's face is buried in my hair. His tongue is in my ear and some part of my circuitry goes haywire. My limbs fail me and he has to get me through the door and up against something before I slide, useless, to the floor.

I am at a loss to understand Jim. How can he be in such control? Why is he not desperate?

We back up against an open window that overlooks the intersection of Hawthorne Boulevard and Essex Street. It's a busy street with stoplights, a crowded, loud Irish bar across the way, and lots of traffic. I can easily see the museum from here. It's very hot in this old hotel with an HVAC system that knows no subtleties—just hot and cold. We push the window open all the way.

He has my blouse off. He has my bra off. When did all this happen? I'm naked from the waist up in full view of anyone who cares to glance up. Is this a Fellini movie? We're kissing each other like the end of time is on the other side of the door. We kiss like this for ten or fifteen minutes until suddenly Jim stops it all. He steps back. He pulls my skirt over my hips. He takes my hand and places it on his penis.

Just as a cold wind blasts through the window, just as I think I've been slammed by a sledgehammer, Jim grabs me, lifts me onto the bed, and in one swift breathtaking move, slides his penis into me.

. . . .

It is a long night of no sleep. We are not total animals. We take rest breaks for our picnic and a comedian named Lewis Black.

One time in the night we fall back, exhausted. Let's sleep, we agree. There is only the sheet that covers the mattress and our two naked bodies on the bed. We look for pillows and we try to find ways to lie that might lead us to sleep. Impossible.

Jim gets up from the bed to pee. He switches on the light, looks back at me, smiles. I hear him mutter as he pees, "That was great, even for me."

. . . .

I shower, pull on winter running tights and a warm shirt, and go out. It's sleeting and the ice is beginning to coat the streets and brick sidewalks. I am careful and I am tired and I am wired. I run down to Salem Willows, on the ocean, and get lost on the return trip. I find myself by the Salem Bridge and slowly make my way back over the icy streets.

Jim is waiting for me at Red's, a busy breakfast place in town, and I slide into a booth across from him.

I smile at the sight of his beautiful face as I sip hot coffee. How good this all is, I think.

Thank you, I say. I am so happy he walked over here in the icy rain to meet me, that he came up on the train from New York City, that he brought his dress shirt to wear to meet my staff, that he spent the night fucking me.

Thank you, he says. It's my pleasure.

"I WANT TO GO UPSTAIRS"

CHAPTER 14

On a crisp, clear Sunday afternoon in late March, Jim and I sit quietly across from each other in Rockport. As is often the case, he's on the couch and I'm in my reading chair. I scan the *New York Times* book reviews and he's online on his laptop, browsing various news websites and blogs, including his favorite, *Emptywheel*. He reads to me—something Marcy Wheeler writes about Vice President Cheney. A strong light turns the sky a paler blue than wintertime and floods the windows directly behind Jim. The seasons are changing. Bright sun glints off the ocean and warms the attic bedrooms. Temperatures still drop at night but the sun will now keep the bedrooms warm into the fall.

Later this afternoon Jim will carry his small suitcase down the stairs and head back to New York City. As usual, we don't mention the pending departure. Until he stands, zips the suitcase, pees one last time, and kisses me goodbye, we go about business as usual. He's here;

he's gone. One minute there's laughter and talking and arguing about the ways Al Gore and Sandra Day O'Connor fucked over this country; the next minute it's me, sucker punched, wondering what the hell just happened. It's always the same. The door slams at the bottom of the stairs and silence swamps me like a rogue wave. It's all encompassing: a chilly, dark embrace I eventually relax into. I sink into silence and note the nature of this nothingness. I'm never in any hurry to surface because this, at least, carries the residuals of Jim.

. . . .

Jim arrived Saturday around noon and he's leaving a day later, in early evening. He's abbreviated this visit. Though he doesn't say so, I suspect it's because I keep the house at sixty-two degrees to conserve fuel oil, doubly cold when you live in a superheated New York City apartment and routinely have to wear shorts and T-shirts in winter. And Rockport in March doesn't have the appeal for him that New York City does. Though he never complains, this small town isn't where his life is based. A cold house on a windy New England coastline in late winter doesn't have a lot to recommend it unless you fancy living a survival drama.

I offer these rationalizations up as excuses for Jim; frankly, a long drive for a twenty-four-hour visit feels like fuck-and-flee to me.

Fortunately I don't have to seriously question the brevity of the visit because we've got plans. In nine days I fly to Miami to rendezvous with Jim and drive to Marathon Key. I will introduce him to my friends who have a home and a boat there. These are good, old friends whom I enjoy tremendously and see every winter during their annual Florida stint. Just as important, though, Jim and I are going to spend five days and nights together—a significant entry on our growing list of firsts.

I'm about to ask Jim if he'd like some more coffee when he looks up from his laptop. "I want to have a drink and go upstairs."

Oh.

For a few seconds my mind blanks. What is he talking about?

Oh.

Now I get it. *It's nice and warm upstairs in the attic bedroom. I've been waiting for this. It doesn't look like I've noticed but I have. It's springtime and the angle of the sun has shifted and now it's pumping its rays directly into our little love nest. I've been sitting here thinking about what I want to do to you. Come on Rae. Let's get buzzed and naked and have the kind of hot white light, magnified by window panes, that transforms lovemaking into graphic porn. Let's have lots of sweaty sex the way I like it. And what's wrong with a traditional Sunday brunch bloody Mary? I want you naked and I want you open. All the way open. Open wide. Swallow this booze. Suck my tongue. Do you like my dick?*

Of course he doesn't say this but he's thinking something along those lines. I guess he hasn't caught on yet. He doesn't get it. But I'm committed to my vow. I'm not going to say no. This won't be easy for a modest woman, age fifty-eight. Raunchy sex in broad daylight. Wet sheets. Pillows hurled across the room. Semen and perspiration and saliva running down my legs. A taste of blood from what? Reckless kissing during reckless fucking?

"Sure," I say. "Let's have a drink and go upstairs."

After all, that's what this relationship is all about.

. . . .

Jim's not in my bed. He's not even in the bedroom.

"Jim?"

"I'm here," he calls. He's in the guest room, prostrate across the larger bed that better accommodates him.

His long white body, naked on top of a navy blue flannel sheet, glows incandescent in this light. And I see he's been expecting me. His erect penis, as pale and flawless as his skin, lies upon his lower abdomen. Mmmmmmm. I can almost taste it.

Jim's grinning at me. It's as if he's saying, *Look. We're ready for you. We want to have some fun. Join us!* He seems boyish and sheepishly proud of himself, like he's just dug up a pint of quality earthworms or eaten the whole chocolate cream pie.

I smile at Jim, letting the surprise of finding him here instead of the other bedroom show. I wrinkle my brow a bit as if to ask, *What's up?* But I don't say anything because I'm a little numb from my drink and I have tasks to attend to: take off my clothes while standing, stay upright and balanced, appear undaunted, summon courage.

My eyes drift back to Jim's penis as I undress. He's watching me with more interest, not so much because I'm undressing but because he knows I'm getting into his penis right now. He sees my focus shift. He reaches down and takes it in his hand, proclaiming ownership, saying *Hurry up, come on,* demonstrating possibilities. His eyes momentarily drop to watch what he's doing. Good god. There is nothing more male than a gorgeous man holding his erect penis for you. He lays it back down and clasps his hands behind his head, eyeing me more seriously now. *Come and get me. I'm all yours.*

No.

It's funny how you can love a man's penis separately from the man. His is smooth and beautiful and hidden in the sense that its physicality, its behavior, even its taste are tricksters. It's all so languid and benign as it stretches along his belly.

Then it flexes. An invitation.

No.

Not yet.

I can be possessive. Jim's penis is really my penis. He's up there somewhere, in his head, getting off. Jim has nothing to do with this. He's the recipient of whatever fun I have filling my mouth with his penis, enjoying the surprise of steel rigidity or running my tongue along the washboard bands that seem like hard, flexed muscle. This is not the soft, seductive penis lying there as it is right now, winking, lifting, summoning. This is the interactive penis that talks directly to me. We correspond. If Jim had his way, he'd get right to my vagina. But his penis likes me and I like Jim's penis. So I choose the penis.

"Come here."

Jim reaches an arm to me to indicate that I'm to climb on top.

No. Not now.

I step out of range of those long tentacles and climb between his legs, pushing his hands away several times. He always wants it his way.

I love this. I love the soft fleshiness. I love the smooth sweetness, nipple shaped, rocking in the crook of my tongue, pressed up against the hard palate of my mouth, rolling gently, side to side. I have all the time in the world.

I love the moment of its awakening, the way Jim's penis begins to take on a life of its own, summoning its resources and distributing its great powers. I love this give and take. Blind sympathy, deeply felt. We are so sensitive to each other's every twitch and tick. I feel as if it's here that I take my sensitivity training. I feel it's here I learn the power of myself. Every single motion we make elicits consequences, some intended and some unintended. I take the penis from its dormancy to its cathartic release.

I understand a whore could do this. I understand he could be imagining Nicole Kidman, the waif-woman whose look he especially enjoys. These powers—sprung from tongue, touch, and resonance— are everywoman powers. I close my eyes to shut out what I know, to get closer. To find that primal link. The primary chord. To get animal.

Here are two bodies, letting go of thought, turning to a richer, deeper, darker correspondence. Hands. Teeth. Mouths. Feet. Hair. Butts. I lick the head of this gorgeous penis and I draw back, wait. See what it wants. Feel its pulse on my cheek. Hold its tip between my soft lips. Let my saliva wash over it.

It's me here and me now. I am the only woman.

I love the way the genitals are the path to the lover's heart. I choose this. The direct route. His joy matters.

The erotic heart is ephemeral because ecstasy is chemistry. Good sex is not love. Jim says, "There are so many parts in your sandbox."

Perhaps he would agree. Unencumbered sex is when you are fucking your playmate, not the mother of your children, not the holder of your sad secrets, not the payer of bills, and most certainly not your best friend.

True. Everything is foreplay, as long as *play* is the root word.

I love the way the soft smooth luscious head pushes out in all directions like an umbrella unfurling in the wake of the imminent opening up of the skies. A furious storm is coming. I feel it. I love the way that first drop, the early scout in search of true north, settles in the grove of my tongue, trapped, salty, and thin. I swallow these little scouts.

I love the way every touch of my tongue pumps him up, elicits little boy sighs, turns the thighs rock hard, reaches into the throat and rips out surprises expressed in guttural tones, arcs his head backward into the pillows as if electroconvulsively shocked. I love the whole-scale rigidity because it's me, just me, the tip of my tongue, the edges of my teeth, the vice-grip in my hand, pulling him up and out of himself. Come here.

For a while, his hands reach for me. I don't like that. I push them off, bat them away. Leave me alone. I'm busy.

• • • • • • • • • • • •

I'm in the Connecticut River, maybe twenty miles south of the Canadian border. I'm up to my waist, at least, in this cold and forceful current that pushes pushes pushes. I don't know how I'm standing and cannot think beyond this moment because every single thing I possess in terms of knowledge and muscle memory and skill is working right now, right here, to keep me upright.

Behind me somewhere is my fishing guide, who urges me to cross the river, get to the other bank, and cast from there. This is impossible. The next step takes me deeper into the maelstrom. I root myself, instead, right here where I stand, smack in the middle of the river I love, dream about, make pilgrimages to, take pictures of in all weather and all temperaments, describe endlessly to friends, rhapsodize about in my journal. I fish here to become one with the river, to know it one more way.

I wedge my feet between the slippery rocks. I insist. Eventually my young guide relents and lets me be. I begin to relax, breathe, note where the trees bend into the river, see the clouds of gnats, watch leaves make shadow patterns, listen to wind rile surface tension, lick bitter tannin off my lips, warm to the river. I cast, aiming toward the far bank, the languid pool, the wild speckled trout that understands this water, these shadows, the eddies and water bugs and reflections of dragonflies and the hand-wrapped fly cast clumsily, in violation of nature's sensibilities.

I cast again and the line jerks. I jerk back. I have him.

I feel his muscle relax, flex, test the limits of his range. I give a little, tighten up, marvel at the conduit between fish and me, transmitting intent, fear, ferocity, cunning. I empty my mind, close my eyes, and take my cues from the filament till it's my turn to act. I bring in one salmon, one brown trout, and one speckled trout. I catch them, wrap my fingers around their muscle middles, slip the hooks from their jaws, and let them go. I slide them back into an astonishing unknowable world I touch only in that one instant when I hold the muscle body, bring him below the surface, open my fingers, and release. It's a joy we share.

. . . .

One night I get home from work and find a call on my answering machine. Something about the mammogram I had the week before.

The woman leaving the message talks fast and runs her words together. She sounds bored, as if this is a message she's left a thousand times before.

I play it back again and again until finally I get it. "There's an abnormality in your breast tissue. Call me back right away." Shit.

It's 8 PM. What was she thinking? I wait through the long night, wide awake and terrified. I have no inner reserves for this, not after the latest acrimony between my boss and me, Eli's continuing decline, and the long-distance love affair.

In the morning, while having coffee with two good friends from work who insist on sitting with me, I call for an appointment and the woman at the "breast health center" tells me to get in touch with my gynecologist to get the full story. This takes a day. All she does is read me what's on the report, which boils down to "abnormality in the tissue of the left breast."

"Everything will be alright," she says in a flat voice. She's busy and irritated. She knows what I want—to hear that this is all just one big mistake—and she knows we live in no such fairytale.

I tell Jim. "In for a penny, in for a pound," he says. Not *too bad,* not *how awful.* Just the one thing: *I'm right here.*

I remember the technician having trouble and redoing the test twice. She said it was a fold in the skin. So why this? Why now? It takes another three days before I can be retested but when I am, the radiologist reads the digital scans immediately. My daughter has driven up from Newton to be with me. We both hear, at the same time, that everything is normal.

For now, I think. Sooner or later the news will be bad. That's the nature of living.

. . . .

This incident is, for some reason, close to unendurable. After some thought, I call Jim. "I've taken a week off work. Can I come down and work and write? I want out of here. I want to get away."

He hesitates. In terms of the passage of time, his hesitation lasts less time than it takes for a hummingbird to flap its wings, but I'm sensitive right now and I understand that I'm asking for a lot. This isn't foreplay. This is Rae wanting something very different. Normalcy. Quiet and companionship. Regular living. He comes through for me. "Sure," he says. "I'd love it."

. . . .

One evening during my quiet week of working and writing at Jim's apartment I take a shower after a late run. Everything is fine. It's exactly as I'd envisioned it—long days at the little writing desk he made for me that includes shelving, a printer, and Wi-Fi; takeout salads and soups; runs; a couple of walks to the Strand bookstore and Barnes & Noble; lots of reading, sometimes to each other. It's easy and relaxed.

After my shower, I put on a big yellow seersucker shirt his son gave me and I walk into the bedroom. I see that Jim has turned off all the lights, drawn the curtains, lit seven or eight small votive candles, and set them around the bedroom.

He sits on the edge of the bed and catches my hand as I walk by. Come here. Sit astride of my knees. Take off this shirt. Put your arms around my neck. Be sure to hold tight. Good. Good. Now, kiss me. Yes. I like your lips. So soft and big and wet. See the way I suck your upper lip? I pull the luscious lip into my mouth, run my tongue under your lip, suck it harder, dart the pointed hard tip of my tongue into your mouth, shove it in all the way. I like to fuck your mouth and would like to do this with my penis. Not now, though. Now, let me suck your nipples. Like this. Oh. Perfect. I suck a little harder. Give me something, Rae. Show me how much you love this. Now, let me slide my legs apart a little. Yes. Like that. Is this okay? I am going to suck your nipple and put my fingers on your clitoris. Like this. Your legs are spread wide the way I love it. Love it. Love it. Sit down all the way. That's it. Relax. Did I say I love this? I have full access. Hold on tight. I can't help you there because I have to use both hands. That's it. See how I brush my fingers lightly back and forth across your clitoris. Lightly. Lightly. No worries. Plenty of time. I need to push your labia apart. And let me spread your pubic hair. I do this gently, like opening a curtain. Yes oh yes. Let me open you up all the way. Now I'm going to reach my fingers into your vagina. I need to get those sweet juices. I bring them out, paint you liberally till your labia, your clitoris, your vagina are runny and juicy. Ah. So good. Now I can speed this up a bit. Your little motor is running. I feel it. Is this right? Is this good? I'm going to spread my legs a little further now. Careful. Hold on. I'm going deeper now. Fucking you with my fingers. Rubbing a little harder. Come on baby. You can do it. Come on. Let go. I like the taste of this nipple. Mmmm. I'm going to bite down a little. I won't hurt you. I like the way my teeth feel on your hard nipple. Yes. Hold on. Let me pull my fingers out of you. Don't worry. This won't take long. I need to taste you now. Oh yeah. This is good. Now kiss me. You can have a taste, too. Come on. Lick my fingers. Suck. Oh this is so good. I'm back in now. Everything's okay. Go ahead. Go for it. You are so hot. You are so wet. I need to go just a little harder. I can't help myself. And a little faster, too. I won't hurt. I promise. My hand has this power. I'm like a machine. Oh yes.

. . . .

Jim is my man. I don't think of him tenderly. He is the one holding his dick out to me. I am the one deciding how I want it. When he says, "I do love you, you know," I think he says it to let me know I'm not just the cunt he plays with. When he says, "I do love you," I think he's talking to himself, reminding himself that there's more to me than my cunt.

. . . .

Jim and I have a fight. It's huge. It's wordless. The worst kind. It lasts two weeks.

The fight starts when he comes to Rockport for a long weekend, during which time we visit friends of mine and have martinis in the late afternoon because, as my friends say, "Jim makes a fine martini," and they like to drink martinis.

They talk about golf and I tell them about the fabulous golf course up near Pittsburg, New Hampshire, where I hike. I tell them it would be great fun for all of us to spend a weekend at the Balsams Hotel in Dixville Notch. They can golf while I hike the hotel's trail system, which includes one rock climb that's designated "acute pitch." I tell them I did this on my fiftieth birthday and it was a fast but scary climb that required both hands. Jim, a former rock climber, says, "What's the rating? Five? Six?" I don't know what he's talking about and tell him, again, the trail map's designation for level of difficulty. Something I've said has irritated him because he keeps grilling me about the level of difficulty. It doesn't stop till they get up to watch golf on television. I go into the kitchen and wash all the dishes and try to figure out what just happened. When we get home, I tell Jim I didn't like what happened. We make love, but I see that he's withdrawn. He pulls the sheet up to his chin afterward, like he's in need of protection, from me, and I feel wretched.

He doesn't call me. He doesn't email. Nothing. When he finally calls, he's pleasant but says little and gets off the phone. Again, a day or two goes by with no communication. This behavior is perplexing and frightening. I tell a friend, "I'm losing Jim." By Thursday I'm inconsolable. I decide to call Jim on my lunch break. I ask him, "What's wrong?" This has to be one of the worst questions you can ask someone. It's backfired on me more than once.

Of course something's wrong. You're what's wrong.

Jim's irritated. He tells me he's driving and he's going into a tunnel. "I'm losing you," he shouts. His voice is loud and shrill. I'd never heard anything like it from Jim. I'm stunned and tell him so. He gets angrier and tells me he has to hang up and he'll get back to me at some point.

I still don't see my part in this. I check with my friends. "Did you think Jim was aggressive in his questioning of my rock climb? Did you notice how I argued back? Did I seem rude or mean? Did things seem odd or off to you?" Their reply: No comment.

While I guess Jim's withdrawal has to do with the way I talked to him after the martinis, I don't know. He won't say. Another friend tells me what made him angry was my decision to wash the dishes. "Your place is with him. Not sulking in the kitchen." I am shocked to hear my actions interpreted as "sulking" but I don't fight back. If she sees me that way, maybe Jim does, too. She tells me to back way off. "Leave him alone. Men don't like to be pushed."

I'm miserable. I sit on the beach and stare across the water, dazed. I try to read and can't. I try to eat and can't. Naturally I can't sleep either. I run and find myself bawling halfway through.

And I stay away from Jim. I don't call him. I wait.

I tell a good friend what's going on. She says, "I did notice that he's very self-contained."

Great. "What does that mean?" I ask.

"You know."

I guess I do. He doesn't need anybody.

Jim doesn't call three times a day like he used to, but he begins calling again, once each evening. We chat about our day but little else. He says, "Everything's fine." Eventually he says I should come to Chelsea, as we had planned before our fight, and we can talk about what happened. He tells me he needs a little time to think through his feelings and put words to it. Even though I agree to see Jim while in New York, I feel only marginally more hopeful that all is not ruined. He's not the type of man who would break up over the phone. I guess I half expect him to greet me with, "It's over. You're a good girl but I just don't need all these complications at this point in my life."

. . . .

I stand in front of Jim's apartment door, debating whether to use "my" key, try the door, or knock. He's expecting me but I'm not sure how to proceed. Whenever I start thinking like this, I stop. Never play games, I tell myself. Say the most truthful thing you can think of. Do what comes naturally. Speak, don't sulk. On and on. Who would believe that at fifty-eight I'm still working this hard at being a grownup?

So I knock, try the doorknob, and find that Jim has cracked the door open for me. I immediately sense that whatever this fight is, it's not lethal. Possibly, I'm still listed in his Frequently Called phone queue. I relax just a little.

We walk down to the liquor store to buy a bottle of wine. We never say so out loud, but the usual get-together martini is out of the question. We open the wine, sip it slowly, and make small talk while eating a salad that Jim has ordered from Moonstruck. I'm extremely tense. "Let's walk down to the liquor store again," I say. "We can buy another bottle of wine. Just in case."

We walk arm in arm, like old times. It doesn't seem possible that we had a fight, especially a fight that involved no words. To me, nothing is more excruciating than to be made to remain silent.

Jim says, "It's like I'm starting over again." I try to imagine what this must be like for him. I decide this starting over is a good thing. I argue to myself that I make the quality of his life better; I argue back: He could give a shit about quality of life.

* * * * * * * * * * * *

Later that night, after lovemaking and food, he brings up our fight again, as he promised he would. At the time, I'm lounging on the bed, facing him, and we're making hesitant small talk. It's midweek and I have a press check on Long Island early the next morning. He switches subjects and says, "We said we'd talk. Well, I guess you're not the only one who feels vulnerable. I have fears and insecurities, too."

I can see that he's embarrassed and uncomfortable, but he maintains eye contact. He's not so much afraid of this conversation as he is out of his element. "I'm sorry," he says. I look at him. He made me miserable for two weeks but in those two weeks, I remind myself, he maintained contact, albeit sparse, and he did assure me that everything was going to be fine. I also recall his statement, early on, "I need time to understand my feelings. I hate to say anything before I've worked it out for myself. I don't want to fuck this up."

It's challenging to work out problems when you're 250 miles apart. Like email, so much of the interaction between two people is invisible when you problem-solve by phone. The touch of his hand on my knee means he cares about what I'm feeling. The way his eyes soften and blink tells me he's listening. By the time our big fight happens, we're already in the habit of setting aside serious matters for our face-to-face meetings. Thus, this miserable event plays out over weeks, not hours or even days. In the process, I gain a great deal from the experience. I learn not to hound. I learn I don't need to fix everything. I focus on the positive. I assume the best. It hasn't been easy for me. I've needed to be the watchdog, the fixer, the peacemaker, the healer. I have to ditch all that at fifty-eight and just be. So I let go of the fight. I make a decision to drop it, to wait and see. I trust my instincts and I'm happy I do. I discover that instead of running from conflict, Jim confronts perceived issues head on. I, in turn, don't want to put Jim in the position of mining my emotional state, so I speak out quickly on the little stuff. Bigger issues, I think about, pull apart in my journals, and talk about with Jim. He tells me, I like the way we fight. I do, too. Because Jim stays in the moment, he hasn't spent time concocting scenarios or harboring resentments. I, on the other hand, feel safe and strong bringing issues forward. Jim says, I respect your thoughts. It feels like you're my partner."

. . . .

One Monday evening in the summertime, I call Jim. This phone call comes after another of his visits to Rockport. We had a wonderful time but now that he's gone, I know what's going to happen. He's going to withdraw to his Manhattan life and though our phone calls will be lively and fun, they will be guarded, especially at first. We have to protect ourselves. It will be four weeks before we see each other again.

I tell my girlfriend, a woman who also had a long-distance love affair: This is very hard. It's exciting and intense as our visits draw near. Afterward, it's a letdown. We travel all the time. It's a lot to manage.

I also tell her: There are two Jims in my life. There's the phone-Jim and the real-Jim.

Jim doesn't see it quite like that. He says Phone-Jim is in service to Real-Jim. Phone-Jim makes the relationship possible by keeping it going while we're apart. Because of the distance between us, our love affair remains fresh and exciting. Because of the distance, misunderstandings can be doubly bad. Long-distance love affairs require faith to work. Long-distance lovers need to focus on the positive and keep it upbeat. I understand that this experience is perfect training for me and I see that I'm learning and changing. I follow Jim's lead. Just as my Lama suggests, I'm letting Jim be my teacher. Right now he's teaching me more than patience. He's teaching me what confidence looks and feels like.

That's the trouble with teaching. I do gain trust. I do grow more confident. I do ask for more.

I think I can trust that we'll get through the ups and downs of the long-distance cycles but it's tiring. Even more tiring is the commuting from Rockport to work to Amtrak and back again to work. For a while my visits are more frequent as I have a few work-related trips that bring me into Manhattan.

"I'd like to know if you think it's possible for us to live together," I ask Jim that Monday night. I do this right after a visit to forestall the inevitable withdrawal. While in Florida, he suggested that I quit my job and write. "Enjoy the free fall," he said. So on Monday night I tell him I could do this for several months because an unexpected windfall came my way, a small amount of money from a retirement plan I didn't even realize I had.

This time, he doesn't hesitate. He says, "Okay. Let's make a plan." This was the last thing I expected to hear from a man who says, way too often to suit me, "I'm most comfortable living in the moment." And though it's a long way off—six months to a year, I begin making lists of questions to ask Jim: Won't it be boring to live with someone who faces a bedroom wall and writes all day? How will it be when I have nothing to talk about except word count and rejection slips? Do you think we'll still have hot sex?

When I first met Jim he said, "I'm not mate material." Back then, it didn't matter what he thought. Now, of course, I have to ask, "Why aren't you good mate material?"

"Well, I'm good at beginnings and endings. But I suck at middles."

"Are we close to the middle yet?"

"No, but when we are, we'll have to stay on top of things and work at it."

"I guess I can do that," I say. I have no idea, of course, what I'm talking about. I do know my confidence wavers considerably. The middle, after all, is where most of life gets lived.

"DO IT AGAIN"

....

CHAPTER 15

I spot Esther Perel's *Mating in Captivity: Reconciling the Erotic and the Domestic* on Jim's bookshelf. Ugh. What's he doing with this book, anyway? Brilliant title. Ugly message.

I gobble it up despite the annoying alarms jangling my nervous system, despite my brain messaging me with urgent prompts to *stop reading now and toss the goddamned book down the incinerator*. But, possessed, I read to the end.

Oh boy.

No wonder all of humankind is in constant turmoil. No wonder we suffer. The book's one-sentence summary goes something like this: We aren't wired to mate happily while in captivity, yet we are driven toward exclusivity in our relationships. Put another way, the sexual tension we love in the courting stage is the sexual tension we extinguish in the cohabitation stage.

If pandas weren't proof enough, now there's Esther Perel weighing in on the woman-man (or man-man or woman-woman) conundrum. Our essential core unit is basically unstable.

Wars, bad grades, overeating, AK-47s, pedophilia, priests in confessionals. It all makes sense now. Yet I admire us for our optimism and our persistence, for in persistence we devise solutions. On the other hand, in denial we exhibit lunacy. Just as I overrode impending-pain alerts and read this book, we humans override all knowledge of divorce rates and the anecdotal evidence provided by family and friends and we, nonetheless, attempt to prove that we can do it—manage an exclusive relationship over the long term.

I'm alone in Jim's apartment with this book, which is like being alone when your worst nightmare breaks through the twilight zone and cozies up next to you. I close the cover and slide *Mating in Captivity* to the other side of the bed, where I have been reading in a fever sweat.

I wrestle with a powerful urge to flee to Rockport. I need to get my bearings. I must rethink this relationship. Or, maybe, all I need is a lot of wine and space to convince myself that Esther Perel is full of shit.

Too late. I've unwittingly had my consciousness raised a rung by an attractive, smart woman with plenty of confidence and a rather European, more enlightened take on life and love. Jim, too, has read Perel. He heard her speak on the radio and ordered the book. A bachelor for more than two decades, Jim may well have purchased Perel's book to possess tangible affirmation of his lifestyle choices. Until now, that is. If I have my way, if I overcome the odds, Jim is going to mate in captivity. Repeatedly.

Perel posits a fresh view of humankind's age-old dilemma—dependence vs. independence—as it douses the flames of our hot sex.

In *Mating in Captivity* she enlarges upon what I intuitively know—chances are slim that Jim and I can sustain this high level of sexual tension if we cohabit. Key is the word *tension*. Our sexual tension results, in part, from our chemistry; in part, from the 250 miles and the weeks that separate us; in part, from the anxiety of the unknown (Who is she lunching with today? How high is that scaffolding he's climbing in this photograph he emailed me on his phone? Hey, it's after nine. Why hasn't he called?). We have managed these uncertainties well, so far, funneling the tension into sexual energy and titillation, rather than jealousy or worry or recriminations. Maturity certainly has its upside.

How would we handle a sudden and unending diet of each other's face and penis and vagina after a year or more of desperate longing? Damn. I like Esther Perel for her intelligence and her artful writing and, I suppose, for her heads-up. But why must the thing I love so much—our passionate love affair—be the very thing I intend to jeopardize? Is this tendency to risk what we love yet another weakness in our human nature? What stops me from simply letting things ride as they are?

The answer is simple. Chemistry. My hormones, thus far, derail rational thought. My command center is corrupted.

According to Perel, there's a trade-off that some couples prefer: intimacy for passion.

No thank you. I'm not in the market for a growing and meaningful intimacy at this time in my life. I've raised my child and, for some reason, the need for intimacy now feels far less propulsive.

I simply don't want whatever intimacy connotes. I don't long for intimacy the way I long for Jim's long arms to simply encircle me. He makes me feel safe. Because of the sheer strength of his embrace, I find I have greater courage. It's as if actual muscle memory is being reprogrammed. And since I've never felt safe before Jim, I've never felt courageous even when I was called upon to act courageously. Courage excites me now. I see potential in courage. Intimacy bores me. Without Jim there would be no free fall. I was stuck and now I'm free.

I think of Jim and wonder what intimacy would mean for him. He's so energetic and impassioned and restless that images of intimacy with Jim don't even come up for me. In these ways, moreover, he's entirely hidden. I want something akin to coexistence with sex. I want periods of parallel play with moments of coming together. I want all this till the in- evitable happens, as it will, and soon. I see intimacy supplanted, in fact, by vulnerability. Age necessitates this shift. Our bodies will need each other just to get to and from the bathroom in the middle of the night.

For now, forget intimacy. Forget Valentine's Day. Forget anniver- saries. I don't want the hazards of merging and the expectations, the needs, and the inevitable ennui. I want Jim to operate in a free zone, where he can breathe in deeply and not smell me circling the perim- eter. And god save me from circling the perimeter.

There is such urgency. I assume it's my age but realize the age ar- gument is the love drug talking. The imperative—acting now because we have so little time left—is a feeble excuse. Anything can happen. I could be hit by a falling brick when I run out to check the mail. At fifty-eight I could be nurturing the mother of all brain tumors every time I eat one of my delicious salads. I could be hosting a melanoma that lurks between my toes and not even know. It happens.

Jim invokes his "we were separated at birth" pronouncement ev- ery time we find ourselves reaching for the same avocado or laughing in tandem at a toddler's antics on the subway. I trust this. We can fuck like animals, frolic like kids, laugh till we wheeze because we understand something about who we are. We both separate sex from the rest of it. He says, one morning on his way out the door, "We'll have sex at four." Shocking? No. Fair warning. He's telling me it's almost time to switch channels, access the inner child, head for the sandbox. There we unleash those sweet, undaunted souls who still know something about recess and joy and physical pleasure.

I want Jim for the laughing and talking and reading to each other and railing about the war in Iraq and most of all, for the fucking. I want what we have now, just more of it. And I want less of the travel and the expense and the exhaustion. So, I ask myself as I shove *Mating in Captivity* back onto the bookshelf, why can't I have an enduring and pleasurable sexual relationship?

There's no one who dares say no to me. And I, in the thrall of my chemically induced love affair, would need a sponsor in Narcotics Anonymous to seal me up in a straitjacket and ship me off to detox for fourteen days. Maybe then I might conjure an image of what a rational relationship with Jim would look like. Right now though, like all addicts, I'm in denial.

* * * * * * * * * * * * *

For me, says Jim, sex is service.

What does he mean?

I don't always want to have an orgasm. After an orgasm, I lose interest for a while.

But I like his orgasms.

You can't imagine how much pleasure I get to have when I play in your sandbox. You have no idea.

I have wanted women. I can imagine the fun but I can't know.

I do my best. It's my highest art. My craft. I am extraordinarily pleased when I am successful. There's nothing like it.

I'm beginning to see.

It must be hard to understand.

All this talk is making me horny. Must he go on?

I want you to do something for me.

This is interesting. He asks for practically nothing. His voice is rough, as if he's angry. And here I am, naked on my back in his bed, the light of eight votive candles flickering, amassing, practically klieglike. What? What does he want?

Take your fingers and put them into your vagina.

Oh.

Two fingers. That's right. All the way. Slowly.

What oh what.

Okay Rae. Deeper. Mmmm. Now take them out. Easy easy. Good.

Jesus god.

Put your fingers in your mouth. Yes. Like that. Taste yourself.

Anything.

Very good. Now do it again. I want you to do it again.

. . . .

In a large meeting that includes my boss and several of the other museum's deputy directors, I announce that I've hired a new staff photographer to replace the one I let go.

"I realize some of you had some problems with our previous photographer," I tell them. "You'll find that Walter is skilled, personable, and experienced." I talk a bit about how my new photography department has grown since it started a year ago and about Walter's impressive digital expertise. My hope is that they'll forgive our missteps when they see that we're alert and responsive.

I also remind them that we will continue to work with Dennis, a talented photographer we retain part-time through a contractual arrangement I negotiated. Dennis is creative, advanced in his use and understanding of technology, and well liked.

When the meeting ends, my boss and I leave together for the museum atrium across the plaza, where two of my staff members will join us to talk about new atrium directional and program signage.

As soon as we're out of hearing range of the Museum Office Center, my boss says, "What were you thinking?"

"What do you mean?" I turn my head in his direction and see that he's angry.

"You have no business calling your new hire a staff photographer. You misled everyone there. He's nothing more than Dennis's assistant."

"Of course he's the staff photographer. That's the title on his job description. That's the position he fills." Not to mention, I think silently, none of this would have happened if my boss had allowed me to hire him a year ago, as I had initially requested.

"You must not let people think he's the staff photographer. You are not to use him in that way. He is not the staff photographer. You are not to use those words again. He has to earn that distinction."

Since my boss approved the hire this time around, I can't figure out what's going on. "He earned that distinction," I say, "by producing an impressive body of work over many years."

"You heard me. He's Dennis's assistant. You are to use him as Dennis's assistant."

"I need a staff photographer to get the work done. I can't function without a staff photographer. We've got a ton of jobs lined up, waiting for him. We've got a studio to build. And we've got to start mending fences. He is capable. People are going to like that."

"This isn't fair to Dennis. You owe Dennis. You are not to call Walter a staff photographer. He is Dennis's assistant and that's the end of it."

After five years of these outbursts, I should have developed skills for this. But I haven't. My heart pounds. I sweat. And I'm frightened by the surprise and force of his anger, and by the way he keeps repeating himself when he gets like this. Where is this coming from? What did I do here that's so wrong? I acted quickly and decisively to protect our department and meet the museum's large needs for photography.

I hate sounding defensive, so I don't say much. Over the years I've done a lot of peacemaking and accommodating with my boss, which is probably a mistake. To him I look weak.

Adam Phillips and Barbara Taylor, who published "On Kindness" in 2009, would most likely agree. They detail the decline of kind behavior in societies that are made up of people who scorn one of the sincerest forms of pleasure. They say, and we all know, that performing acts of kindness brings us much joy.

"An image of the self has been created that is utterly lacking in natural generosity." This image, they say, shows us "deeply and fundamentally antagonistic to each other." Our motives, in this familiar model, are "utterly self-seeking" and our sympathies suspicious "forms of self-protection."

I look at my boss as he rails and wonder where he gets his support. The model of a society suspicious of kindness could be hackneyed if used to describe the corporate mind-set in this country, a mind-set adopted more often these days by museums and their corporately backed benefactors. Things change. There are still museum staff members here who remember when they used to gather at a round table in the afternoon and have tea.

You can be kind and tough, but what will be seen first is the kindness. With my boss, I do not relent on the key points. I say instead that I am genuinely respectful of Dennis and would do nothing to threaten his status at our museum.

As we head in hot silence toward the museum entrance it occurs to me that my boss has just demonstrated an impressive fit of fucked-up transference. He feels emasculated and, for some reason, he sees me as emasculating Dennis. In going to the mat for Dennis, a man I obviously value since I hired him, my boss endangers even his position at the museum since he is ultimately responsible for the visual presentation of our museum and its art and programming. His dislike of me gets in the way of his common sense, which only compounds his rage.

It doesn't end there. Once inside the museum atrium and its cafe, he strides over to my staff members, a graphic artist who will design the new signage and an editor who tracks signage, and he huddles with them. I walk around my boss and my two employees, attempting to hear the conversation since signage is my responsibility. Impossible. My boss angles away from me at every turn, keeping his back in my face. At one point, I give up and take a seat right there, in the café. Eventually I make myself stand up and I force myself between them. I tell them we need to include the deputy director in charge of exhibition design, since he is working on atrium exhibition signage and he asked to be included in the meeting. "We need to include Fred in this discussion," I say. "He's supposed to be present."

"I am in charge here," my boss snaps. The exchange heats up and a museum visitor, a man having coffee right beside us in the atrium café, stares, mouth agape. My boss is now livid. I look at the visitor. He's clearly alarmed. What does he think? Nonetheless, I persist. I don't go away again, despite the backs turning into my face another time.

I say something about the signage they're imagining as the three of them point to the second-level India galleries. My boss has marginalized me, my employees do what my boss wants, and I fight against all of it by holding my ground. But my boss has had enough. "You're dismissed," he yells. Out of the corner of my eye I see my staff members edging away uncomfortably. "You are dismissed," my boss repeats. "You are to leave this museum right now. I am dismissing you."

I walk out, call the director of human resources, and demand that they fire this offensive man. Now I'm livid. She says she's heard enough and will insist that he get, at the very least, some serious coaching. I take no hope in this since he's been coached before. I restate my demand. I want that man fired. He is a liability.

The next day I am called to an arbitration session in which I'm told that I'm not forthcoming, assertive, or direct. What? Since when is this about me?

And yet I have to admit, to some degree, this is true. I'm mired in a dysfunctional relationship. I'm conciliatory but I refuse to cave. Yet this turnaround on the part of HR—everything that happened is my fault and he never ever said I was dismissed because the word *dismiss* is not even in his everyday lexicon—is shocking and it takes me time to realize what's happened. I want to say, *Let's look at the video of this,* but I've lost my fight. The director of HR tells me that if I want my staff to give their impressions, it will backfire on me. I wonder how that could be but, again, I don't ask. I feel I've been threatened. The truth has been rewritten. Two hours into this, I'm exhausted and disgusted.

I now understand that I must apologize to end this misery. I leave the director's office and, when I see that she's calling me on my cell phone, just a few minutes later, I ignore the call. She tries again, this time on my work phone. I go home early and listen to her message from the safety of my reading chair. She says she's driving to Cambridge and she wants to know if I'm okay.

Absolutely.

I think of Jim. I think of Eli. I think of my boss. I'm done with the rancor. I need never again be the object of someone's fervid scorn. I will never listen to another unwarranted accusation. I decide that in the fall, I will give my notice. In the winter I will leave the job and all of the abuses behind. It's over. Finished. Goodbye museum. Goodbye Eli.

Free fall?

I jump with both feet. I see no bottom but know that I leap toward strong arms and a new beginning. I hear only the sound of the wind whooshing. Ahhhh. I think of the March winds I loved so much in Santa Barbara that brought me the scent of sea salt and eucalyptus and chaparral. I realize it's no coincidence that these are the very aromas that Jim adores.

Finally, in the midst of free fall, I have clarity.

"I'VE TRIED SO HARD"

CHAPTER 16

It's 2:13 AM. My eyes open to the crimson numbers on the clock radio. What is it? Then I hear the ringtone, the gentle strum of a harp. The night is black and red. I grope for my phone.

I am alone and everyone I love is somewhere else. Somebody must be in trouble. Please god make this be a dream. Strum. Strum. Strum.

It's Eli. Drowning in his own words.

I just can't do this anymore. I've tried and you know that, how hard I've tried. I've worked so hard and nothing, just nothing, gets better. Howard and some of the people from the sangha have been helping me. I said I'd go to McLean, the psychiatric hospital my doctor contacted for me, but when we got there I just couldn't do it, couldn't go in there and admit myself like that, and we left and they said it would be okay for me not to go to McLean. I told them, what's the point? Is there any reason for me to go on? Give me one reason. I just need one. I asked each one of them, why go on. Give me a reason. None of them could. Not one reason.

What does that tell you? So what about you. Can you do it? Give me one
reason and I won't kill myself.

Oh Jesus.

I stall. Where are you? What time is it? Are you alone? I want to
ask—Are you drinking? Have you been taking your meds? Did they
change your meds lately? These are inflammatory questions for Eli so
I stay neutral and try not to show how I feel. I will fail Eli again. This
time it will be for good.

But I don't need to ask him how. This part I already know. He
will do it with a piece of rubber tubing that he will attach to his car's
exhaust pipe with duct tape and he will run the tube into his driver's
side window, which he will then seal with tape. He carries these things,
along with ice melt and a window scraper and a couple of cans of engine oil and a collapsible snow shovel, in the trunk of his car. I don't
need to ask him how because he's tried this before.

My mother taught me what I know about suicide. Some people,
when they say they mean it, mean it. And if they mean it they're probably going to do it no matter what you say or do. You cannot stop someone who is determined to die. I tried stopping my mother. I stood in
front of the car. She put her key into the ignition, started it up, inched
forward. Her or me.

Not me. I stepped aside.

I do not give up on people who ask for help. I will never give up
on Eli. I sit up in bed, desperate to stop him because what I hear in his
voice is fear, loneliness, a genuine cry for help. He has too much time, a
crushing depression, and no one to talk with. The night blares red and
black. Eli's scared to death.

"Eli? Are you there?"

"Yes I'm still here."

"One reason? Well here it is, your one reason. You're calling me. That's your reason. You're calling me, therefore you don't want to die. You must honor your deepest wish, even if it's hidden to you."

I've tried so hard.

Oh, yes. He tries. He's not like my mother, angry and hateful and determined to hurt others. He's a pure soul, 100 percent honest and earnest. He deserves none of this. I have to save him.

Now 2:57. The red numbers. The pitch black. Red bleeds to nothing. Me all pounding heart. Eli way too quiet now. 3 AM. The crisis concentrates, amasses, swells. This is all there is.

"Eli."

I'm losing him.

"Eli."

Dear god.

"Eli."

"What."

I ask him if what he'd done, inadvertently and with disastrous results, was to pose a trick question for the Buddhists. These devout Zen practitioners believe in reincarnation and karma. Death is so temporary. In their thinking Eli will be back. We will always have a version of Eli.

Do you want to be a barnacle next time, I ask him. Or the West Nile virus? Or an eleven-year-old Muslim girl, raped by the village men, awaiting her stoning? Even now, when there's nothing worth living for, there's still karma to consider. Don't ruin it for your next life, I say. Be kind to that person. Let the truly reprehensible take the shape of a mollusk. You work on bringing Eli to the next level right here, right now, as my own Buddhist teacher would say. Be here now.

But he's not thinking Buddhist thoughts at the moment. He doesn't give a shit about karma and worms and reincarnation. He wants to get rid of the pain.

Where are you, I ask again, but he won't say. I can give you hundreds of reasons why you need to live, I tell him. But that's not what you want right now. You just want to make this feeling go away. If you wanted to die, truly wanted to die, I'm the last person you'd call. You know me. I love you and want you to get better. You called me because you want to hear that you are entitled to feel better. Yes. I agree. You deserve more than this. Go back to McLean. That's where you can get help to feel better. Right away you'll feel better. You'll be safe. It feels good to feel safe. You haven't felt safe in some time, have you?

This goes on for an hour. He's exhausted. For long times there's nothing on the line. Just Eli thinking: Live or die. What will it be?

Eli? Are you asleep? Where are you? How far away from McLean are you?

I'm a long way away.

Does he mean that literally? I ask again, How far?

A long drive.

I see. Well, can you make it if you drive? Are you too tired? Can you drive up to the door, get out of the car, go in there, and tell them you want to feel safe?

He tells me he can't go back because he'll need another doctor's note to admit him. He says there's a lot of red tape and it took all of them a lot of running around and a whole day to get the admission request.

I ask Eli to wait while I call McLean. I shake so hard I can barely press the buttons on my phone. A nice woman with a calm voice and lots of love in her heart answers and tells me she's waiting for him.

Right this minute, she says, she's waiting for Eli. She says she's expecting him to arrive at any time. She has all the paperwork completed. All he has to do is pass over the threshold and he's home free.

Of course I cry. I didn't know someone could be so calm or so nice. I ask her if she'll talk to Eli for me and say something to help him come in. She says yes and she calls Eli. In five minutes he calls me back and tells me he's moving now, en route, driving to McLean. He tells me he'll call me when he gets there.

Promise me you'll drive safely.

I promise.

Call me when you've seen that nice woman and when you feel safe. That's when to call me. I hang up and wait. I sit in the bed and never move. I wait for Eli to decide to live.

. . . .

Two hours later I get two phone calls, one immediately following the other. First it's Eli, saying he's safe. He sounds so much better. He sounds normal, like maybe he could just go home, rent a video, have a burger and a cup of coffee. But this is just a momentary release of endorphins. He's experiencing profound relief.

The next call is from the nurse. She tells me Eli is safe now. They have him and he's safe.

. . . .

Eli endures nine hospitalizations in twelve months, only twice at the same institution. Two hospitalizations have to do with enormous swelling in his legs and feet. He cannot wear his shoes or even socks. Both times he's discharged without any resolution and both times, he exits in the throes of emotional trauma.

· · · · · · · · · · · ·

The institutions and the psychiatrists, working independently of each other, can find nothing to help Eli manage his bipolar episodes, which recur continuously. His cycles are short and acute and unrelenting. Up and down. Up and down.

I visit Eli at McLean, the first of scores of visits to these rundown psychiatric units with their linoleum floors, scuffed walls, and echoey corridors. I pass addicts, the morbidly obese, the psychotics and Iraq vets, the young crazies and the old-timers. Some are cheery but many seem the same, with the same vague look in their eyes, the same odd gait. As they say in NAMI, "It's all the same drugs, no matter what name you give it—bipolar, depression, personality disorder."

I knock on the door of Eli's room. He's alone.

"Stay away. I'm murderous."

"Eli?"

"Don't come near me." He's yelling.

I open the door and look in. He's standing in the middle of the room. There's only him and a bed and a wooden desk. His arms are covered in claw marks, scabs, and bloody gashes, and there is a fat black-and-blue lump just above his right eyebrow. His scalp is bleeding.

"Get out!" he shouts.

I pull the door closed and rush to the head nurse, whose office is just across the corridor from Eli's room.

"Don't you know what's going on in there? Hasn't anyone checked on Eli?" I am furious. They open the door and the nurse eyes Eli. She yells at him. "Why didn't you tell me about this?"

I can't understand what she could possibly mean.

Eli lurches at me. I step out of the room and they tell me to go and wait in the lounge, located down the main corridor. When I'm allowed back in, Eli is half asleep, mumbling hello, saying he's pissed his pants. McLean releases him a few days later, after they put him back on lithium. The next psychiatric hospital pulls the lithium. His kidneys are going to fail if they don't.

At one of these places, they give him something that causes him to have symptoms that mimic Parkinson's. One morning he tries to walk to the bathroom and falls flat on his face like a felled tree. He says he wasn't expecting his legs to be stiff like boards. When I see him, his arm is tucked into a sling, he limps, and his nose is swollen and bloody.

. . . .

Eli finally lands in Beverly in late summer, where he asks for electro-convulsive therapy after every drug he's tried seems to have failed him. They hold him for several weeks while he's taken off all medications and while they wait for a slot to open for the rounds of ECT treatments.

By the time he winds up in Beverly, Eli is all bones and hair. His beard is ragged and long. His stringy hair grows past his collar. Wiry hairs spurt out of his ears and nose. He doesn't want food. He complains bitterly about everything. "The eggs are powdered," he hisses. "The toast is cold and the coffee is decaffeinated piss."

He sits for hours, head drooping and shoulders slumped—a cliché. He looks like every crazy man ever portrayed on film. It's as if someone sucked the marrow out of his bones. He's collapsing in on himself. We sit together in the common area, where he slumps, shaking his head slowly back and forth, muttering no, no, no.

At first, I find that little treats like chocolate pudding or a Coke get him to lift his head slightly, take a bite, murmur "Good." Soon enough he tells me to stop bringing anything to eat as he has lost his desire for sugar and his appetite for food. I try magazines, hot black coffee, newspapers, *The New York Times* Sunday crossword puzzles. Eli settles into this holding pattern until it's his turn to undergo a series of electroconvulsive shocks, spread out over a few weeks' time.

. . . .

In early spring of the following year, Eli drives up to our house in Rockport. By this time, he's been able to get into subsidized housing in Melrose, about forty miles west of Rockport. He has his own place, with a kitchen, living room, and bedroom. Jim gave me money so that I could help Eli furnish it with a new bed, television, computer, and some appliances. It's not the same as Rockport with its dramatic ocean views, big office just for Eli, woods paths, and woodworking shop in the basement, but it's safe and sweet and Eli has made it a lovely, accommodating home.

Jim watches from the living room window for Eli with the knowledge that Eli was gracious and loving when I told him about Jim. One very hard year has passed and Eli and I are both changed. The evening after I talked with Eli about Jim, he called and said, "I want you to know that I am happy for you and that I love you."

When Jim sees Eli pull up in his station wagon, he goes downstairs. They have not seen each other, and spoken only occasionally, since my love affair with Jim began.

They embrace, shake hands, and together they walk to our favorite restaurant, Brackett's, to have lunch. Old friends looking for new common ground. After they leave, I slip out and take my run.

I decide on the same run I took a year and a half earlier—that warm December day when Jim and I spoke on the phone for the first time.

I knew back then that something was coming. Something bigger than winter and nor'easters and changing jobs. I imagine how I must have looked after the telephone call, as I stood up, stretched, walked over to the beach, and breathed in the luscious sea air. I felt tall. My legs felt firm, rooted. My eyes held on to the horizon. I had known something was coming. I had known it was pointless to worry. I was at peace. Relaxed. Open.

I stand in the same place fifteen months later. Another wave breaks high up, close to my feet. As the water slides back over the small round rocks, I hear that jangly rattling sound I love so much—like a thousand xylophones playing at once. By now I get it. Change is sure, as the tides are sure. Sometimes you can postpone change, as Eli and I did. The longer you do, the harder it gets. But we did it. The three of us did it.

. . . .

I run straight to the restaurant, duck into the ladies room to clean up a bit, and then walk into the dining room with its astonishing view and the sense of welcome. Jim and Eli are having coffee and dessert. They're not expecting me.

"Hi," I say. "Do you mind if I sit down?"

They tell me they're fine, the food was great, and they were just about to take a walk down Bearskin Neck. I eat a few cold french fries from Jim's plate, he pays the bill, and we head out for a bracing stroll. The winds have picked up but we are used to this.

. . . .

We take the same walk a few months later. June. Eli has Daisy, his adorable little mutt, on a leash. It's crowded on the Neck and everyone, it seems, needs to bend over and pat that cute head of hers. We get out to the end of the Neck and the three of us sit on one of the granite benches. It's a beautiful day. A man stops by, pets Daisy, says hello. He says something funny and the three of us laugh out loud. The man, pleased with himself, moves on.

Eventually, we quiet down and note the fine quality of this day.

"Great view," says Jim.

"Nice day," I say.

"Yep," says Eli.

We just sit, staring out over the Atlantic, settling in to the way it is now, feeling the pleasures of this new configuration. I call it family.

EPILOGUE

CHELSEA

F inally, after a month's separation, I'm just where I want to be, in Jim's bedroom, sitting on the edge of his bed. Jim has pulled his office chair into the room and he sits, facing me, talking. The chair has wheels and every time he gestures, which is often, the chair shimmies to and fro. These little twists and squirms turn up the tension, as if at any second he will let go and roll right over to me. I think of that, of him sliding toward me. *Do it please.* It's been over a month. Yet Jim talks, talks, talks. I feel a little lost here, in this interim moment, in civilized foreplay, where I perch so properly, embarrassed by the abject want, the wet crotch, the inability to focus on the words themselves. I want to please him. I want to do the right thing, to play along. I latch onto his eyes, his smile, his happiness, and I hold on.

In my life, there is nothing I take for granted. Everything good is a gift that can be wrenched away from me.

So that even now, after a year of tumult and ecstasy in which Jim has held fast, I still find the idea of removing my shoes in front of him, in his home, upon my arrival after a long day at work, and five hard hours of travel in packed trains, to be presumptuous—as if I must be invited to make myself at home, relax, unburden myself. I need this verbal cue from Jim, even though I know full well what's coming. Sometime this evening, at a time Jim decides, I will be expected to stand, take off my blouse, my skirt, my bra, my panties, open my legs, let him in with all the light and the big hazel eyes wide open and me, a yawning, gaping thing of want and little else.

Between us right now is a couple of yards of floor space, seemingly unnavigable, jammed with the weeks and miles and hours and hours of living and all the retrenched inhibitions wrought by age and longing and need and then, finally, this last bit, the attention to foreplay, and the one last question: Is the other still willing?

It's been a year since he yelled over the phone in the middle of a bitterly cold winter night when I drove hysterically in search of medical supplies for Eli: *Don't you know what I want by now? I want you naked.* Nothing's changed between us in all these months. Me, naked. That's the bottom line.

I'm so happy to finally be here even if I do tremble like a scared virgin. I return Jim's smile so often my face hurts. I'm reminded of how it is when babies coo and grin—you cannot resist their sweet joy.

But this is no nursery and we are no innocents cooing for mother's milk. The tension in this room has a smell—heat and musk and something sweet. Sun-warmed earth in April. Wine newly uncorked.

I sip my merlot. Yes, the smell in this room is a little like this wine, a distillation of heat and sugars and yeast and us. It's a lusty brew, an earthy perfume we lay down everywhere we go. I bury my nose in Jim. I roll all over Jim. I slide to his side of the bed the instant he rises to get water or go into the bathroom. I taste, suck, lick. I flash through all this as I sit and wonder, what is going to compel me, finally, to slip off these shoes? I cannot stand the feel of these shoes.

Jim slides closer, but not close enough to touch, and lifts the wine bottle from his nightstand. He pours a little of the merlot into my glass, asks, "Are you comfortable? Do you feel at home?"

Of course. I'm in my second home now. I have a key and a side of the bed that goes empty when I'm away and my own flourless bread in the freezer. Of course. So I bend carefully while in my chair, slide off my shoes, slowly, with one hand, a shoe at a time. I take a breath. Then another. Sip the merlot. Settle in a little.

I've known this apartment for a year now. To even call it a bachelor apartment, with those connotations of wide-screen television, the well-stocked bar, leather furniture, the condoms in the nightstand, is misleading. Though Jim has a shop in Brooklyn, this place serves as his office and has evolved into a satellite shop. There's very little space for actual living outside of the bedroom. Here Jim has deposited bits of old window frames, panes of glass, lead weights and heaps of chain, cans of paint, color samples painted onto flat pieces of wood, toolboxes, drill kits. There are printers, a fax machine, phones ringing, filing cabinets, desks, tables strewn with discarded batteries, flashlights, chopsticks, and a printout of an e-newsletter called *CounterPunch*. Yet I see my place here. My desk, my lamp, my printer, my bookcase, my nightstand, my carrots and apples Jim stocked in the refrigerator for me, a pair of running shoes I leave in a closet that's cleared out a bit for me, in case I want the space. I'm just where I want to be. I'm undaunted by a flashlight on the dining room table. I don't care about shoes tossed off in front of the TV. There is a man here I like very much. I will hold on, persist as I always do, hold open the way to whatever's coming.

Every once in a while Jim will say, "Look at me. I'm almost seventy and I'm starting over." I look around. I nod in sympathy. Yes you are, Jim. But I'm pretty sure this will be a good thing. Try not to worry.

I'm not worried. I'm not going to give up. This feels new. Untried. Interesting and fun. In truth, I've never done anything like this, never done anything I wanted, just because I wanted it. I want this. And as long as he wants it too, I'm going to persist. Persist. Persist. My life's mantra.

. . . .

Jim's talking to me. I must pay closer attention because I can't help but notice I am at the center of his universe. There is no one and nothing here but me, I see, by his focus that is trained so directly and intently on me that I feel enfolded in a force field. My face throbs and it's a hot flash, all right, though not of the menopausal sort. The sparks are exploding all over this bedroom.

He's happy and animated and his eyes are full of his smile. His hands talk to me, too. They flutter, fold, unfold at the ends of long outstretched arms. Jim's awesome wingspan—they say your wingspan matches your height and he's six feet five inches tall—commands the room. Talking for Jim is a full-body expression, like the things he does to me. I think of birds, the way they dip forward, spread their wings before they launch into flight. Jim's fingers spiral out from his palm, a winged unfurling. He is doing this for me.

What's this story he's telling me? I try to pay attention to the words, but only in case they have something to do with the real drama that's going on between us. I prefer watching him. I like basking in the electricity. I resist thinking, processing, mustering coherence. Christ. Can't he just kiss me?

Months ago, when it was just beginning, he said, "Everything is foreplay." The way he slides his long fingers under his right outer thigh and lightly holds his leg when he drives is self-contained and private and achingly sensual. The way he barks into the phone to one of his subcontractors, "Hold on! Hold on!" makes me crave his angry dominion. The way he stops and smiles in the middle of this story literally suspends all animation. Ah, but he's just teasing me.

Jim's relating an experience he had, earlier this afternoon, after descending subway station stairs somewhere in Midtown Manhattan. He says he swiped his MetroCard, pushed through the turnstile, walked onto the platform, all the while feeling a bit distracted by business, by concerns about a check that should have arrived, by wondering what to have for food for us and whether he needed to pick up some grapefruit juice for the morning. He pauses and smiles at the mention of morning. Suddenly, he says, returning to the subway story, he heard a sound so surprising and so clear and so insistent that all his thought clutter just fell away—just like that. He snaps his fingers.

Holy shit. There in front of him was a five-piece mariachi band, dressed in black as if the musicians were background to their music— three horns and two guitars. He says they were giving it their all, serenading like he and his commuter cohorts were would-be sweethearts, like all of procreation depended on it. The horns sang out as clear and tender as first kisses. Dear god, I think, at Jim's mention of kisses, for it seems that all I have thought about for all my waking moments in the last month has been Jim kissing me, which needs, in fact, an entire month of dedicated consideration because his kisses are varied and complex and precise and hot and hungry.

I see that it's not the exuberance of the music that's got him bouncing in his chair and calling up every colorful detail for me. He says the band's performance, so unexpected and raucous and full of life, was a spirited reminder that he's blessed. He chose New York City at the age of twenty-one, having hitchhiked cross-country, having stepped into Greenwich Village at midnight and seen, not the indifferent, empty black of night, but hundreds of people from every walk of life all busy doing something, going somewhere. This was not the bleak and boring Los Angeles suburbs he came from, where endless rows of identical tract housing drained all the specialness and color out of a living landscape. This was someplace big enough for a man of his monumental wingspan. Suddenly anything was possible and surprise was the constant.

"I couldn't believe it," he says. "A goddamned mariachi band right there, right fucking in front of me!" With that he stops, looks at me with all that elation and possibility, and says, "I thought of you, how you would love it." And I try, in that instant, to stop emulating a throbbing sex organ. I try to understand what he means.

Jim thinks I love surprise. He thinks I love the press of people and the chaos of rush hour and the satisfaction of a long workday and the disorienting upheaval wrought by the unexpected. He thinks I can take all this in and still want more, the sensual overload of the red and blue and green and purple of the serape spread at the musicians' feet, the light and airy pile of crumpled one-dollar bills, the three horns and two guitars and five tenors imploring the virgin on the balcony to come to them, to give it up. . . .

I watch his eyes, his face. I feel his energy. The story accelerates, starting slow and low, like percussive bass notes at first, then moving up the scale as he gets going, until that same will and cunning and coy winking seduction I hear in the horns is all about me as I sit on the edge of the bed. All right. I get it. This is seduction and all I have to do is be.

. . . .

The front door to his apartment clicks closed. A deadbolt lock snaps into place. Jim's son, who'd stopped by to pick something up, has left. Jim stands and so do I. "Want to watch a little television?" he asks, grinning. I step toward him. Finally, we kiss, and I am overpowered by his strength, his stature, and the full-length press of his body. Here I can forget that I am nearly six feet tall, that I am a boss and an adversary to my boss, that I am a disciplined writer, a single mother—the one calling the shots.

Now I want this, a counterbalance. Show me what's really important. Show me something new. Let me let go.

He slides his massive hand under my blouse and spreads his fingers against my back. Finally I am where I want to be, overtaken.

. . . .

Later that evening a shocking moment of reckoning shatters the thrill. I have the perfect man buried deep in my vagina. There can be none other than Jim. Ever. I am sobered at the implications.

ACKNOWLEDGMENTS

Free Fall has asked a lot of many of my friends and loved ones. It is deeply personal and takes up subject matter not commonly broached among friends.

After I forwarded two early chapters to my daughter, a library manager, so that she could help me research related literature for my book proposal using her library's databases, she said, "Mom, this was not easy to read. But I love your writing." Spoken like a good daughter and a true librarian. Books are our passion. I'm proud and grateful to have Ardis Francoeur in my life and I thank her for her enthusiastic support of my work.

Many people close to me have read drafts with unflinching grace. They did so because they are true friends, they knew they were needed, and they live their lives in service of the written word. Among these lifelong friends and astute readers are Lynn Harnett, a writer, editor, and book reviewer who somehow managed to read whenever I asked despite her weekly deadlines. Her feedback and encouragement have been invaluable. Betsy Marro, an avid reader with instincts I need and trust, also devoted herself to the task even though her own book is taking shape at this time. What impresses me is how these two smart women can look beyond the personal to the bigger picture. They are dear friends and consummate professionals.

My friend and downstairs neighbor, Stephanie Hobart, has been a guiding light. Early on she encouraged this project. And she has continued to share her joy and good sense with me. She, too, is a wise and accomplished reader. Many times, while writing, I have taken great comfort and joy from the fact that she is downstairs, fully engaged in her own creative endeavors.

My writers group is a special story. They write and publish mysteries and true crime, yet they allowed me to join at a time when I, as a writer, was particularly isolated. They have been immensely caring and polite as I've worked through drafts far more raw than what you will see here, in works both fiction and nonfiction that are clearly not of the mystery genre. These are talented, committed writers and editors: Margaret Press, Susan Oleksiw, Joy Seymour, Larry Griffin, John Urban, and Bill Joyner. They have spent scores of hours with me on this book, even when the word *censored* popped up where the tasty bits should have been.

Others who have been very important to me include my dear friend Marilyn Conover, an artist and writer herself. I hold her in the highest esteem. I view my father's daily practices of good humor, stamina, and persistence as the most precious of gifts. Claudine Scoville and Lisa Kosan are best friends, always there, ever wise and fun-loving. Hope Coffman, director of the Rockport Public Library, and her skilled and warmhearted staff, along with Eleanor Hoy and the Friends of the Library, have allowed me to use Rockport's exemplary library as if it were my own private treasure trove. Hope, along with Toad Hall bookstore manager Amy Pierson and her staff, work together to offer free literary programming in Rockport that rivals what's available in Manhattan. I am indebted to them for allowing me to be part of their team.

My agents Jane Dystel and Miriam Goderich are among the most positively oriented, most professional literary agents working in these difficult times. I am grateful for their support, their experience, the systems they've developed, their feedback, and their invaluable know-how. The same is true of my editor, Krista Lyons, at Seal Press and Perseus Books. Krista, Jane, and Miriam have been ideal readers. The positive way they frame their feedback and their intelligent guidance couldn't be more empowering for a creative writer. Also, I am deeply honored to publish with Seal Press: *By women, for women.*

Eli is the best kind of friend, allowing me to be myself despite the difficulties it causes him. He's a master writer, a pitch-perfect editor, and enviably well read. I've relied on his literary sensibilities for more than twenty years. Early on his gentle, carefully selected feedback provided me with the training I needed to dare to write fiction and creative nonfiction. I hope I've done justice to his goodness in these pages.

Every once in a while, I'm struck by the similarities between Jim and Eli. They are both generous, loving men who choose to support rather than govern. They are unique personalities, cast in a ribald and passionate era. They've retained their demanding politics and their beautiful passion. They both give what they have, whether it's the scarce dollar in their pocket or their glorious enthusiasm. Jim has delighted me in all ways. This book, in great part, is meant to honor that delight. In Jim I have my own personal cheerleader. He teaches me new ways to love. Jim is a smart, naturally gifted editor and reader. I'm not surprised, as his grandfather founded and ran a newspaper in the Midwest. Jim does surprise and amaze me, however. He's been able to step outside of himself and read this highly personal manuscript with tremendous calm and an amazing lack of self-consciousness. He remained grounded and supplied the feedback necessary to keep the book accurate and true. He's profoundly positive and unfailing in his trust and compassion.

Please note that I've changed the names of those whose privacy needs safeguarding. The story is true, however, and as accurate as memory allows.

AUTHOR BIO

© Ruth Schneider

R ae Padilla Francoeur is a journalist and editor. She writes book reviews, essays and nonfiction articles, short stories, and novels. She organizes and moderates literary panels and workshops, and worked for several years at art museums producing magazines and marketing materials while directing an award-winning creative services department. She was a newspaper reporter and, later, managed a number of magazines and newspapers. Most recently, Rae founded New Arts Collaborative to help artists and nonprofits build brand, enlarge their audience, and spread word of their work. She divides her time between Rockport, Massachusetts, and Manhattan, New York.

SELECTED TITLES FROM SEAL PRESS

For more than thirty years, Seal Press has published groundbreaking books.
By women. For women. Visit our website at www.sealpress.com.
Check out the Seal Press blog at www.sealpress.com/blog.

Better Than I Ever Expected: Straight Talk About Sex after Sixty, by Joan Price. $15.95, 978-1-58005-152-1. A warm, witty, and honest book that contends with the challenges and celebrates the delights of older-life sexuality.

Tango: An Argentine Love Story, by Camille Cusumano. $15.95, 978-1-58005-250-4. The spicy travel memoir of a woman who left behind a failed fifteen-year relationship and fell in love with Argentina through the dance that embodies intensity, freedom, and passion.

Good Porn: A Woman's Guide, by Erika Lust. $17.95, 978-1-58005-306-8. Fun, fact-filled, and totally racy, *Good Porn* is an unapologetic celebration of porn—and a guide for both women who like it and those who don't know what they're missing.

Rescue Me, He's Wearing a Moose Hat: And 40 Other Dates After 50, by Sherry Halperin. $13.95, 978-1-58005-068-5. The hilarious account of a woman who finds herself back in the dating scene after midlife.

Dirty Girls: Erotica for Women, edited by Rachel Kramer Bussel. $15.95, 978-1-58005-251-1. A collection of tantalizing and steamy stories compiled by prolific erotica writer Rachel Kramer Bussel.

For Keeps: Women Tell the Truth About Their Bodies, Growing Older, and Acceptance, edited by Victoria Zackheim. $15.95, 978-1-58005-204-7. This inspirational collection of personal essays explores the relationship that aging women have with their bodies.